Charles King

The General's Double

A Story of the Army of the Potomac

Charles King

The General's Double
A Story of the Army of the Potomac

ISBN/EAN: 9783744747066

Printed in Europe, USA, Canada, Australia, Japan

Cover: Foto ©ninafisch / pixelio.de

More available books at **www.hansebooks.com**

Charles King

The General's Double
A Story of the Army of the Potomac

ISBN/EAN: 9783744747066

Printed in Europe, USA, Canada, Australia, Japan

Cover: Foto ©ninafisch / pixelio.de

More available books at **www.hansebooks.com**

THE
GENERAL'S DOUBLE

A STORY OF
THE ARMY OF THE POTOMAC

BY

CAPTAIN CHARLES KING, U. S. A.

ILLUSTRATED BY
J. STEEPLE DAVIS

PHILADELPHIA
J. B. LIPPINCOTT COMPANY
1898

Copyright, 1897,
BY
J. B. Lippincott Company.

TO

ROBERT ELIOT,

MOST LOYAL OF UNION MEN, MOST

PATRIOTIC OF CITIZENS, MOST PATIENT OF READERS,

AND MOST PERTINENT OF CRITICS,

THIS STORY OF THE WAR DAYS

IS

𝔇𝔢𝔡𝔦𝔠𝔞𝔱𝔢𝔡.

LIST OF ILLUSTRATIONS.

	PAGE
Bareheaded, with his coat torn open from throat to waist	12
"Drop them, sir, instantly!"	101
"Back with you, captain! Ride like mad"	220
Blushingly holding the wine-glass	442

THE GENERAL'S DOUBLE.

SOME LETTERS.

THE ADJUTANT'S.

In Hospital, Washington, D. C.,
August 2, 1861.

George Lowndes, Esq.:

My dear Sir,—The colonel has received your letter asking for the full particulars of the death of your gallant son, one of the last to fall on that fatal Sunday afternoon. I am spending the morning at the bedside of my commanding officer, for he himself is flat on his back, disabled by his wounds, and he has asked me to reply.

The papers have told you how hopefully we marched from Centreville, and with what enthusiasm the attack began. Of course, we know now that it was intended that General Hunter's column should open the ball much earlier in the morning, and that the heights back of the turnpike should have been assaulted soon after sunrise, but it seemed nearly noon before our brigade commander led us through the ford and we pitched in to the support of the attack. You have read, too, how successful we were at first. Really, as we swept up the slope in line, we saw no enemy at all, only a smoky ridge, topped by open fields in which two regular batteries were banging away in front of the Henry house, making tremendous noise and smoke, and setting us to cheering like mad. But we had hardly gained the crest, and were pushing forward, when the opposite woods blazed with fire and we could see mounted officers waving the rebel flags and rallying their men, and then came crashing volleys from over beyond the batteries, and the next thing we knew those Fire Zouaves were tearing through the right of our line utterly demoralized. Captain Arnold was hit in the leg by a rifle ball just as we reached the top, and had to fall out, and that threw Jack in command of his company, the right flank. Oh, Mr. Lowndes, I know very little of the circumstances that led to the estrangement between you and your great, brave boy, but if you could have seen him raging at those running Zouaves, hacking at them with his sword and damning them for cowards, calling meanwhile on his men to keep their line, you would have been proud of him, and you couldn't have helped it. He was the handsomest fellow in the line of officers anyhow, and that day he seemed inspired. He looked a head taller and grander and braver than any man in the regiment, even our giant color-bearer.

It was no use trying to stem that rush to the rear, though. Those fellows swept all over the right company, and then, as we could catch a glimpse through the smoke, we saw that horses and men were dropping in dozens all among the guns and caissons, and the bullets came whistling through our ranks like hail. We couldn't see where to fire, couldn't hear what to do, until, as we got about half-way over the field, the rebels rose like a gray wall at the edge of the woods and began pouring it into us. I own my heart jumped up into my mouth, and I thought it was all over with us then, but when the men of that first company began to waver, for the fire was hotter on that flank, there was Jack shouting and collaring them and shoving them back into line and waving his sword, and the colonel was shot just as he rode over to praise him; and then things seemed to melt away anyhow. We carried the colonel off the field, and we made a stand at the edge of the bluff, but everywhere the lines were going. You could see the rebels swarming through the guns and dancing on the caissons and yelling like mad, and then that fresh line of Johnston's from the Shenandoah came crashing and volleying in from the woods, and that ended everything. It seemed as though nothing could hold the men. They felt that they had been tricked, outwitted, sacrificed, misled. God knows, perhaps they were; we only obeyed orders,—and then down the slopes went everybody with a rush, and presently everybody was mixed up with everybody else.

But to the very last Jack was there with his company, shouting, urging, praying, threatening, and though they got the full force of that flank fire, I'm bound to say his company was the last to break and go, and all because of him. My God! I see him now, glorious in his rage and daring, and his utter contempt of danger. I see him bareheaded, with his coat torn open for air from throat to waist, ripped in two places by whizzing balls. Another had cut away the tassel of his sash in such a manner that the strands of the silk were trailing like so much blood down his left leg, and all of a sudden, as I was running to the right with the order for them to fall back fighting, for the general saw it had to be, Jack suddenly reeled, clasped his hands to his breast, and then plunged heavily forward on his face. I screamed to some of the men to raise him. Sergeant Haney and Lou Willett strove to lift him, but his head fell on his chest; his face, which had been reeking with sweat a moment before, was now plastered with mud. We did lift and carry him down the hill, but he never gave a sound or a sob, never spoke, never regained consciousness one minute, and Haney cried out, "My God! he's shot dead!" Then what could we do? Such ambulances or wagons as we had were gone in mad panic and rush for the Stone Bridge. The men had got started on the run, and were throwing away knapsacks and blankets, cartridge-boxes and everything. It was all mad flight, climbing over one another's heels, pushing, pulling, swearing,—yes, some poor fellows were absolutely crying in terror. And then the yell went up, "Look out! look out! Black Horse Cavalry!"

and Sergeant Hancy saw it was no use, and, dead though he was, poor Jack was propped against a low wall just south of the pike, and there we left him, shot through and through, the blood soaking down his shirt front. We were barely in time to save our own skins, for half a dozen were cut off and captured not ten yards behind us as we got in sight of the bridge.

And that is all I have the heart to write. We were strangers, your son and I, until chance brought us together in the same regiment, but a more soldierly fellow never lived, despite the recklessness that seemed to possess him when camp life grew monotonous. He did not like me at first, because I had to be the writer of occasional missives ordered by the colonel, who is a strict disciplinarian, but I was drawn to him from the start, and we soon became warm friends. Duties prevented my seeing as much of him as I could have wished. The colonel was hard, perhaps, when we lay around Washington, for Jack was drawn thither, I fancy, by a fascination he could not resist. But from the time we got across the Potomac and well out towards Fairfax he was a model officer, and we all swore by him. Bull Run would have made him a captain had it not killed him. There isn't a man in the regiment that doesn't mourn his loss,—that doesn't seem to think our best soldier was killed in our first fight.

I wish I could send you some token or relic, or the papers to which you refer, but there was no time.

I did try to unloose his sword, but the knot was looped tight about his wrist, just as he had worn it so gallantly, and it seemed as though he resisted the effort, and I let it go. We pray that your quest may be successful and that your friends can ascertain for you just where poor Jack was buried, and I need not say that we would gladly aid in the search were it permitted us. In any event, believe me, dear sir, in sympathy and sorrow,

Faithfully yours,
Esmond Harkness,
Adjutant —th Regiment New York Volunteers.

P. S.—To be accurate as to the spot where we left him, I should say it was just about due north from the Robinson house and at the edge of the turnpike.

THE REGIMENTAL COMMANDER'S.

In Camp near Alexandria, Virginia,
August 3, 1861.

George Lowndes, Esq.,

  No. ——, Fifth Avenue, New York:

Dear Sir,—Agreeably to your request, I send you the enclosed extract referring to your son from my official report of the battle of Bull Run.

"The rout began to our right and the fugitives came rushing through our lines despite all efforts to stem or turn them. Captain Arnold having been wounded, the command of the first company devolved upon Lieutenant Lowndes, who instantly sprang to the front, and by voice, example, and personal effort did everything in the power of man to check the fugitives and hold his own company in line. In this he was successful only so far as the company was concerned. They fell back as ordered, with steady front, keeping up their loading and firing until we reached the crest again, and here the volleying from our right front seemed to redouble. The regular batteries were silenced and captured, the rebels were swarming all over them, and with everything gone to the right and left of us I had to order retreat. Just at this juncture, Lieutenant Lowndes received the fatal bullet that entered his breast and probably penetrated the heart, for he fell on his face and never spoke again. So long as there seemed hope of his life his comrades bore him down the slope, but were compelled to abandon the body on reaching the pike. Thus died a brilliant soldier and heroic man, who would doubtless have risen to high rank had he been longer spared to his country's service."

It would have been easy to add words of higher praise for this young man, and, had I consulted my own desire, I should not have withheld them, but such praise might have been considered a reflection upon my superior, who, earlier in the campaign, at least, seemed to find it difficult to overlook certain absences, etc., to which I would not now refer but for your own allusions to them. From the time our onward march began Lieutenant Lowndes was a model soldier.

I deeply regret that it is impossible to comply with your request that further search be made for papers, etc., supposed to be in the possession of your son. Everything except what was on his person at the time we went into action was carefully packed under the supervision of Major Murray and sent to you by express. If there were other papers of importance, they fell with the body into the hands of the enemy.

Accept the tender of my sympathy in this deep affliction, and believe me, dear sir,

Very truly yours,

LEROY P. FITCH,

Lieutenant-Colonel commanding —th New York Volunteers.

A SISTER'S LETTER.

No. — FIFTH AVENUE, NEW YORK CITY,
August 4, 1861.

Your letter has reached me, and answer it I suppose I must; and yet how can you expect me to write calmly at such a time? Jack loved you devotedly, and all might have been so different if you could only have been more kind. That last dreadful quarrel between him and father, when father found that he was here in New York again, instead of attending to his duties at Monadnock, and all because you would not answer his letters and the poor boy craved the sight of your face,—that last quarrel, I say, would have killed mother had she lived to see it; and from that awful night when father ordered him out of the house, out of the home where we had been so happy, I never saw my darling brother's face again. God forgive you, Belle Heatherwood; I cannot—yet. I know that he was reckless, improvident, that his college days were failures, but mother always spoiled and shielded him, always gave him money when father denied him. He was a different man from the day you first came to this house as our guest and my trusted friend. He became your slave, and he worshipped the very ground you trod on. He abandoned all his old companions and devoted every hour to you. I was even jealous to see my brother's love so lavishly poured out, but if I had supposed you could refuse him it would have been a thousand times worse. Admitting that he had been reckless, intemperate, and played cards and bet, and—did other things that worried mother and infuriated father, that was all in the past, and it was all the fault of the fast set with which he had been thrown from the start. At heart Jack was ever a gentleman, full of sweetest impulse, kind, brave, and generous, even to the men that made a wreck of his life. But all that old life, I say, was changed. He became a totally different man from the moment he met you. At least he was, and would have remained so, so long as you were kind to him. If you really were in love with Floyd Fairfax I would not have blamed you, but you weren't—you told me again and again that you were not. Then why couldn't you think of Jack? O God! O God! it's all over now, and my heart's broken. Father sits all day in his study and broods. I know he'd give anything—*everything*—to call my brother back and bid him forget the bitter words—my great, gallant, noble brother. Belle, Belle, no matter how you may sympathize with this wicked rebellion, no matter how many kinsmen you may have on the Southern side, even your cold heart must beat with pride when you read how superbly brave Jack was, how gloriously he died, fighting for our beautiful flag—my hero brother, my noble Jack!

There, I've stopped—I *had* to stop or blur this letter so that it would be utterly unintelligible, but I am calmer now. You were my dearest friend, Belle, and I have tried to put myself in your place and think for you. I try to believe all you tell me of your sorrow and sympathy. Father commands me to say that he deeply appreciates your letter and a very sweet one that came from your dear mother from some place over in Virginia, where she had gone to be near your wounded—there was no one, *no one*, to give my Jack a drop of cool water in his dying agony. I wish I could write in some other way, but I can't, and if you're hurt I can't help it, Belle. You would have my answer, and this is the best I can do. You ask what our plans are, and I reply that we shall remain here in New York for the present. Aunt Eunice is here with us, but father expects to leave for Washington to-night, perhaps, in hopes of recovering Jack's body. It was your picture that lay on his heart when he died. Father bids me say that you and your mother will be welcome now or at any time that you feel ready to come, but I cannot dissemble. I will only pray that your brother may not be taken from you as was mine from

Florence Lowndes.

A WOMAN'S LETTER.

— Eutaw Street, Baltimore,
August 6.

Again I write you, dear Florence, not to upbraid you for the reproaches in your letter which reached me last night, but to explain some matters wherein you must have been misinformed. God forbid that I should resent any word you may have written when so sorely stricken. I tremble to think that at any moment I, too, may lose the brother I deeply love. Florence, you have your father still. You have many friends and relatives who have taken no part in this cruel war against us, against our hearths and homes, but all of mine,—every man of our name or kin is now enrolled in the Confederate army. All of ours are gone. We are utterly alone. Mother, as you know, is now at Warrenton nursing our wounded. Mrs. Fairfax, Floyd's mother, is with her, and cousin Belle (Mrs. Tighlman), and not a word has reached us from them for over a week. It is her purpose to return when she can be spared and to live at Heatherwood, which Major Thomas guarded for us until recently, but which has, nevertheless, suffered not a little.

And this will be the more painful to me because of all its association with Jack. Two months last year, September and October, he was with us almost all the time, and if I was unkind to him, Florence, it was because he was angering his father and ruining his own prospects. Thrice mother brought me letters Mr. Lowndes had written, blaming her because Jack would not obey him and return to his duties. I pleaded with Jack to go, and he would not. I did behave to him with coldness at last, and told him his presence there was a distress to us all, but he would never have misunderstood my motive if Floyd Fairfax had not happened just then to arrive. Jack did leave our roof and went to visit Frank Waddell at Leesburg and the Tighlmans at Frederick, but every now and then he would reappear while Floyd was here, and from the first they seemed hostile to each other, and poor mother was bitterly distressed. Finally, as I say, I had to tell Jack that I would see him no more. There had been words between him and Mr. Fairfax that day, and a bitter letter came from your father, and I was harsh and unkind, perhaps, but when I saw how utterly he was stung, when I learned that he had gone, really gone, then my heart misgave me. They told mother he was at the Club in Baltimore a whole week, and she presently followed him there, to try and persuade him to go home; and then we heard other things,—of his breaking down, and it nearly broke my heart.

Florence, we had to go to New York last winter again, we had promised that visit to the Bells, and I did write to Jack telling him how I grieved over the harsh words I had used, and begged him to forgive me and be friends, and he misunderstood it all,— thought I wanted to call him back, and so he came to New York again and stayed, and you know the rest. I, too, implored him to return to Monadnock, but he hated the place and told me of troubles he had with your father's lawyer, Mr. Clarke; and then your father came and accused me of luring Jack there and holding him there. It was that night that I told him either he or I must leave New York. And that ended everything.

Then came the news of Sumter, and you know all the rest. Time will acquit me of your charges, Florence, but this I will tell you now; even though he died battling against all I hold dear, against kith and kin and home, I did glory in his valor, and I wept for days over his death. I am weeping now. But for one thing I think I would have said yes to him a year ago, and if it could recall him from the grave, even in that uniform,—I know I would say it now.

BELLE HEATHERWOOD.

CHAPTER I.

The sun had gone down over the bold blue heights towards the Shenandoah, and all the broad valley of the Potomac lay in shadow. Bursting from its mountain gate-way to the west at Point of Rocks, the river came rippling and swirling about the huge boulders that dotted its bosom, and then, abruptly bending, swept away in long, shadowy, willow-fringed curves towards the south. Over on the northward,—the Maryland shore,—where the placid waters lay mirroring the cloud fleet sailing across the summer sky, faint columns of bluish smoke went drifting aloft among the white tents at the ferry landing, and the voices of the guard, clustered about a motley batch of mud scows and pontoons moored under the shelving bank, came drowsily over the intervening waters. Here, on the Virginia side, a squadron of grimy cavalry had dismounted in the dun-red dust of the roadway and was silently awaiting the result of its leader's parley with the opposite shore. Some of the troopers, passing their reins through the headstall of a comrade's horse, had thrown themselves on the scant herbage by the roadside and, with their caps pulled over their faces, had gone instantly sound asleep. Some few, with the bight of the reins looped about a blue-clad arm, were squatting or lying in the soft dust of the trampled thoroughfare, reckless of contact that might increase the volume but could not add to the effect of the besmirching soil. Some few, well up towards the head of column, confident, apparently, of their young leader's approval or at least never seeking audible token thereof, had led their weary steeds to the water's edge and were busily sponging out their dust-clogged eyes and nostrils. The bearer of the silken guidon was one of these, and, leaning the staff against the blanket roll at the cantle of his saddle, he was sousing his own sun-tanned visage in the stream when something sent the little standard clattering down upon his broad back, off which it bounded and splashed into the now turbid waters. It was fished out in an instant, and the young corporal cast an anxious glance at the slender form of the squadron commander, as though expectant of reprimand, but that usually "snappy" officer was busily studying the opposite landing through his field-glass and concentrating his sharp sayings on the sluggish movements of the ferrymen. The horses thus led to the riverside had plunged their muzzles deep in the refreshing flood and, after slaking their thirst, were tossing their heads from side to side and lashing the waters into spray in keen relish of their own privilege as being at the head of column, and in equine triumph over the less fortunate bulk of their comrades deeper down in the command. A grizzled sergeant, true to the old dragoon tenet of watering only when you can water all, had indeed interposed a growling protest against this undisciplined proceeding on part of the men, but the silence of the senior sergeant had given consent, and the work went on. Other troopers, not yet asleep, profited by the example of the few in front, and they, too, came leading down to the water's edge, seeing which, the first sergeant, with perfunctory touch of the hand to his cap visor, briefly addressed his commander:

"Can we water, sir?"

A nod was the only response. The lieutenant was too busy to waste his words. The trumpeter, at a glance from the sergeant, wriggled out of the dirty, yellow braided cord by which his brazen clarion was hung between his shoulder-blades, clapped the instrument to his mouth, ground his heels into the yielding sand, fixed his eyes on vacancy, and essayed to sound "water call," but so parched was his own gullet that the resultant discord was a burlesque of the stirring peal to which the troopers were accustomed. Some of them growled a soldier anathema on the luckless performer. Some contented themselves with casual and comprehensive reference to the hottest region known to them. Some few, not utterly tired out, laughed or chuckled audibly over Schmitz's failure. One young rider jocularly addressed him. "If it was beer call could you sound it, Dutchy?" he asked, as he tossed his carbine backward over the shoulder, letting it hang there by the sling, while leading his drooping horse down the somewhat steep incline to the shore.

"He could answer it, begad," spoke a tall corporal, who followed closely at the weary charger's heels, "and so could I if it were only Baltimore brew. Tumble up here, Larry," he continued, launching a kick from his spurred boot at the recumbent form of a comrade at the roadside. "It's little you look like a light dragoon this day, if you are the beau of the troop. Larry, I say!" he continued, stopping short and prodding the victim with his foot. "It's water call. Don't you hear?"

"Aw, leave Beau alone, Jimmy. Don't you know he was orderly to old Foulweather all last night? Sure he hasn't slept out of saddle for forty-eight hours."

"Fact," answered Corporal Jim, remorsefully. "Here, give me his horse, too. I'll take him."

But already the trooper referred to as "Beau" began to find his legs, yawning sleepily the while and rubbing his red-rimmed eyes with the back of a worn gauntlet, an article owned by not half a dozen men in the squadron. It needed but a glance to determine that in this tall, slender, yet stalwart man was a creature of somewhat finer mould than the run of his comrades. Standing nearly six feet two, with broad, muscular shoulders and deep, massive chest, lean in flank and slim, comparatively, at the girth, with head well poised and carried almost proudly, if not even haughtily, erect, with straight, broad-nostrilled nose, overhanging eyebrows, oval face, and clear cut chin,—all was fine even through the coating of dust. Underneath the matted brows and lashes a pair of keen blue eyes flashed forth, bright and piercing despite the sleeplessness of the nights gone by. A blond moustache, red-bronzed now by the Virginia dust, the hirsute adornment then called an imperial, and close-cropped, light-brown hair completed the framework of these attractive features. A battered forage-cap of the style then known as McClellan, with the crossed sabres and regimental number in tarnished brass upon the overhanging crown and the unbound visor turned up instead of down, sat jauntily well forward on his head. The high collar of his trooper jacket, heavily trimmed with tawdry yellow worsted lace, was unhooked at the throat and destitute of stock, but a dark-red silk handkerchief was loosely knotted about the neck, and half-way down the front the jacket itself was unbuttoned, showing the coarse gray flannel of the shirt. His straight, sinewy legs were cased in cavalry trousers of light-blue cloth, and thrust deep into a pair of top boots, much finer than those of government make. Over his shoulder passed a broad black leather carbine sling, its buckle tarnished, its steel swivel coated with rust, and the carbine swinging therefrom was weather-beaten and rusty too. His waist was girt about by the "buff leather" belt then worn in the service, supporting holster and Colt revolver at the right hip, and a dangling, battered, rusty sabre and scabbard on the left side. A common brass spur was strapped to the right boot, but its mate was missing. This, barring the silk handkerchief and the handsome boots, and the fact that most of them had two spurs, was practically the costume of every one of the ninety men who made up Hamlin's squadron of the ——th regular cavalry,—two troops whose captains were commanding brigades of volunteers, one of whose lieutenants was leading a regiment, another languishing in Libby, another on staff duty, leaving only Bob Hamlin to command the array.

A good soldier was Bob, one of the not too many in whom a capital sergeant had successfully borne his elevation to a commission. Not yet twenty-six years of age, he had served in the cavalry in Texas and on the plains when such service was full of hardship, peril, and isolation, had won his way to the chevrons after a spirited brush with Comanches, and when half the officers of his former regiment went with their State in '61, and that regiment, with most of the others in the army, was sorely depleted as to the commissioned list, the vacancies were filled by the appointment of civilians and the promotion of scores of intelligent non-commissioned officers who bade fair to show fine mettle and ability in their new grade. Mettle was never lacking, though the ability was sometimes questioned, but not in Bob Hamlin's case. "There's a fellow who can get almost anything out of his men," said an admiring brother officer, "and I believe it's because he never nags them."

And yet Mr. Hamlin was one of the strictest young officers in the service. For many months of the first year of the war his troop had been stationed in and about the city of Washington, and was noted for its spick and span neatness and style. It was a sight to see it on Pennsylvania Avenue on sunshiny days in its trim-fitting uniform, with glistening shoulder-scales, buckles, and scabbards, riding up to the War Department or head-quarters of the army. Its horses were marvellously groomed and cared for then, and this being before the days of big bounties in the volunteers, not a few enthusiastic young soldiers in the ranks of State troops succeeded in getting transferred to this particular troop of regulars, while on more than one occasion there appeared at the lieutenant's office young civilians who had seen, perhaps, too much of higher life, and now sought admission to the ranks of the cavalry, and one of these was Larry or as he was borne upon the muster roll, "Lawrence Bell."

At first Mr. Hamlin had refused to enlist him. "I know your kind exactly," he had not unkindly said. "You are a man of social position. You've had trouble, and now with an alias you come here to enlist and bury yourself in the regulars. We buried two of your set after first Bull Run,—fellows who thought they ought to stay and whip the whole South when the rest of us were falling back on the Potomac. I'd rather not take you."

"Very well, sir. Then I'll enlist at the Capitol

Barracks," said Mr. Bell, neither affirming nor denying the lieutenant's theory, and, finding him calmly determined, and being furthermore a bit inquisitive, Hamlin himself yielded, and "Beau Bell" his recruit became before he had been with the troop a week.

But now it was mid-October, '62. Antietam had been fought, and Lee allowed to make good his retreat to the sacred soil. His army had pushed on southward, taking it leisurely, while McClellan, timid and irresolute, was hovering along the Potomac, deaf to urgent pleas for action, pursuit,— anything rather than standing there all the day idle.

Hamlin's squadron had been scouting along the east front of the curtaining range, peeping through Aldie and Upperville and the Gaps at the dust clouds of the slowly retiring hosts, far over beyond the Shenandoah, and "not once did Beau Larry turn a hair," as Sergeant Shaw expressed it. He had stepped into his uniform and swung into his saddle with the easy grace of a born cavalryman. He said nothing of what he knew of soldiercraft, yet proved to be better "set up" and better drilled than some of his instructors. He didn't like the balance of the carbine at first, and from the fact that with this one weapon he seemed awkward, and only this one, the old sergeants concluded that he had learned the manual with the musket in hand. But he could groom a horse and give some troopers points in the care of the hoof. He kept his own counsel, minded his own business, sought no intimacies, repelled none who sought his, yet dismissed them with his blessing and abundance of tobacco. He had money, or it came to him frequently, and he showed some discrimination in loaning it, as speedily nine-tenths of the men importuned him to do. He avoided discussion, contention, criticism of every and any kind; was patient, even conciliatory in manner towards his new comrades, who bored him very much, despite their interest in his doings. He was frequently one of the show figures of the troop, and could have been detailed for permanent duty at the quarters of some big functionary in Washington had he not almost excitedly urged that he might never be detached for any such purpose. On campaign, in the field, he said, he would take his chance as orderly for any of the general officers who might desire, but he drew the line at Washington. He rejoiced heartily when hurried off to Yorktown with the transport. He was eager in the pursuit to Williamsburg, and foremost at the start in the famous charge at Gaines's Mill, but ere they had fairly taken the gallop his horse went down and pinned him underneath, saving his life, perhaps, but nearly breaking his leg. A veteran cavalry general had him assigned to duty a few days at his head-quarters and was astonished when the young soldier begged to be relieved. But now under other skies and other soldiers Hamlin's squadron was scouring the Virginia roads, nimbly dodging the heavier bodies of Southern horse and swooping fearlessly in headlong charge when numbers were anywhere near equal. And on this particularly dry and sun-baked day in October it had been marching and scouting since early dawn, and was now sore hungry for supper.

"Are you looking for your horse, Beau?" asked a jovial Irish boy, rolling the quid of "plug" into the other cheek. "Will ye lend me the price of a pint till St. Peter's pay-day if I find him?" for Beau was just beginning to see that his charger was gone and that his comrades were slowly leading down to water.

"Faix, it isn't the horse Larry's lookin' for," chimed in a second, an ill-favored specimen; "its the off side saddle-bag. Isn't it now, Larry? Sure ye niver yet told us what's in the tin case, and that's what the corporal's looking through now."

Bell started as though stung by a lash, sent one piercing glance at the speaker, probably flushed red under the red dust coat of his skin, but only the sudden blaze in his eye betrayed it. Then down the bank he went, finding the corporal indeed tugging at the strap of the saddle-bag, yet only, as he promptly explained, to fasten the thing because it had come loose. But the corporal turned and curiously studied the tall soldier who had so suddenly roused himself and was now standing glowering angrily, suspiciously, at his side. With scant ceremony, Bell himself seized the strap, almost jerking it from his comrade's hands, unbuckled what had just been buckled, raised the flap and, interposing a broad back between the bag and the by-standers, thrust his hand within the folds as though to satisfy himself that certain items were there, and then, withdrawing it, raised the flap and reassured himself by a long peep.

"You're no end particular about that saddle-bag, Beau," said the nettled non-commissioned officer. "I was doing you a friendly service, man, and you look as though you thought me a thief."

"There's nothing there worth stealing, corporal," was the reply, in a voice that lacked all ring of heartiness. "Yet it's mine and no other man's, and I gave fair warning when Devlin tried it that I'd have no tampering with my possessions. One of the men said you were opening it, and I'm glad to find you were not. That's all there is to it."

"That isn't all there is to it, Bell, and you may understand it now, first and last. I'm not the man to pry into your affairs, nor am I one to take any threats. You can't handle me as you did Devlin."

"Not while you wear those, at least," answered Bell, with significant nod of his head at the chevrons of faded yellow. "Not while——"

"Not while they're either on or off, Bell," was the spirited reply. "No man in this squadron can say I ever crawled behind a corporal's warrant to shy a fight. You insinuated a dirty thing when you virtually accused me of prying into your affairs. Damn your saddle-bags and you, too."

"That'll do, there, you men," came in sharp, imperative tones the voice of the first sergeant. Even the lieutenant had lowered his glass and turned about to see whose voice it was that angrily broke the drowsy silence of the late afternoon.

"You can find me whenever you want me, Bell," continued the corporal, in low tone, "and there'll be no chevrons when we strip." And with that, both angered and hurt, the young soldier turned away, and the troopers that had begun to gather about the two led on to water, leaving Bell, with gleaming eye, restrapping his saddle-bag and loosening the girth. Any one could see that he was annoyed far more at himself than at Corporal Dixon. It is when a man realizes that he has wronged another and made an ass of himself that his temper is most apt to be snappish and peppery. Moodily he led his weary horse to one side, found a place to water him in a little pool among the rocks a few yards farther down, let him drink his fill, then flung himself again upon the bank.

"The Duke's got his dander up again," tittered the Irish trooper who had told that Corporal Dixon was trying to open the saddle-bag. He was one of those ill-conditioned creatures whose happiness seems to consist in setting other people by the ears. "Him and Dixon'd make a fine match anyhow, wouldn't they?"

"Shut that ugly mug of yours, Feeney," snapped the nearest sergeant. "You've too many snarls to answer for now. There'll be no fight between them two for all your trying. Even Devlin wouldn't have got into his trouble but for your naggin'."

It was an old story in Hamlin's squadron, though it had happened barely a month before,—just as Lee and Jackson came splashing through the Rappahannock on their famous dash around Pope's right flank, and Hamlin's squadron was disembarked at Alexandria and ordered to push to the front. Somehow, somewhere in that sleepy old Southern town the Irish troopers got a canteen of whiskey. It was soon empty and three men were drunk. For joke, as he said, Feeney had persuaded Devlin that he would find liquor in that off saddle-bag of Bell's, and Devlin was just drunk enough to search, to drag out a tin box tied with silken cord, and to be caught in the act by the angered owner just as he was in the further mischief of striving to untie the cord. They left Devlin in hospital that night when the squadron rode for Centreville. He wasn't well enough to rejoin when they came trotting back to the Long Bridge the first week of September, and had not been able to catch them since, but he sent a message—an Irish message —by one of the men who managed to see him a moment. "It isn't Bell I've got it in for. I'd perhaps ha' done the same by him. It's that blackguard Feeney I'll drub if the devil doesn't get him before I get back." Devlin had had some reputation as a fighter before his impromptu match with Bell, but the whole troop saw how utterly he was outclassed when Bell drew off his gauntlets, slung them in the marauder's face, peeled off his trooper jacket, and sailed in. A straight, clean, scientific hitter was the beau, an educated hitter, and when the brief, bloody battle was over and Devlin, like a human chopping-block, was borne off to the hospital tent, there was no man present who cared to take up the challenge. Bell was panting a little. He was very pale, but his eyes were flashing; a tiny stream of blood was trickling from his under lip, and his white fists were clinched hard. "I disturb no man's belongings in this troop," said he, "and no man shall touch mine. Some of you have put that young fellow up to prowling in my saddle-bags. If they'll dare step up and own it, I'll take the biggest of the lot right here and now." There were some glances at Feeney, some murmur of applause, but no takers.

"Then I give fair warning," said Bell, "the man I catch tampering with these saddle-bags of mine will get a lesson he'll never forget."

And now here, once more, on the banks of the Potomac those saddle-bags had come in as a factor in what, for the moment, promised to be a very pretty quarrel. They were all hungry, were the men, and more or less savage as a result. They were more in mood for fight than frolic, as troopers are wont to be after hours of jog-trot on empty stomachs. But they had begun to fancy the "Duke" in spite of themselves—in spite of himself, for he courted neither friendship nor popularity. They had always liked Dixon, and knew him to be a plucky, brainy fellow, with far more prospects for the future and much less mystery of a past than were Bell's possessions. In all their number, Feeney, probably, was the only man who would have thought of stirring up strife between them. Dixon had come into the troop only a week ahead of Bell, and had won his stripes within three months, whereas Bell stood in his own light and apparently would not have them. Mr. Hamlin had called him up at Harrison's Landing when he rejoined after three days' duty at General Kearny's head-quarters, and told him promotion was sure to follow such a report as Kearny's chief-of-staff sent in, whereat Bell had deliberately told his squadron leader that promotion was the last thing he wanted,—it involved too much responsibility. All the same, Hamlin named him corporal on the way to the Long Bridge, and that was the last he saw of his new non-commissioned officer until the provost-marshal's people handed him over four days later, arrested in the streets of Washington without a pass and apparently majestically drunk. To all questions as to his regiment, etc., he had persisted in saying that he belonged to the New York Seventh (which was mustered out of service before first Bull Run), and that he had been left behind when they went home. But the provost-marshal's people were regulars, and some orderly riding by recognized Beau Bell of Hamlin's squadron, "Chickahominy" Bell, as some one started to call him, and Beau, erect, dignified, unabashed, had begged the patrol to come around to a certain stable and permit him to examine his saddle-bags and establish his own identity. Thither they escorted him, and found his horse and equipments all right. Beau gravely handed out a ten-dollar bill for his care and keep, proposed to his captors a joint visit to the bar at Willard's, where he would gladly set up the champagne for such charming companions, and professed much surprise and disappointment at their refusal. He was perfectly quiet and gentlemanly, said they, never used a cuss word or gave the faintest trouble, only he did want some champagne despite the war tariff then beginning to soar. Hamlin received his semi-deserter with official sternness, and told him the corporalship was revoked. Bell promptly thanked the lieutenant and asked if, that point being settled in his favor, he might now go and groom his horse. Hamlin didn't know whether to be angry or amused. He concluded that Bell was an original who would bear watching. He had only recently learned that it was he who used up Devlin.

Full twenty minutes had elapsed since the arrival of the squadron at the ferry, and still the clumsy scow that did duty as a ferry-boat had not reached them. The river was not so low as to make fording a comfort, besides, Hamlin's orders were not to cross. Late as it was, weary as it was, the day's work for his command was not yet done. All he asked for was a quantity of coffee, sugar, bacon, and bread which was now being ferried over. His men could cook their own supper among the trees along the south bank and be off about their business before moonrise. He stood impatiently tapping his booted foot upon the rock at the shore and commenting audibly upon the draggy movements of the ferrymen when his first sergeant again approached.

"Trooper Bell, sir, asks permission to speak with the lieutenant."

"What's he want?"

"I don't know, sir. He said he preferred not to say except to the commanding officer."

"Well, let him come."

A minute later the Duke stood erect before his young commander. It was their first interview since just before the brush at Crampton's Gap, on which occasion Bell had begged to be relieved from duty with the wagons, where he had been kept under a cloud since the Washington episode, and permitted to go in with his troop.

"I understand that the squadron merely cooks supper here, sir, and then rides on. May I have permission to take my horse and go back with the ferry-boat and be gone three days?"

"Certainly not, Bell. I'm surprised at your asking."

"Well, sir, I can bring more information from that side in three days than the lieutenant can get on this in a month."

Hamlin's eyes looked angry. Neither the words

nor the tone were such as he was accustomed to from his men. "You speak boldly, Bell, and not too respectfully. One would suppose you knew all about my orders. How do you know what information I need?"

"Because, sir, I was the major's orderly all yesterday and last night, and because the man you're looking for—isn't on this side of the Potomac."

CHAPTER II.

An hour later even the tiny cook-fires that had been glowing along the southern bank were smouldering into ashes. The troopers had silently remounted, men and beasts weary yet refreshed by the bountiful supply of rations or grain. The ferry scow still swung at her moorings from the Virginia side, and as the squadron filed away into the darkness of the wooded bank, Lieutenant Hamlin stood at the water's edge, pencilling some lines in his note-book. Then tearing out a leaf he handed it to the infantry officer who, with a file of the guard, had come over to meet the troopers and inquire for news from the front.

"I have signed receipts for forage and rations, captain," said Hamlin, "and have written a brief report to the commanding officer at Frederick. Will you kindly take Trooper Bell over with you and pass him back should he return this way?"

The older officer hesitated in some surprise. "I don't quite understand," he said. "It has taken a general officer's authority to pass a man over, so far." And he looked at the simple shoulder-strap of the young regular in some perplexity. Even so late as the second year of the war there were volunteer officers who thought that the regular knew more about the minor details of service, at least, than the lately commissioned amateur. Hamlin saw his embarrassment and smiled.

"It's all right, captain, and I'll be responsible. I've written him a pass, and I have no superiors, as you see. I'm my own colonel and brigade commander to-night. Now I must ride after my men. Bell, report to this gentleman. Good-night, captain." And with that he turned. The German trumpeter promptly led forward the reluctant horses; Hamlin swung lightly into saddle and rode briskly up the steep incline. "Dutchy" got his foot in stirrup, as his own horse started in pursuit, and went clattering after his commander, clinging to the pommel and mane, and only settling into his seat as he disappeared over the top of the bank. Then even the sound of hoof-beats died away in the gathering darkness, and only the plash of the water broke the stillness of the autumn night. By the gleam of his lantern the infantry officer stood poring over the scrap of paper Hamlin had thrust into his hand. It read as follows: "I have given Trooper Bell authority to remain on the north side and to visit friends down the river after having delivered his despatches at Frederick. If he should not be back in three days oblige me by sending a squad to the Heatherwood place, a mile below you, to make inquiries. It will bear watching anyway."

Twice the captain read this missive over, and then peered into the gloom in search of Bell. The trooper's tall figure was only faintly outlined. He stood there in statuesque silence, a firm hand closed on the bit of his uneasy horse, now pawing impatiently and striving to see what had become of his companions. Finally the captain spoke.

"Come this way, will you?" he called, hardly knowing how to address this tall cavalryman, and Bell silently advanced a few paces and again stood at attention, his horse once more tugging and pawing and switching from side to side, yet never shaking loose his master's hold.

"You are all ready to start?" said the captain, doubtfully.

"All ready, sir."

"Then I suppose you might as well lead aboard."

"After you, sir," said Bell, and waited until the officer had stepped across the hinged staging before he followed. The boatmen swayed down on their rope, the stage was hoisted, and they shoved off across the placid surface of the stream, all dotted now with faint, phosphorescent night lights, the reflection of the peeping stars. Seeing that the trooper remained at the stern of the slow-moving boat, patting and reassuring his steed, two or three of the guard ranged backward towards him and began their soldier scrutiny. The captain himself turned and listened. They were men of a far New England regiment, serious-minded fellows, deeply imbued with the solemnity of the duty which had called them so far from home and into scenes so strange.

They were but a few weeks from their native hills and new at campaigning, and this was not only a veteran of many fields and a cavalry soldier at that,—a something strange even to the farmers' boys among them,—but a something stranger still, a "regular," a thing no one of their number had ever seen before that day, and that some, indeed, had never heard of except as wearing a British uniform, and being drubbed at Concord Bridge and Bunker Hill. They stood somewhat awkwardly by, closely watching Bell as he passed his hands over girth and buckle and curb and rein, and then rubbed his horse's legs as though to see that all was in readiness for a night ride. There was sympathy and deep interest in their gaze, but, though all were eager to question, no one of the number seemed to care to be the first to speak.

At last as Bell straightened up and looked about him, first at the nearing watch-fire on the northern shore, then at the night lights gleaming aloft in the autumn skies, one of the party, a farmer's boy who knew whereof he spoke, took the best road he could think of to a trooper's confidence, and diffidently bestowing a friendly pat on the charger's shoulder, as diffidently remarked, "Look's though he'd had no loafin' time lately."

"Devil a minute," was the laconic answer, but it was enough. The ice was broken. The others drew nearer. The bearded captain—a school-master at home—came close to the group. The stranger had used an expletive, and thereby established a desired fact,—he was not of superior mould.

"Been fur to-day?" asked the first speaker, presently.

"Well, not so many miles in a bee-line, but we've had a good deal of dodging and prowling and scouting to do." Bell's stomach was warmed by coffee, or was it the unexpected nip from Hamlin's proffered flask before the start? and he had grown affable. He knew these fellows for recent levies at a glance. Their uniforms had not lost their gloss or buttons. Their belts and buckles and cap ornaments were unbattered, and few old soldiers can resist the joy of adulation from the new. Well he understood what else they wished to hear, and so went on: "There's quite a force of rebel cavalry screening the enemy's left flank. He's marching south, and their fellows are well out this way, popping through the gaps in the range every now and then, and we've been stumbling into them for the last three days."

"Had any fighting?" queried the captain, chiming in now, as interested as his men.

"Well, nothing to speak of, sir," answered the trooper, facing instantly towards him and bringing heels together and hand to cap visor at once, a something that afforded the officer unspeakable comfort. It was just what he wanted his men to learn, yet hardly knew how to teach. As for them, they noted the action as promptly as did their captain, and exchanged quick and appreciative glances. Later that night they were showing comrades at the camp-fire how the regular did it.

"We lost a couple of horses shot near Aldie, sir," continued Bell, "and left two rebs and one of our fellows wounded at a farm-house under the heights. You see there is nothing but cavalry over there,—of our side, at least, and not too many of us. I don't suppose we've three hundred all told, and our squadron's about used up."

"Where were they going from here?" asked the captain.

"I don't know, sir, exactly. Back to join the main body, possibly. I suppose we're expected to cover all this front out here to prevent their coming through the gaps and appearing suddenly across the river opposite you. May I ask your regiment, sir?"

"—th New Hampshire. We're guarding the ferry and the bridges along the canal hereabouts. We've only been here a few days, and it's pretty novel work to my boys. I—'spose you've been at it a good while."

"Not a year, sir. That is," and here the trooper faltered a bit, "not a year in the cavalry. I saw something of the first month or two of the mischief."

They were nearing the northern shore now, and could dimly see that a little group of shadowy forms was gathered at the landing awaiting them.

"We had an idea," said the officer, after a pause, "that most of the rank and file in the regulars were foreigners,—Irish and German,—uneducated men, but, excuse me, you're an American, and *you* haven't lacked schooling."

Bell's gravity gave way to an amused grin. "We're every kind, sir," said he, without answering the hint as to himself. "Mostly reprobates like myself," he added, inaudibly.

The boat came slowly grinding upon the shelving shore, and horse, trooper, and his interrogators all lurched at the interrupted way. "I presume the lieutenant showed the captain my pass and it's all right for me to push ahead at once," said Bell.

"It's all right," answered the officer. "I may have to explain to our colonel, who's just back here a piece across the canal, but you can tell him what I can't. We'll go right over to his tent." So saying, the captain led the way through a group of silent, but inquisitive soldiers, dimly visible in the starlight, and Bell strode after him, his horse following at his heels. They passed some scattered tents, a brightly blazing fire, about which, standing or sitting, or stretched upon the ground, were a dozen armed and belted infantrymen, one or two of whom essayed a half-sheepish salute, and then gazed curiously at the captain's convoy. They crossed the dry bed of the canal by a heavily arched wooden bridge and came in sudden view of a cluster of white tentage where men were whistling, singing, lolling, or skylarking about, and, passing through a bustling canvas village, following a necessarily irregular camp street, they halted presently in front of a large and more pretentious tent where paced a sentry and within whose guarded walls could be heard manly voices in lively chat, while the shadows of stalwart forms were thrown upon the screen of its sloping roofs. The captain tapped at the tent-pole, and evoked no reply. The flaps were down, so he pushed one aside and inserted his face.

"Colonel Clark," said he, "can I see you a moment?"

"Hello, captain! That you?" answered a ringing voice. "Come right in, Frisby. Come in."

The instant Trooper Bell heard the name of the commanding officer, he stopped short in his tracks. The instant he heard his voice he was restored to action, sprang to his horse's side and thrust his left foot into stirrup.

"I can't very well," answered Captain Frisby. "I've got a courier here whom I brought over from the cavalry party. He wants to push right on in the direction of Frederick, but I said he must see you first. Can you come out a moment, sir?"

"Certainly," was the hearty answer, and the officer came striding massively forward, the tent floor creaking and bending beneath his weight. "Where's your orderly?" he asked, as he threw open the flap and gazed out into the night. Captain Frisby turned quickly to where he had left Bell but a moment before,—and horse and rider had vanished.

Not five seconds later, out under the stars to the northwest, there was sudden shout, challenge, order, and warning all jumbled into one.

"Who comes there? HaltorI'llfire! Halt! HALT!" And then—*Bang!*

All to no purpose. Far to the northward, spurred to mad excitement, galloping as though for life, a horse went tearing through the gloaming, reckless of pursuing shout or shot, and when rider Bell drew rein and calmed him down, and wiped his own heated brow, he muttered malediction on his luck, listened a moment to assure him no pursuit was to be dreaded, then, quitting the northern road and reining abruptly to the right as he came to the first crossing, he once more urged his horse to a lope and muttered between his set teeth, "Not for a fortune—now."

CHAPTER III.

THE bees were humming about their hives in the old orchard. The sun was sending slanting beams through the leafy branches and painting the slopes in shifting patches of gold and green. There was on every side the drowsy sound of buzzing insect life, and from below the languorous plashing of waters. Away off to the northwestward, beyond the broad, fertile, hamlet-dotted valley, a deep rift was cut into the long chain of blue hills that stretched from north to south, and from this rift a silver ribbon came winding through the middle distance, joined from the heart of the northward valley by a slender thread, shining and shimmering as itself, that poured into the larger only a mile away and seemed so potent a force as to bend the great river in almost abrupt right angle. Aloft the vault of heaven burned unclouded. Southward a soft haze seemed rising above the dense groves of timber, fringing the banks of the broader stream as it swept towards the sea. Westward, as though backing the barrier range, heavy masses of cloud rolled up against the blue. Creeping slowly southward along the smaller stream, a long train of white dots seemed on its way towards a thick cluster of other white dots, nestling in the timber at the water's edge, while parallel with the broader river there wound and curved and twisted the long, snaky bed of the old canal, ruined, for the time being, by recent raiders in Confederate gray. Here and there, in the timber at the water's edge, thin columns of bluish smoke curled upward through the tree-tops, and farther away across the valley, in heavier masses and from different points, lazily drifting smoke clouds thinned and finally vanished in the upper air. Away off to the southwestward there rose, in several places, between the eye and the blue-black line of the heights, dull, dun-colored masses of cloud that were drifting slowly southward, despite the fact that not a breath of wind had rustled the forest leaves since dawn. Down in the meadow underneath the slope on which was perched the orchard a dozen cows were drowsing in the shade, and the faint tinkle of bells came floating like far-away music. Somewhere, just beyond the hedgerow of wild-rose-bushes, at the northward side, over whose tops the roofs of some barn-like structures could be seen, a horse had been browsing but a while ago, for the swish of his tail and the impatient stamp as he strove to drive off the winged pests that hovered about him, and the occasional *b-r-r-r-r* that told of equine peace and contentment had frequently been heard, but he, too, seemed to have lain down somewhere for a snooze, and was heard no more. Over across the orchard, on its southern side, a venerable wooden paling was peeping in spots through the bushes and shrubbery by which it was well-nigh hidden. Here and there were gaps in hedge and paling both, evidently utilized in by-gone hours by animals both two- and four-footed, resentful of the fact that no gate-way broke the defiant line. Barbed wire was unknown in those days, and the gaps stood open now, available either for marauders or defence, and the stripped condition of the trees too plainly indicated that the former had had the better of it thus far. Only a few high-perched apples or pears remained to tell the story. Bounding the orchard at the east was another hedge and paling, and a dislocated gate that swung, cat-a-cornered, from its upper hinge and could not close at all despite the persuasive powers of a ball and chain, and through the yard-wide gap of the gate-way and the thick foliage beyond, occasional glimpses of dingy white wall, whiter columns, and one green-latticed window were had,—the westward gable end and southern portico of an old-fashioned Southern mansion, one that unquestionably must have known far better days, and that now, like nature all around it, had gone placidly, contentedly to sleep.

For over an hour not a human being had been seen or heard about the barn, out-houses, or orchard. Once or twice, somewhere down along the old towpath that skirted the canal, some drowsy voices had been uplifted, and a big hound with flapping ears and a face expressive of general benevolence had roused himself from a cool bed he had pawed out under the bushes, and cocked his head on one side as much as to say, "I wonder who can be fool enough to stay awake at this hour of the day;" then as the sounds subsided he, too, dropped back to doze. It was long after four o'clock, so told the mouldering face of the old sun-dial on the lawn in front of the colonnaded portico, and even the voices down along the canal had drowsed away. The shadow of the copper arm was crawling close to the antiquated V when at last the silence was broken. Somewhere across the lazily flowing river there rang, sharp and clear, the report of a rifle, a report that went echoing down the broadening valley. Somewhere down along the towpath there was quick stir and excitement, and an authoritative voice was heard in brief order, "Fall in the guard!" Somewhere at the rear of the mansion a door slammed aggressively, and a feminine voice, shrill and piercing, was heard in confident summons, in answer to which, rubbing his eyes and stumbling sleepily into the sunshine, a big, burly negro, clad only in loose cotton shirt and trousers, appeared in front of the wood-shed and humbly answered, "Yeassum."

"Miss Belle wants that horse saddled right away."

"Yeassum."

"Don' you go to sleep again while you're 'bout it, now."

"Nome."

And then the hitherto invisible lady advanced from the regions at the rear, tripped briskly through the garden at the west side of the house, and came with a vivacious, bouncing step between the decrepit gate-posts, dealing a contemptuous kick at the gate as she did so, and once fairly in the orchard poured forth her soul in song.

It could not be called a musical voice. Neither in style nor execution could she be considered a pleasing singer. Her lay was one of the folk-songs of the ante-bellum days, descriptive, as were most of them, of the matchless charms of some village maid whose early dissolution, told in most pathetic verse, seemed the invariable penalty attached to such preternatural gifts of mind and person. Following, as did this rural ditty, so closely upon the recent silence, its effect was intensified upon the hearers, who were fortunately few.

> " 'Twas a ca-am still night and the moon's pale light
> Sho-one soft o'er hill a-and va-ale,"

she began, and the old hound moved uneasily. A black felt hat with a straggling feather in it loomed up across the hedge towards the south, and a sunburnt, fuzz-covered face peered eagerly through the bushes, but the girl gave no heed. She was walking rapidly through the orchard as she sang, and gazing expectantly down the slope towards the little grove that lay close by the water's edge to the west. Reaching the boundary of the enclosure she stopped short and, louder, shriller than before, gave voice to the chorus.

" Aw Lillay—sweet Lillay—dee-ur Lillay Day-ul,
 Aw the wild rose blossoms awer the little green grave
 Whey-ur lies sw-ee-eet Lil*lay*—uh Dale."

And then she paused and listened, and the fuzzy face under the black hat at the fence gazed more earnestly than at first, for the girl was worth seeing, even though she couldn't sing.

She certainly was not more than eighteen. She was short in stature, but plump and round and wholesome as a ripe, sound winter apple. She was erect, and she moved with a vigorous, natural ease and grace. Her cheeks were rosy, her eyes and hair almost jet-black, her lips red and full, and her little teeth milk-white. She wore a loose summer jacket, open at the round, white throat. Her skirt was shaped, after the fashion of the day, like one of the beehives,—round, inflated, and voluminous. A broad-brimmed straw hat dangled upon her arm. Her little feet were cased in queer, shining, black silk gaiters that laced up the side and ended abruptly at the ankle. Her hair, parted in the middle, was brushed down low over the temples, puffed out over the ears, and done up in some kind of a knot low down at the back of the neck. The slanting sunbeams dazzled her; she shaded her eyes with her hand, which was not as white as it might have been, and in so doing revealed a plump little arm that was as white as her pretty teeth. She was an impatient little body, as any one could see, and the man under the black hat did see, for she stamped her foot on the wooden bench to which she had suddenly mounted, and said, "Botheration!" most emphatically, and then when it looked as though she were just about to begin to sing again, the black hat came poking through a hole in the hedge, the fuzz-covered, sunburnt face came after it, and finally a tall, slim sprig of a soldier boy, dressed in the uncouth, single-breasted frock coat of the early war days, straightened up and strode towards her, ducking under the lower branches as he came. Not until he was close to her side did she hear him. First she gave utterance to the beginning of a squeal, then switched off to contemptuous, even indignant personalities.

"Aw, here you are! I thought you'd *nevuh* come."

"That's what I've been thinking of you for a whole hour," was the mild response.

"Well, *I* have something to do, I'll have you know," was the majestic rejoinder. "You have nothing, but eat, sleep, and make believe guard a rotten old bridge. Why didn't you speak when I called?"

"Didn't like to interrupt your song. It was real—splendid," said the tall youth, with lavish admiration in his eyes.

"Well, better late than never. Least it will be if you do what I tell you. What's the captain's name down at the bridge?"

"'Tain't a captain. It's the lieutenant,—Homans."

"Well, you tell Mr. Homans Madam Heatherwood wants to see him before sunset, and the quicker he comes the better, and don't let her catch *you* in this orchard or round these premises, or she'll set Patsy on you sure as your name's—well, what's your real name, anyhow? I believe you're trying to fool me. Who ever heard of a man's being called Reuben Pettingill?"

"That's my name, anyhow—prove it by the parson any time or by the muster-roll. Now, aren't you going to tell me yourn?"

"Mine, as I told you," very majestically, "is *Miss* Wad*dell*. Don't you dare call me Waddle, as that horror of a captain did. He'd better not show his ugly face here again. *Our* young man's back from the wars, I'd have you know, and when he's here no Yankees need apply."

" 'Tisn't your last name I care for," persisted Private Pettingill. "That'll be changed soon enough, I guess. What's the first name? Kitty, Patty, Sally?"

"Sally—your grandmother! D'you think my people had no sense of decency when they named me? You cla' out now and tell your captain what Madam Heatherwood said, and you can't fetch him up here any too quick."

Then once again, sudden and sharp, a rifle-shot rang out across the placid waters, and the echoes, as before, crashed away down-stream. The girl started nervously and anxiously and gazed back at the house. "Do hurry, Mr.—Mr. Pettingill," she pleaded, "and I'll tell you my name next time."

"But—Gosh all hemlock! Say, don't run away yet," he begged, as she started as though to leave him. "I've been waitin' all day to see you, and maybe they'll shoot me dead for not bein' there when the guard fell in a while ago."

"Fell in what?" she asked, and then, as with sudden rejoicing, "the canal? That would do some of them good."

"Fell in ranks," he exclaimed, cubbishly trying to seize her sunburnt hand, a proceeding which she readily defeated, even though letting him come dangerously near success. "There's no use in my telling the lieutenant to come up now. He knows all about your having wounded rebs in there. They're both paroled, or exchanged, or something. He told us fellows all about it two days ago. They can't do the Union any harm laid up as they are, but the lieutenant says if any of us fellers get shot over yonder," and with a nod of his black-hatted head the soldier indicated the opposite Virginia shore, "we needn't think to get out of prison to be cared for at our sweetheart's home———"

"'Course not," interposed Miss Waddell, with pert promptitude. "What lady down South would be having a Yankee beau for a gift? *I'd* have to be hard up for a lover even here before *I'd* think of such a thing." And here the damsel shot a sidelong glance from the depths of her saucy eyes. How much could the fellow stand, she wondered. Not much more, apparently. He was vexed already, and seriously, too, for he turned sharply away, dropping instantly the slender wrist of which he had just managed to possess himself. Was he going to leave her like that, disenchanted, disenthralled? No woman on earth could stand that.

"Wait one moment," she faltered. "I forgot another thing Miss Heatherwood told me to say." But Private Pettingill had already got half-way back to the hole in the fence. "Mr. Pettingill, don't be—silly. *I* didn't mean anything—Reuben," she continued, and the Reuben mollified him. He turned with rapture in his eyes and came striding back.

"Say it again," he said.

"Say what?" she asked, in wide-eyed innocence, —"that no Southern lady'd have a Yankee for a gift?"

Again he turned from her.

"Or was it only just"—tantalizing pause—"Reub-en?"

And before he could reply, "Bang!" the third time, and clearer, sharper than before, the rifle-shot rang out beyond the river, and gazing across the stream both girl and soldier could see where a faint little patch of powder-smoke was sailing aloft in the dense timber. Almost immediately another voice, a woman's voice, clear, bell-like, penetrating, rose upon the air,—

"Laura! Where are you?"

"There, now, you've made her come hunting for me. You've got to go. Mind you don't forget—to-morrow." And with this parting piece of coquetry, away she ran, bounding up the worn pathway, through the ruined gate, and out of his sight. Almost at the same instant, too, the negro came forth from the stable-yard, leading a tall bay horse equipped with cavalry housing of the United States army. The dark-blue saddle-cloth edged with yellow, with the regimental number in the corner, was new and glossy. The bridle and breast-strap were black and polished, so were the holsters at the pommel. Even Pettingill, volunteer infantryman of a few weeks' service, knew at a glance it was a cavalry officer's horse and equipment, and suddenly, as the girl would have started round to the back of the house, the big front door was heard to open and out upon the broad porch came a tall, distinguished-looking officer, and with him a tall, graceful girl, whose eyes were upturned to his in silent pleading and farewell. The sight was too much for Laura. She turned in her tracks, ran to the end of the house, and, barely exposing half her pretty face, peered eagerly around the corner, saw him hand the darky groom a *douceur* that made that humble servitor bow and grin and scrape with delight, and then, bending forward and taking both the slender white hands of the tall girl in his own, the officer kissed her white forehead, turned suddenly away, sprang to his saddle, and rode clattering down the pebbly drive to the road below.

"My sakes alive!" exclaimed Miss Laura Waddell. "If Captain Tighlman was to see that, wounds couldn't keep him abed. And to think of Belle Heatherwood kissing a Yankee, even if he is an officer!"

Meantime, Private Pettingill had made the best of his way down the wooded slope, and presently found himself among a curious knot of his comrades, all demanding explanation of his whereabouts when the guard formed a while before, but the soldier parried all inquiry by saying he had been away on a mission for the lieutenant and must report to him at once. Another moment found him standing before a serious-looking young man in the dark-blue frock that, but for its brass buttons and shoulder-straps, would have been declared the coat of a country parson, so utterly clerical, so totally unmilitary, was its cut. Leaning against a tree close at hand were the officer's sword and belt and the crimson sash so soon discarded when once the wearer fairly took the field.

"I was asked to tell you that Mrs. Heatherwood wanted to see you up at the house before sunset, lieutenant," said the soldier. "There was one of our officers there."

"One of ours?" asked the lieutenant, in much surprise. "When did he get there? When did he come?"

"I don't know. He rode out not ten minutes ago, down towards the east. He belongs to the cavalry."

"And we have guards on every road," exclaimed the lieutenant. "Are you sure, Pettingill? Describe his dress."

"Just like yours, as far as I could see from a distance, only I saw the yellow border to his saddle-cloth before I started. Say, here he comes now!"

Surely enough, out from a wooded aisle close at hand, at easy, quiet gait, came riding the same tall, stalwart officer, dressed in trimly fitting cavalry uniform. His cap with its crossed sabres, his equipments, his glistening scabbard and hilt were all as handsome in quality as his dress and the high, well-made boots. His face was oval, deeply tanned and clean shaved but for the light-brown moustache and imperial. His blue eyes were full of intelligence and fire. His form as he sat erect in saddle was splendidly modelled. He looked the picture of the officer and the gentleman, and his cordial, ringing voice, the moment he spoke, intensified the pleasant impression he made.

"Good-evening, sir," he said, courteously raising his cap to the young commander of the detachment. "Let me introduce myself. I am Captain Belden, of General Hooker's staff, on my way to Harper's Ferry after a mission to Washington. I heard that firing across the river and turned back to ask what it meant."

"I don't know," was the slow reply. "We can't get over from here. A boat with a patrol crossed a mile above us about twenty minutes ago, apparently to hunt up the cause. The second bullet came right over here somewhere. Our men could see no sign of the fellow who stirred us up."

"Odd," said the horseman. "I heard three shots, I think, and turned out of my way to inquire. I knew you had pickets every few hundred yards along here. Well, good-evening to you. Oh! would you mind passing me out, as some of your sentries are vigilant and suspicious both?"

The infantryman picked up sword and belt and said, "I suppose it's all right. Er—will you come this way?"

At the outpost the corporal of the picket was duly notified, and the captain passed on out of the lines.

"Beg pardon, sir," asked the officer of the guard, "but what name was yours? I may have to give account. I didn't quite catch it."

"Belden—Grosvenor Belden, at your service. Thank you a thousand times. Good-evening, lieutenant."

"Grosvenor Belden," muttered the lieutenant, as the trooper rode away. "And what was Grosvenor doing at old mother Heatherwood's? Now, if I weren't new to this business I should say a fellow ought to show his credentials, or something, riding away from his regiment as he is. But he couldn't have come thus far without being overhauled time and again. If the provost-marshal's people have passed him along I suppose we can."

Instead, however, of returning to the main body of his little command, the young volunteer stood there at the turn of the country road, following with his eyes the graceful figure of the horseman, as he rode easily and leisurely away. He had passed out from the shade of the grove, and the golden sunshine, slanting almost to the horizontal, poured forth upon the soldierly form and upon the powerful, spirited horse. The brilliant steel of the new scabbard glistened like a mirror and threw off dazzling flashes of white light, and the lieutenant wondered how it was that this young gallant should look so trim and spick and span when all other officers who had happened to pass with their commands were dusty and travel-stained. Something was queer about it, but he couldn't tell what. It was too late to question now. The vanishing horseman, still riding leisurely on, was swallowed up in the shades of another grove, three hundred yards up-stream, and at last was lost to view.

And then the lieutenant bethought him of the message brought by Pettingill. Turning slowly away, he went back to his tent, left there his sword and belt, and then clambered the wooded bluff across the road. The path was old and worn, the ascent was steep, and once at the top and in sight of the portico, he stopped to recover breath. The sun was just ready to dip behind the screen of the distant Loudoun heights, and the shadows of the fluted columns were thrown far across the eastward lawn and the pasture-field beyond. Above and below many of the windows of the mansion were open to receive the soft, flower-scented air, and at one of these, on the main floor, a woman sat, a woman with silvery hair and a face high-bred, refined, yet worn with care and anxiety, if not with illness. Evidently she was looking for his coming, for she rose at once and presently appeared at the main hall-way, beckoning her half-reluctant visitor to approach.

The lieutenant hesitated a moment, cast a backward glance down through the thick growth of timber that covered the steep bank, as though to assure himself that all was well with his little camp, then came forward to meet the lady of the house. He raised his forage-cap as he stood before her, simply saying, "You sent for me, madam."

"I did, sir, and to ask a favor at your hands. Forgive me for referring to the fact that the officer who preceded you in command was here so long as to become quite one of the family, and to visit us frequently, and now that he—Captain Ainslie—is gone we feel very friendless. I know we are necessarily objects of suspicion, especially since the battle and my boys were brought here wounded, but whatever their sympathies and mine, we are disarmed, we are harmless. My son's wounds will keep him on his back at least a month. My nephew's are less severe, but he has given his parole. We can't be very dangerous, can we?" she asked, with an almost tearful smile, looking pleadingly into the young volunteer's troubled face. "You have your own mother at home, have you not? Can't you fancy how she would feel with you brought back to her roof as I brought my boy from that wretched farm-house at the Gap, and if our soldiers were keeping guard over your home as you are over mine——"

"Surely our guard has been a protection, Mrs. Heatherwood," he interposed, a little stiffly.

"In many ways, yes," she answered, "yet of late it galls—sometimes. What I have to ask is such a little thing, yet it means so much to us. You heard—those shots across the river, did you not? They meant no harm to you, no wrong to your government, but they mean there is news of serious consequence to us. Laura's home—my niece's home—was over there towards Leesburg. Her father took up arms with his State when Virginia seceded. Her mother, my only sister, has been dead many a long year. Her two brothers are in the Confederate service, in the cavalry. The old home is abandoned except by faithful family servants. It is one of them that has come to the opposite bank, and has been striving to call our attention. He has letters for Laura. You may read every line, if need be. He brings us tidings of her home, of her father and brothers. Surely it isn't giving too much aid and comfort to an enemy in distress"—and here flitted about the lines of her mouth the same sad, pleading smile—"to let that poor child hear from those she loves? Our boat lies down there under the willows. May we not send our negro over?"

The officer hesitated. "My orders are strict," said he, "to allow no communication with the opposite shore. I cannot let him go. I could not go myself; but I'll tell you, Mrs. Heatherwood, they sent a boat over from the post a mile farther up-stream. They are sure to find that messenger, if he wants to be found, and I will go or send up there the moment we see them coming back. Will that answer?"

A shade of deepest disappointment, even of deep distress, swept over her face. "I fear not. He'll never give his letter or messages—to your comrades. Oh, think——" But her plea ended abruptly.

Again from the southern shore rang out the report of the rifle. Again the echoes went reverberating down from bank to bank, and then gave way to new alarm, for fierce and sudden the crash of a volley of musketry woke the echoes anew, and with blanching face Madam Heatherwood tottered within her threshold, while the Union officer, springing to the bank, went plunging down the steep to join his men.

CHAPTER IV.

AGAIN the sun had sunk behind the distant jagged line of heights, its parting rays thrown aslant through a red-gold haze of dust rising far to the westward beyond dense groves and copses. From somewhere among the trees up-stream along the Virginia shore a heavy cloud of blue-black smoke had risen and hung awhile, then, drifting away before the slow, sluggish breath of the coming night wind, had given place to eddying volumes, pallid and gray, telling that the conflagration had spent its force and that there was nothing left to consume within the ruined walls of some homestead, sacrificed within the hour upon the altar of the god of war. All along the banks of the canal bed little groups of men in Union blue were gazing curiously and excitedly across the swirling river. Above at the ferry, and here underneath the wooded steep on which was perched the old Heatherwood place, the guard still stood in ranks, and among the tents of the New Hampshire regiment, to the east of the Monocacy, Colonel Clark still held his strong battalion under arms, awaiting further development from the southern shore. Somewhere over there opposite Heatherwood, beyond the thick woods at the sharp bend, there had been a savage fight of over ten minutes' duration,—a cavalry affair, undoubtedly, for mounted men in the yellow-laced jackets of Uncle Sam were even now twinkling in and out of the forest aisles, some leading spare horses, some aiding wounded comrades, some riding eagerly down to the water's edge in search of a drink for themselves and their thirsting steeds. Up-stream at the landing the flat ferry-boat was still moored at the Virginia bank, and several of the patrol recently sent across to investigate the cause of the single shots were seen slowly returning, leading with them two or three men in dusty gray, men who limped or faltered painfully, and officers on the Maryland shore were curiously studying these groups with their field-glasses and commenting on the situation.

At the ferry, Captain Frisby, whose company was of the guard, had unhesitatingly announced the Union troopers to be men of Hamlin's squadron, the same that appeared to them the evening previous, for he had recognized Hamlin himself; but who on earth were their opponents? The yells that followed the volleying outburst were unmistakable, so were these few uniforms, but Stuart, with his bold column of raiders, was believed to be far away at the moment. Only old "Foulweather," as the troopers designated the field-officer commanding the detachment of Union regulars scouting east of the Loudoun range, was supposed to be in that section of Virginia. Yet the fury and volume of the firing, brief though the engagement had been, and the enthusiasm of the enemy as shown by their exultant yells, were proof enough that Confederate cavalry had managed to force some gap in the screening ridge to the west and come exploring down to the very banks of the Potomac, right here to its sharpest elbow, almost directly opposite the mouth of the Monocacy.

And old Foulweather had got wind of them only just in time, too. The curtaining ridge lay barely five miles away to the west, and Leesburg, where Bob Hamlin had left his leader on the previous day, could almost be seen from the upper windows of the Heatherwood house, nestling in the heart of the beautifully wooded country just beyond the next great bend of the Potomac, where once more the majestic river swept eastward to the sea. Foulweather was a weazel who slept, when he deigned to sleep at all, with one eye open and the saddle for a pillow, and Foulweather had need to be alert, for every hamlet in Loudoun, Fauquier, and Fairfax Counties teemed with active sympathizers of the South, women who had given husbands and fathers, sons and brothers, to the cause, and would have given their heart's blood as well. Men there were none left to offer old Foulweather battle, but he would have met them by battalions, single-handed with his own old squadron, rather than a group of those rural Virginia dames, armed only with their wits and tongues. Somewhere among those farms, hamlets, or stately old colonial homesteads there had been in hiding ever since Antietam one of the boldest leaders of Virginia horse. Slightly wounded in some cavalry affair of outposts, he had been left behind when Lee made his first leap into Maryland. A negro bearing letters to him from comrades in the First Virginia Cavalry had been captured by Foulweather's scouts, but when that burly leader swooped with his squadron on Leesburg and surrounded the home of the young gallant, he found no foeman worthy his steel, and his ears buzzed for hours through the vituperation excited by his unbidden call. Foulweather's temper was never the best, neither was the court language of the old-time dragoon, and he said things that made Bob Hamlin blush for him, and that disgusted his occasional orderly, Trooper Bell. Foulweather had gone back towards Aldie with most of his force, sending Hamlin with orders to communicate with the pickets at the Potomac opposite the Monocacy, and then to scout the little valley west of the first range, for Foulweather was bound to capture Captain Fairfax if fighting, scouting, or searching could do it. And even in the midst of his schemings, into the midst of his force, in fact, Captain Fairfax's own troop had burst through Clark's Gap, swept like a whirlwind into Leesburg, followed their guide to within sight and hail of Heatherwood when they found their captain no longer there, and then had been met and grappled by Hamlin's squadron, galloping back to intercept them, and had stemmed and held and fought it like men until enabled successfully to withdraw, Bob Hamlin storming and old Foulweather swearing at their heels, with only a few prisoners to pay for all their trouble.

The sounds of strife had died away to the west. The pursuit was feeble, for the Southerners were fresh and few in number, the Union troopers worn with long days and nights of scout and sleeplessness; their horses, too, were "leg weary" and jaded. When darkness settled down and the ferry-boat came drifting over with its cargo of wounded prisoners, officers and men intermingled, as was the fashion of the early war days, Colonel Clark's New Hampshire soldiers swarmed along the bank, eager for details of the exciting event. There were nearly a dozen Union troopers shot or sabred. There were only five Virginians in their gray cavalry jackets and gayly plumed hats. Four of these were sabred, one had been dragged by a wounded charger. All were suffering, but all were silent. With a later boat-load came old Foulweather himself, exhausting questions and threats in vain effort to extract from the prisoners information as to whether the dash had been successful, whether Captain Fairfax had indeed been found, rescued, and hurried away by his triumphant men. The Virginians grinned, partly from pain, partly from pleasure, and would only say that they believed and would bet the result was all that was hoped for. They couldn't say for sure their beloved captain was actually carried away; they wouldn't say where he was in any event. All they agreed upon was the remark, extracted from one of their number, "If Captain Fairfax did get away, you'll know it inside of twelve hours, sure as you're born." And this did not comfort Foulweather in the least.

An ugly man in his talk was Foulweather, as has been said, and he was the madder for being tricked, baffled, and outdone by that little troop of Virginians. Knowing every bridle-path and rabbit-track, these natives had easily evaded his patrols and scouts, had taken prompt advantage of the splitting up of his command, and had swooped down from the heights the moment he and Hamlin had, between them, uncovered the ground they sought to penetrate. Only by chance did Hamlin get word of the dash, and, wheeling about, had headed for Leesburg at the trot, sending couriers 'cross country to his superior, urging that Foulweather cover all the roads to the Gaps and thus cut off the Confederates' retreat, while he, Hamlin, attacked them in front when found. He found them several miles nearer and many minutes sooner than he expected, and got a volley before the mêlée of the charge that followed.

Hamlin had brawn and grit, discipline and numbers to oppose to the daring and enthusiasm of Southerners fighting on their own soil, and speedily bore them back. But when he had them fairly headed for the Heights again, and rejoiced at thought of the trap into which he was driving them, lo! Foulweather came lumbering up from the south to join in the pursuit, having followed the enemy's trail rather than a comrade's advice. And so the chance was lost. A single troop of Virginia horse had dared and outwitted three squadrons of regular cavalry. No wonder Foulweather said and Hamlin thought unpublishable things. But while Foulweather audibly damned his luck, Hamlin silently damned his chief, and with better right. One thing was certain, Foulweather had not found Fairfax; the Confederates probably had, and this was the result of his communication to Colonel Clark when the two detachment commanders met as the tattoo drums were beating along the Potomac, while up on the bluff, at the Heatherwood place, two hearts were beating harder still, those of Belle Heatherwood and her patrician mother.

Not a light was visible in the old Maryland mansion when, towards ten o'clock, Lieutenant Homans climbed the narrow pathway, piloting a puffing and much-disgusted major of Union cavalry, who never appeared to good advantage out of his proper sphere, the saddle. Behind them trailed an adjutant and a brace of orderlies. Once clear of the shrubbery, the New Hampshire lieutenant stood well out on the lawn, pointed to the ghostly white columns of the portico and the dim façade behind them, unbroken by the twinkle of a solitary candle.

"You can see for yourself, sir, they're all gone to bed, and I don't like to disturb them now."

Foulweather came panting to his side, spread his

booted legs well apart, braced his gauntlets on his hips, and gazed. Presently his adjutant followed, a tall young man, who seemed out of place in the clerical-looking frock coat of the day, and had little of the dragoon about him in form, face, or manner, and then the orderlies, and all stood and waited for the major to open his oracular lips. Foulweather continued to breathe hard and stare about him a few minutes, and finally said, "You know the way. Go and knock at the door."

Lieutenant Homans drew back in apparent distress. "Of course I'll do it if you say so," he hesitatingly said, and it was evident that the young soldier had been too short a time at the front to learn much of the realities of war, "but I don't like waking people up who have had so much trouble. It seems mean, somehow."

"It's business, all the same," was the gruff answer. "I've got to see that old lady before she's a night older. So bang away."

For a moment Mr. Homans looked irresolutely into the grim features of the veteran regular, then slowly turned from him and tiptoed his way along the worn gravel path and up the low flight of steps, as though reluctant to make the faintest noise until compelled to wake the echoes with the old-fashioned brass knocker. The field-officer slowly and bulkily strode across the lawn, and then with his eyes upon the dark windows, his hands braced on his hips and his sabre trailing, he again planted his sturdy legs wide apart and awaited results. Behind him in silence the tall young subaltern and the two cavalry orderlies ranged themselves and listened. The night was still and starlit. Sounds of soldier song and mirth had come floating up on the soft night wind but a few minutes before from the camp-fires upstream, but now the signal for lights out and silence had been sounded and even the distant bay of watchdog had died away. A lone whip-poor-will earlier in the evening had piped its plaintive song from the forest depths across the waters, but had tired of its unsupported effort and apparently dozed to sleep. Far over towards Frederick Junction the rumble of heavy freight trains could be dimly heard, telling that the rents and breaks torn by Stuart's raiding troopers had been repaired, and that supplies were again being trundled to the front. Somewhere, closer at hand, the muffled stamp of horses' hoofs was heard on hollow wooden flooring, and Homans whispered explanation as they climbed the path together. There was a superannuated steed belonging to the estate that dozed and dreamed about the orchard by day and was stabled in the mouldering barn by night.

And just as Homans disappeared into the shadow of the portico, still tiptoeing, the muffled stamp was heard again, and all of a sudden, as though in eager answer, or equally eager inquiry for a night's lodging, from somewhere over among the dim slopes and night shades at the east, came the shrill neigh of a tired horse,—a sound stifled almost as suddenly as it began; and it was this abrupt stop rather than the neigh itself that caused old Foulweather to turn sharply to the east, mutter, "Hullo, what's that?" and then, in loud stage whisper, to call to Homans, "Hold on! hold on! don't knock."

Then tiptoeing in turn, the veteran picked up his sabre and hastened over the dew-laden turf towards the hedge, dimly visible beyond the winding carriage-road that circled the eastward gable end of the house. Close to the hedge he halted, peered over, and listened attentively. Noiselessly his little party followed him, Homans coming last of all, and by the time he reached the others the sound of a horse's hoofs was distinctly audible, and that horse was coming swiftly up the road that wound through the groves and fields rolling away northeastward under the shining stars.

"Follow me," whispered the major, as he turned quickly towards an old gate-way that stood bowered in vines and shrubbery a dozen yards away. "We must halt that fellow as he comes through."

The gate stood wide open. Not for months had it swung on its rusty hinges. Beyond it lay the winding road, dark and sombre and overarched by luxuriant foliage only just beginning to thin at the touch of the autumn frosts. Almost like a huge letter S the road twisted through the trees, sloping to the level of the northward valley, and when first heard the hoof-beats came from the outermost sweep. Now as they listened the coming steed could more plainly be heard, the hoofs, occasionally striking some loose stone, beating on the second curve of the roadway. One more complete turn, and, though dim and shadowy, the unlooked for visitor would be close at hand. They heard the hoof-beats quicken an instant, as though responsive to impatient touch of spur or jerk of rein.

"He's just at the turn now," whispered Homans. "He'll be here in a second." But the second, ten seconds, twenty seconds came and no horse, no rider, no further sound. Not fifty yards away they had plainly heard those hoof-beats, and now a silence unbroken by even rustling leaf had fallen on the night.

"He's halted there at the other turn," whispered the old officer. "Is he reconnoitring, do you think?" No one could suggest an explanation.

"Keep in the deep shadows each side of the road and follow me," whispered Foulweather. "Not a sound now," he continued, and out through the broad gate-way groped the little party, down the first stretch of the S to the northward, around the turn that bent the roadway again to the south. There it emerged from the grove and lay bordered by slopes only sparsely dotted by little fruit-trees, and not a vestige was there of horse or horseman. Bending low, Foulweather struck a match, and the feeble flame suddenly broadened and illumined the roadway.

"See!" said he, in excitement; "see! here and

here,—fresh hoof-tracks all going up, not a sign of one going down. He's left the road between this and the gate, by God! Where's he gone to?"

"To the barn, most like," said Mr. Homans, solemnly. "There's a path around back of the house and a gap through the fence. It's shorter than through the main gate."

"Lead on, then, and be quick, if you know the way," was the old officer's order. And now, following the tall, lanky New-Englander, away went the four, silent, excited, alert, Homans, at least, with an uneasy feeling at heart. Ever since his coming the place had been free from marauders, and not until to-day had a mounted officer or orderly appeared. True, there were pickets on every road leading to the quiet, solemn old place, and current rumor had it that Madam Heatherwood, despite the espousal of the Southern cause by every able-bodied man of her name or tribe, had powerful friends at court in Washington,—friends whose influence with the War Office had placed her and her property under the protection of the Union arms, even to the extent of giving aid and comfort to her stricken son and his fiery cousin Tighlman,—friends who had served with her gallant husband in the Mexican War, and had vainly sought to pull her boy through the scrapes that wound up his career at West Point, where he wore the gray and bell buttons only long enough to get grounded in the soldier art and stranded in mathematics and discipline. Camp talk had it that "Little Mac" himself, *en route* to Crampton's Gap, had ridden far from the bee-line to say a word of kindness to the anxious mother, and certain it was that Colonel Clark had received strict orders to protect her household against stragglers of every kind, even while remembering that her roof was the shelter of Confederate officers, wounded in battle against the national flag. "Yet here," said Homans to himself, "a horseman comes riding in from the north at night, and has taken what only an intimate could have chosen, a practically invisible by-path to the stables." And up to that very afternoon no horseman had appeared about the place since he was placed in command of the little guard under the bluff, not a week before. Then came that handsome, distinguished aide-de-camp of General Hooker's, a cavalry officer and probably a regular. Homans had well-nigh forgotten him in the excitement consequent upon the rattling cavalry skirmish over on the southern shore. And now there came another, and one who must have had authority to pass the pickets.

Pondering these things in mind, the lieutenant led the way up the winding ascent among the trees, following a narrow and almost unseen path, the cavalry commander, sorely tired from his long hours of scout and vigil, panting at his heels, the rest stringing out in single file behind. Through a gap in the fence they stumbled into the barn-yard, then paused to listen.

Somebody was moving about in the barn, and a

faint light was shining through a started seam. Whoever it was, he had come at least five minutes ahead of his pursuers, enough to unsaddle and stable his horse, for before they had fully recovered breath after their climb, the light was extinguished and they heard the barn door close.

"Come on," whispered Foulweather, as he plucked Homans by the sleeve. "I must see who this is and where he goes."

Noiselessly as possible the party pushed on through the roomy barn-yard, Homans leading the way. No sentries, either by night or day, were posted on the height itself. Homans's little detachment down by the canal kept two posts occupied at all times, one of them at the southern gate-way to the estate, where an old, almost unused road branched off from the main drive and led down through a thickly wooded ravine to the edge of the canal. It was by this route, probably, that Homans's mounted visitor, Captain Belden, had reached him that afternoon. But the drive itself circled around to the north through the grounds of the beautiful old estate and joined the highway in the valley of the Monocacy after passing through a gate-way at the northward limit of the Heatherwood possessions. Here a post was maintained by the pickets of the New Hampshire men, and these two gate-ways were the only practical approaches to the mansion for parties either driving or riding, for walls of stone or high picket-fences surrounded it on every side. All this Homans explained in whispered words to his crusty superior, as they cautiously approached the big house, wending their way through a labyrinth of wooden sheds and quarters and outbuildings until presently the leaders found themselves at another fence and a little gate-way leading to the garden at the west side of the mansion; and there they halted, for a light suddenly appeared at an upper window, the casement was thrown open, and a slender form, a graceful, willowy, womanly form, leaned out into the night.

"Who is it?" they heard her whisper to some unseen visitor, shrouded in the black shadows of the house.

The words of the answer were indistinguishable. The low voice was that of a man, an American, the intonation that of a gentleman, and all was evidently satisfactory. "Open quickly," was all that the listeners below could hear, when the form disappeared from the upper window and the light came dancing down the stairway to the lower floor, gleaming from window to window.

"Who was that?" whispered Foulweather.

"One of the ladies," answered Homans, unwilling to mention names, even then, and struggling with a feeling of shame at the idea of his even accidentally keeping watch on a woman's movements. Before the cavalry officer could ask another question there was a sound of sliding bolts; a door opened at the back of the house, and there, with welcome shining in her eyes, despite the anxiety in her face,—there, holding high aloft her candle, stood the fair daughter of the old house of Heatherwood, and there sprang up the steps, bearing on his arm an officer's saddle and housing, a tall, athletic, finely built fellow in the uniform of a captain. The door closed behind him the instant he was admitted, and Foulweather turned quickly on his guide and grasped him by the arm.

"Did you recognize that man? Have you ever seen him before?" he asked, with almost fiery eagerness. "Speak, man, quick!"

"I do, yes," was the slow response. "I saw him to-day for the first time, and didn't look to see him here again, this night at least."

"But his name. Who do *you* say he is?" demanded Foulweather, and Homans noted with surprise that the big, gauntleted hand was trembling.

"Well, the name he gave me," answered the lieutenant, with the caution of the New-Englander, "was Grosvenor Belden, captain on General Hooker's staff."

"And he was here? You saw him?—talked with him here to-day?—you could swear to it?" persisted the veteran, his face working strangely, his grasp on the lieutenant's arm increasing in force.

"Why, certainly, major, if need be, though I don't know anything out of the way about him."

"Never mind that. You saw him and talked with him,—can identify him as the same man we saw enter here to-night. That's what I want to know. You can do that, can you, and some other man in your command? Did any one else see him,—here, I mean?"

"Why, yes, sir, Reuben Pettingill, of my company, he was the first to see him up here, talking with Miss Heatherwood, just before the captain rode away, just a while before the firing began over across the creek," faltered Homans, fearful now of some lapse of vigilance to be laid at his door, and wondering what might come next.

For a moment there was an impressive pause. Foulweather was breathing hard and excitedly. Finally he spoke. "Mr. Wilson," he said, in solemn tones, to the tall subaltern, "I expect you to remember every word of this and to keep it sacred, to speak of it to no one until called upon officially, and then to bear witness that you saw an officer enter the Heatherwood house by the back way and through some understanding or arrangement with its occupants, at nearly eleven o'clock this night, and that Lieutenant Homans, officer of the guard, declared him to be the same man who was here earlier this afternoon when that rebel troop of cavalry came down right opposite here, and were beaten back by my command" (Hamlin's command, thought Mr. Wilson to himself), "and that Mr. Homans declared the officer to be Captain Grosvenor Belden, of General Hooker's staff. Remember it, sir, and be ready to testify to it when you are called upon, and not before."

CHAPTER V.

ANOTHER October day had dawned, crisp and sparkling. The slanting sunshine touched the frosty rime that coated leaf and twig and homely fence-rail and distant steeple, and tiny fires blazed from every surface, yellow, red, and blue, like the flashes from pigmy brilliants. Over the emptied bed of the canal and the shallows in the stream where the waters rolled in sluggish flood the mist rose in fleecy clouds, while the little cook-fires in the clustering camps above the sharp elbow sent the smoke straight rising towards the sky. Down along the worn towpath at the left bank of the river groups of men in light-blue overcoats were sipping from tins of soldier coffee, and nibbling at the morning hardtack, while the sound of jovial chat and laughter rang cheerily from shore to shore. Up on the height at Heatherwood all was silence and inaction, save where sentries were slowly pacing up and down in front, in rear, and at the flanks, wondering what on earth it meant that after midnight they should have been routed from their blankets and set to guarding premises where the only guards posted hitherto were there to warn them off, and what it meant now that they should refuse egress to any member of that exclusive household.

Soon after sunrise old Foulweather, refreshed by forty winks of sleep and as many drops of rye, had ridden half-way up the road with Colonel Clark and held brief parley with an officer stationed there with a guard of a dozen men, and received assurance that not a soul had issued from the house except one old, yawning darky, who seemed amazed and affrighted at being halted by a sentry in blue and ordered to explain his mission. "Only going to the barn to feed and water ole Mistis' pet ole hoss;" and when a sergeant escorted him thither and pointed out to him a second charger, an active little bay, eager for breakfast and friendly hands, the veteran servitor declared himself unable to account for the presence at all, and swore the horse, the halter, the cavalry blanket were utterly strange to him. Questioned as to the arrival of an officer during the night, the negro vowed that so far as he knew no one had been there since the officer gentleman that rode away the previous afternoon. "Marse Belden," he heard him called, and this wasn't his horse at all. All this was duly reported to both Colonel Clark and the cavalry field-officer, between whom it seems there had been a row during the still watches of the night.

Men of totally different mould were they. Foulweather a typical specimen of the old-time Mexican War dragoon, or later rollicking Rifleman of the Santa Fé trail, steeped in traditions of the frontier, a fellow who had known no home but camp or bivouac for a dozen years, blunt, butt-headed, independent, hard riding, hard swearing, hard drinking, with stomach copper-lined apparently, through some occult electro process that coated the mucous membrane with the metal of the still and colored his battered visage with the hues of Monongahela. Daring riding and swordsmanship when he charged the guns with Charley May at Resaca and later sabred a path through the Pedregal had won him the notice of men like Scott and Taylor, a commission in the new regiment of Mounted Rifles, and promotion to a captaincy before the war, a war he fondly supposed could be properly handled and finally won only by men of "the old service," irrespective of the fact that so many of them had taken sides with the South. To him there were never again to be soldiers like unto Scott, Worth, and Taylor, Twiggs, Sumner, and Harney. A general officer in his eyes was hedged in with divinity, until he saw the crop of recently appointed one wonderful day at Willard's in the summer of '61. If such specimens, men who never had set squadron in the field, and some of whom probably never would, could wear the sash and stars of generals, what might not such as he aspire to? Foulweather applied for a brigadier-generalship of volunteers on the spot, was amazed that he didn't get it, was disgusted to read of dozens of hitherto unheard-of citizens who seemed to have no difficulty whatever, and was torn with jealous misery when the honor was conferred on fellow-captains in the line, men whom he had known as subalterns from Palo Alto to Buena Vista, and later on the march of conquest to the city of Mexico, later still in long weary months and years of exile in Arizona, New Mexico, and over the Plains. He raved so rabidly at their preferment and his own retention as an humble field-officer that, officers and men alike, the troopers had begun to speak of him as "The General." As for his real name, one might have served a year in the Army of the Potomac and never heard it, for to every man in the regular service he was known only as Foulweather, and the volunteers were not slow to see the point and follow suit.

But a stanch old fighter was Foulweather. None could deny that. It was his luck, however, to lead into mischief far more often than to victory. He was perpetually charging stone walls, strong positions, heavier forces, and only getting out by the skin of his teeth. He was simply fun for Stuart's light-horsemen, who knew him well, and loved to trick him, and he would rather be riddled following his own devices than ride to glory on the advice of another man.

And now, failing to nab Captain Fairfax over on the Southern shore, and learning from Lieutenant Hamlin that there were reasons for believing that daring and popular Virginian had managed in some way and for some purposes of his own to run over into Maryland, Major Foulweather had come to impart his views and suspicions to Colonel Clark; had received that officer's reluctant consent to make a personal reconnoissance of the Heatherwood place, and had discovered, as he believed, evidence that a certain prominent and distinguished young officer of the regular cavalry, serving temporarily on the staff of General Hooker, was holding secret communication with the inmates of the old mansion, while they in turn were in direct and stealthy correspondence with the enemy. He had roused Clark at midnight and demanded authority to take a company of Clark's regiment, his own men being now away beyond the Kittoctons, and rouse the household, and had run upon a man he could neither blind nor bully.

A typical specimen of the volunteer officer of the best class was Clark, a man who fervently loved his country, feared God, hated slavery, and clearly saw that the triumph of the South meant the dissolution of the Union,—the ruin of the great republic. He was a student, a thinker, a patriot, and a worker. He had inherited little from his father beyond Yankee grit and the sword he wore in 1812. Self-educated, Clark had supported his mother and sisters while he studied law. His youth was one of stern self-abnegation, his young manhood of patient toil and trial. Not until he was nearly forty did modest competence come to bless his labors, and by that time, with a little home and household of his own, a man of mark in the beautiful New Hampshire valley where he had spent his years, he was serving in the Senate of his State, practising law, and looking after the business interests of some wealthy clients in the large cities who had investments in his neighborhood, when Lincoln was elected and the South took fire. Clark's few speeches in the Senate that winter and at the town meetings when the news of Sumter came made him a leader. But Clark held that example was worth more than precept, and he enlisted in the first company raised in the shadows of Monadnock. They elected him captain, and he refused, saying he had no experience and must learn like the rest. Whereupon the command was tendered a veteran of the Mexican War, who held it as far as Washington only. Brains, study, and common sense did more for Clark than war experiences, or a reputation for them, had done for the original commander. The Yankee lawyer, observant, silent, went about from camp to camp, watching the mannerisms and methods of the officers whom he heard described, in the soldier slang of the day, as "lightning." He looked after the diet of his men, the police of their camps, the care of their clothing, shoes, and feet. There were notable drill-masters and tacticians in the division to which he was assigned, and them he watched and followed, "Hardee" in hand, hours at a time, then went back to his tall New-Englanders and patiently explained and exhorted to them. Before ever they got to the peninsula Clark was acknowledged to be the brainiest lieutenant in the regiment. The colonel had a spat with his adjutant and offered the place to Clark, and Clark said he'd do the duty provided he could stick to his company too, whereby he learned the ways of both offices. Then the Mexican War captain fell before the breastworks of Willard's Bar, a vacancy was declared, and this time Clark did not decline the captaincy tendered by unanimous vote. At Savage Station the untried regiment staggered under a terrific fire, and lost heavily in officers and men. Clark, shot through the sword-arm, led on with the other, and though seniors stood to the right and left of him in the battle-line, it was his voice, somehow, that steadied the men. It was his splendid courage and example that restored hope and pluck to the blanched and bewildered faces, that far and near seemed to turn towards the bearded leader of the Monadnocks. Kearny at Seven Pines dashed up to him on foaming horse, spit out "the reins in his teeth," and held forth "the one hand still left," shouting, "By God! sir, what's your name? I'm proud to have such a fellow in my division." And so when Clark went home more seriously wounded after Malvern, his fame had preceded him, and New Hampshire sent him back to the front in the fall of '62, a veteran tried, at the head of a new regiment that bade fair to do as well as did the old. Given native common sense, a legal education, habits of thought and command and one year's experience in the Army of the Potomac, and the possessor was more than a match for any case-hardened old dragoon whose best days had been frittered away in a desolate land. Foulweather thought to carry his point in one impetuous dash, but was brought up standing in the initial charge. Then he started to storm and swear. Colonel Clark calmly suggested that he was talking to a superior officer, and would better conserve his own interests by expressing his ideas in courteous language. Clark as calmly told the irate veteran that his orders were to permit no one to disturb Mrs. Heatherwood, and that, had the major knocked up the household at night, as it seems the major thought of doing, it would have been his, Colonel Clark's, painful duty to place the major under arrest. Foulweather was thunderstruck, but had sense to see that Clark had law and orders both on his side. All he could persuade the colonel to do was to post the guard about the house with instructions to allow no one to leave or enter until examined, and Foulweather had more than sufficient reason for desiring to nab Captain Belden of the Union cavalry in just such a predicament as this.

Belden was a man beloved in the army. Graduated from the Point but a few years gone by, he had risen rapidly to a captaincy when by dozens the Southern officers took their leave. It had taken Foulweather ten years to get his double bars, but he had been rushed through to the majority within the year of the outbreak of the war. Belden and he both commanded squadrons in the spring of '62, and Belden was as brilliant and successful, despite his youth, as Foulweather was blundering. Then came an untoward incident just before Gaines's Mill. Foulweather was a hard hitter and hater; Belden a chivalric foe. The former believed in nothing short of annihilation for the enemy; the latter had many a friend, classmate, even relative, in the Southern lines, and, though loyal to the backbone, dutiful and devoted, he could not stomach Foulweather's descriptives when, one evening at the camp-fire, Stuart's cavalry were under discussion, and frankly told the major so. These were days when the code still held good in the old dragoon regiments and was well recognized throughout the cavalry. Foulweather turned on the younger officer with personal abuse, and got an instant and stinging retort. A veteran cavalry colonel promptly stopped the quarrel, but when Belden's challenge was borne to Foulweather on the following day, he refused it, to the scandal of his fellows. Then came the mad charge at Gaines's Mill, that emptied so many a saddle and consolidated four squadrons into three, and there Foulweather fought and swore too well to be kept in Coventry. Belden had meantime been ordered to staff duty, as the best means of separating them, and the matter might have been dropped and forgotten but for two things,—one was Foulweather's implacable jealousy, and the other the fact that Captain Belden had later been ordered to Washington to explain to the iron War Secretary allegations affecting his loyalty. He stood accused of holding correspondence with certain officers of the Virginia cavalry, notably Captain Fairfax and Ralph Heatherwood. It came just in time to knock him out of the colonelcy of a crack cavalry regiment being raised in Pennsylvania, for Stanton was inexorable. Indeed, nothing but the vehement testimony of generals like Hooker and Kearny saved him from consequences far more serious, for the cavalry had few friends so early in the war. Belden had known Fairfax well in the old regiment, had met him and Heatherwood under flag of truce in '61, and had met them cordially for reasons he would stoop neither to extenuate nor explain, beyond the mere statement that under the white flag soldiers dropped the sword. The "Iron Secretary" bade him go back to duty and remember that he rode with a rope around his neck, and Belden, raging at heart at the injury done him, nevertheless had to confine his protests to calm and respectful words. Stern discipline demanded of him every show of subordination to the inflexible chief of the War Department, who refused him all knowledge of his accuser, but Belden felt beyond all doubt that Foulweather was the man, and longed for opportunity to redress his wrongs.

In no happy mood this gifted officer then had rejoined General Hooker in time for Antietam. "Only be patient and attend strictly to your duties," wrote a friend at court, "and even Stanton can't be proof against such praise as you're sure to get, but he has so many cases of disaffection and even disloyalty to deal with that if you were here you wouldn't wonder." Belden chafed at thought of the loss of that splendid regiment, but his chief consoled him with a promise that it could not be long before there would come another opportunity. "Only," said he, "keep away from that—possibility." And when Belden demanded to know what was meant by "that possibility," the general gave him to understand that it was current rumor in the cavalry that he had been a devotee of Miss Heatherwood while in New York the winter before the war, and, to that fighting commander's comfort and surprise, Captain Belden promptly answered, "General Hooker, I never met Miss Heatherwood in my life."

And so it happened soon after this time that Foulweather was given to understand, in response to urgent inquiries of his own, that his application for a brigade had not been favorably considered, and the story went the rounds in the old regiment that the spectacled monarch, whom few of the officers had ever seen, sent for Foulweather as he passed through Washington and gave him a terrific wigging about something, and there were some who guessed it was because of baseless reports he had made concerning Belden. At all events, having injured Belden in the first place, true to human nature, Foulweather hated him now, and prayed for a chance to prove his words. No wonder then he was nearly mad with excitement over the revelations of the officer of the guard, —that Captain Belden was actually here, here at

Heatherwood, and in close communion with the enemy after all.

It was the possession of this piece of presumptive evidence that nerved him, therefore, to his final demand of the New Hampshire colonel.

"You have treated me with small consideration in this matter, Colonel Clark," said he. "Your rank in the volunteers may outweigh my fifteen years' experience in the regulars in your opinion, but when you see why I insisted on that guard you will change your tune." Then turning to the officer who still stood at the roadside, silently wondering what was to be the upshot of all this mysterious posting of sentries and questioning, Foulweather asked, in civil tone, that he accompany them up to the mansion, as he desired to see the new arrival on important business. The lieutenant hesitated and glanced at his colonel.

"There will be no objection to your doing so a little later, major," said the commanding officer, somewhat coldly, "but as I think I told you last night, Mrs. Heatherwood's household is under our protection for the time being, and I am ordered not to allow her to be disturbed."

"That means robbed or maltreated, Colonel Clark," out-spoke the major, angrily. "It isn't possible that the Secretary of War can have given orders that a house where rebels are harbored and where treason is plotted day and night is never to be inspected, especially when at this moment I know or believe it to be visited by an officer of the regular cavalry, who has only recently been reprimanded by the Secretary himself for sympathizing with this very family and other prominent rebels. What's more, he has been warned officially to keep away from there, and he's here in direct violation of those orders."

But Clark was imperturbable. "I happen to know," said he, "that the Secretary of War considers Mrs. Heatherwood a woman deserving of great consideration, despite the fact of her son's being in the Confederate service, and as for visitors, only one officer has been reported by my pickets as visiting Heatherwood within the last twenty-four hours. He bore the personal order of General Hooker, whom he started to rejoin yesterday afternoon."

"Yes," said Foulweather, eagerly, "and his name was——?"

"Belden—Captain Belden, I believe, though I had not the honor of meeting him. It seems he rode up to my tent just after the fight began yesterday afternoon, then went on up the river."

"The very man!" exclaimed Foulweather, eagerly; "and, so far from returning to General Hooker, he is at this moment under that roof, and I mean to prove it. Ask your pickets at the main gate who it was that rode in at eleven o'clock last night, and——"

A sergeant who had stood silently by listening with keen interest to the exciting talk, stepped quickly forward.

"*I* was there, colonel, from ten till after midnight, and there wasn't a soul came in or went out either."

"I was on the bluff yonder with Lieutenant Homans, of your own regiment. My adjutant, Mr. Wilson, was with me, and two orderlies," answered Foulweather, angrily. "We distinctly heard him coming up the road. We tracked him to the barn and saw him enter the house, and your own officer recognized and declared him to be the same Captain Belden that passed his post down on the other side of the place yesterday afternoon. If he didn't come through the gate it was because he dared not be seen by the guard, because he came by stealth, because he knew some gap in the fence or hedge as he did the secret path through the shrubbery, a short cut to the barn. I tell you, Colonel Clark, that officer is here, after having reported to your guard that he was on his way to Harper's Ferry. Send for Lieutenant Homans if you need confirmation, and I demand the right to call him to account."

For a moment Clark pondered deeply. There was indeed something perplexing in the situation. Then he spoke. "I will ride around to the canal and question Homans," said he. "I can do that much quicker than have him come here. If his report tally with yours, there will certainly be something to investigate in Captain Belden's conduct, but not necessarily in Mrs. Heatherwood's. Will you ride, sir, or do you prefer to wait?"

"I'll join the officer of the guard in a cup of that

coffee," said the major, sniffing eagerly at the aroma that arose from a little cook-fire under the trees, and, dismounting, he tossed the reins to his orderly and straddled bulkily away over the tangled turf to join the squad of blue-coats, that welcomed him none too cordially. It was not music to their ears that an old regular should differ with their hero and commander.

Not five minutes after Clark had gone his way, and while the major was sipping at a fragrant tin of the comforting fluid, a corporal came running down the winding road.

"Lieutenant," said he, never pausing for ceremony, "there's a cavalry fellow just come out of the house. He's raising hell because we won't let him have his horse."

"Here, orderly, quick!" called Foulweather, to the trooper who stood with dangling reins, as the horses cropped away at the grass. "Which side is your cavalry fellow?" he continued, as he set foot in stirrup and swung into saddle.

"West side, sir, next to the barn."

"Come on, Wilson," called Foulweather to his adjutant, who was chatting with the New Hampshire officer a little distance away, and on he went, spluttering up the pathway through the shrubbery he had followed afoot the night before. At the barn-yard he was overtaken by his staff-officer, and together they spurred through, twisting and turning among the out-buildings until suddenly they came to the negro quarters in rear of the house, and there, looking embarrassed and worried, stood a tall New Hampshire lad, in the dress and equipments of the sentinel, holding converse with a tall, trim built, natty looking private of cavalry, in battered forage-cap with upturned visor, in snug-fitting, high-collared, yellow-trimmed jacket, in light-blue breeches and well-made boots and gauntlets, with black belts, carbine, sabre, and revolver, a McClellan saddle and bags on his arm, and a look of disgust on his face, a look that suddenly gave way to one of surprise and dismay, as he caught sight of the coming party.

Instantly his heels clicked together, and he stood at attention as the leading horseman came trotting up and, after one astonished glance in the trooper's face, exclaimed,—

"Bell! Why,—what in hell are *you* doing *here?*"

"Here by order, sir," was the blunt response. "Came over under instructions from Lieutenant Hamlin; carried them out and got others at Frederick last night."

"From whom? Where are they?"

For answer the trooper calmly dropped his load, rummaged in the near saddle-bag a moment, and produced the pencilled memorandum Hamlin had given him at the ferry. This the major took in his gauntleted hand and glared at.

"Mr. Hamlin had no right to grant this, and he knows it," he angrily exclaimed. "But even this gives you no excuse for coming here. What brings you here, I say, and who's here with you? Where's Captain Belden?"

At mention of the name the trooper perceptibly winced, but answered promptly, even hurriedly. "I don't know, sir. I haven't seen him at all. I heard the captain went up towards Harper's Ferry yesterday afternoon, but I was up the Monocacy." Then the major interrupted.

"You haven't answered the question: what brings you here? That's not your horse in the barn. Where is he?"

"Played out, sir; and I got a farmer to swap with me until I could deliver my despatches." And Bell was again at attention and gazing steadily, sturdily into the major's clouded face.

"Who gave you despatches, and to whom were they addressed?"

"The surgeon in charge of the hospital at Frederick—to Mrs. Heatherwood."

"And you've got the answer, have you?" growled the major, suspiciously. "Empty those saddle-bags."

A flush spread instantly over the soldier's troubled face. "There is nothing in the bags that is not my own, sir," he protested. "There is nothing you have any right to touch."

"Well, of all the infernal rot I ever heard!" raved Foulweather, springing from saddle. "Dismount there," he called to his orderly. "You, too, Mr. Wilson. Let's see what devil's work is going

"Drop them, sir, instantly!"

on here. Hand over those bags, sir," he ordered as Bell seized and appeared about to drag them away. "What! Mutiny?" he cried, for a furious light glared one instant in the young trooper's eyes, and he had clinched his ready fists as though to strike. "Drop them, sir, instantly!" And at the word the veteran officer's revolver was whipped from the holster and pointed square in the trooper's face.

One moment they stood there, a dramatic group. The tall, athletic soldier, pale as death now, with beads of sweat starting from his forehead; the flushed and angered field-officer, pistol in hand; the sentry perturbed and uncertain what he ought to do, his rifle at port in his clinching hands; Wilson, the lanky subaltern, hastening to his senior's side, yet sympathizing vaguely with the soldier; the orderly, grasping at the horse's reins and staring over his shoulder at the unusual scene.

"If that man stirs or resists, bayonet him," was the major's stern order to the sentry. "Wilson, search those bags."

"One moment, major," and from a corner of the house, from the little garden at the west side, the words rang calm, clear, and commanding, and Colonel Clark, followed by Lieutenant Homans, came striding through the gate-way. "Pardon my reminding a regular that sentries take orders only from their own officers. You have no authority over my men whatever,—nor on these premises. Is that one of your men?" And at sound of the voice Bell had seemed actually to shrink within himself. Facing his own superior, he stood now with his back towards Colonel Clark, and his head was sinking into his shoulders.

"He is, and I arrest him as a straggler, if nothing worse. Your own sentry halted him here coming out of that house not ten minutes ago."

At this moment the door at the rear of the house swung open, and, as though drawn to the spot by the sound of angry voices, there appeared at the threshold the form of a woman with silvery hair and a sweet, wan, refined face, at sight of which Lieutenant Homans instantly doffed his cap, and Colonel Clark respectfully raised his hat.

"I deeply regret this disturbance, Mrs. Heatherwood," said the latter. "This gentleman claims to know that Captain Belden, of our cavalry, is here contrary to orders, and I find from my officer of the guard that a gentleman giving his name as Belden passed his post on the canal road just before the skirmish across the river yesterday, and that the same officer, or one closely resembling him, entered that door at eleven o'clock last night."

And then another face, witching, saucy, black-eyed, and rosy-cheeked, peered coquettishly around the woman's shoulder, the black eyes dancing from man to man until they alighted on the figure of the accused trooper, standing almost cowering, his back towards them. On him they rested in perplexity.

"No gentleman of that name has honored us with

a visit," was, at last, the dignified reply, yet spoken in gentle tone, "nor do I know any officer of that name,—in either army."

"Then will you explain, madam," loudly demanded Foulweather, stepping quickly forward into the group, "what it means that one of my men, who ought to be with his fellows across the Potomac, is captured here—here where he has spent the night, and what business he may have bearing messages between you and the surgeon at Frederick?"

The instant the major strode past him, Bell suddenly thrust his hand within his jacket, drew forth a little note, glanced quickly, but cautiously, over his shoulder, and saw that the eyes of all men were fixed now upon the stately mistress of Heatherwood. The next instant the note was in fragments, some thrust into his mouth and swallowed, some tossed lightly to the breeze, some ground under foot in the soil. Then up went the hand, and the visor of his cap was pulled down over the bright blue eyes, the neck-handkerchief was dragged up over the yellow-laced collar, and once more he seemed to shrink within himself.

There was a long, impressive pause before the lady spoke. Calmly, almost haughtily, she looked the veteran over from head to foot. The abrupt tone, the suspicious manner, had angered her. When at last she opened her lips it was Clark, not Foulweather, she addressed.

"Any questions Colonel Clark may deem necessary I will answer at any time he desires. May I have a word with you now, colonel, in the parlor?"

"At your pleasure, madam," answered Clark, bowing ceremoniously as though in rebuke to the rudeness of his associate, and then, taking Homans with him, marched back through the garden to the front of the house, leaving the others to settle their own affairs.

For a moment there was silence. Then spoke Foulweather, pointing to Bell, "Mr. Wilson, have that man taken under guard and turned over to the provost-marshal, at once. This thing must be investigated."

CHAPTER VI.

A STRANGE feature of the landscape in the Virginias, in Maryland, and in Pennsylvania is the series of parallel ranges rising, as a rule, higher from east to west until half their number is counted, then similarly falling away to the west. Without exception the trend is from northeast to southwest, and though referred to comprehensively as the Alleghanies, each ridge or range seems to have a name of its own in the State which it traverses. It results that in Maryland and Virginia there is a series of parallel valleys, fertile and beautiful, each one drained by its own stream, each dipping gently towards the Potomac, which, as the collector of the entire system east of the backbone of the mountains, bursts its way through range after range and finally sweeps on through the lowlands in majestic flood, one of the lordliest and loveliest of rivers.

And strange confusion arose at times in the minds of soldiers, Northern and Southern, due to these very ranges and their varying names. Looking westward from the battle-fields around Manassas or the camps in front of Washington, the first range, low and heavily wooded, was known as the "Bull Run Mountains" below Aldie and as the "Kittoctans" above. From the head-waters of the Rappahannock, back of Warrenton, to the Potomac west of the sharp elbow opposite the mouth of the Monocacy, this curtain was, until the last winter of the war, a perennial screen for cavalry. The valley between the Bull Run Mountains and the Blue Ridge was a raiding ground for bodies of horse, Union or Southern, year after year, and fast and furious were the cavalry battles fought from time to time along those picturesque slopes. Aldie, Upperville, and the numerous Gaps—Thoroughfare, Hopewell, and Clark's in the first range, Manassas, Ashby's, and Snicker's in the second—were perpetually being traversed by troopers from one army or the other. Sometimes the advantage of numbers lay with the North, sometimes with the South. At all times the advantage of knowing every inch of the ground and being at home in every hamlet lay with the Virginians and their fellows from below. At no time could the Northern horse rely on information given by the people, for even the negroes often turned out to be more devoted to the interests of "Ole Marse" or "Mistis" than to their own. The very first essay of Northern arms along the Potomac at the foot of the first of the ranges resulted in fell disaster, despite the fact that the best blood and brawn of the old Bay State was landed there in little boat-loads and dribbled out to the triumphant foe in costly sacrifice. Looking southwest from the Heatherwood height, the majestic river rolled away between its wooded shores until, some seven miles distant, it began again to bend to the eastward at the foot of a steep bluff. Midway across to the Maryland shore lay Harrison's Island, and there on the open summit of the bluff chosen detachments of the finest commands ever even Massachusetts had sent to the front, backed by portions of the so-called "Tammany" and "California" regiments, were marshalled in line of battle to be shot down in scores by an overpowering force of the enemy encircling them in the surrounding woods, while from the Maryland shore, a mile away, raging comrades looked helplessly on. For weeks the homes of Leesburg and the farm-houses of the neighborhood were filled with wounded, and the triumph and rejoicing, following such unlooked for victory, were tempered by the sight of suffering such as the kindly people had never known before. And among those who hastened to succor the Southern boys stricken in the fight, but whose tender hearts speedily led them to give comfort to boys as gently reared as their own, now helpless and suffering, was "Madam Heatherwood," who had left her winter home in Baltimore and taken up her abode in the old mansion on the Potomac. With friends and relatives in Leesburg and Aldie, as well as on the Maryland side, this Christian woman had never ceased her labors for the wounded and the dying. And among the wounded, as luck would have it, was a Pennsylvania officer whose name carried weight in Washington, and the story he told when he was exchanged and sent back to the capital five months after the catastrophe at Ball's Bluff brought tears to the eyes of the President himself and a letter from him to the mistress of Heatherwood, and orders to the officers commanding at the Monocacy that they read in some cases with perplexity but in no case dared to disobey. Clark, brigaded for a brief time with the Massachusetts regiments, heard tales of the lady of Heatherwood that taught him to revere her name before ever it fell to his lot to be sent to guard her doors, and Clark needed no stern order over the signature of the "Iron Secretary," much less an explanation for the fact that, at her own home, under her own roof, Mrs. Heatherwood was permitted to nurse and care for her own boy and a kinsman wounded on the slopes of South Mountain when McClellan's men fought their way through to the later grapple at Antietam.

But these were matters that old Foulweather knew little of. Leaving Trooper Bell a prisoner under charges to be taken to Harper's Ferry or Frederick, as the provost-marshal at Point of Rocks might direct, he had recrossed the river immediately after and set out in search of his squadrons, which he found in bivouac over in the valley beyond Clark's Gap. To the west lay the lofty buttresses of the Loudoun Heights, which, torn in twain by the Potomac a few miles farther north, were still further divided on the Maryland shore by a deep rift that ran north and south. They called them the Maryland Heights just opposite Harper's Ferry, but these became the South Mountain a few miles below, and then, still farther east of this latter range and north of the Potomac, the valley was drained by a little stream flowing south into the great river. East of the range and south of the Potomac the valley was drained by a little stream flowing north. The one in Maryland they spelled Catoctin, the one in Virginia they called, and usually spelled, Kittoctan. East of these streams on the Maryland side the heights which hemmed the valley were called Catoctin; east of the valley on the Virginia side they called them Catoctin too, as some did the stream on its west, and thereby hangs another tale.

Foulweather had rejoined, mad as a hornet. He had lost Fairfax after bragging that he had him sure. He had lost Belden after vowing that he had *him* sure. He had lost his battle with Clark after assuming to give orders to Clark's sentry, which he had no right whatever to do and knew he had no right, but presumed on his own assurance and the probable ignorance of raw troops; and finally, he had lost his temper and been caught in the act. He was in no mood, therefore, to dispassionately consider the situation. He found despatches calling for reports as to what he had done, explanations as to what he had not done, and reasons why he did not do things that seemed impossible. This did not add to his serenity.

Short as he was of officers, he had two, at all

events, whose counsel was worth taking at any time, and one of these was Hamlin, but at Hamlin he was angry; first, he told himself, because Hamlin, while temporarily commanding a detached squadron, had passed Trooper Bell beyond the Potomac, but down in the bottom of his heart Foulweather knew Hamlin too well not to feel sure that there was some good reason for his action which he would promptly give when called upon. He knew, too, that Bell was a man possessed of peculiar, even somewhat mysterious knowledge of men and things in this neighborhood, which in itself would account for his selection by Hamlin. He knew best of all that the real reason why he was exasperated and angry and at odds with the world was that by following his own instead of Hamlin's counsel he had lost the chance of nabbing the Fairfax troop if not Fairfax himself, and all because he had followed around by road instead of throwing his men across their trail, and so, being sore on this score, he did not wish to see Hamlin and have to admit it. Being sure that Hamlin could instantly give abundant reason for sending Bell into Maryland, he did not wish to see Hamlin, and have at once to countermand the orders given in the presence of those silent, critical, "damned Yankee greenhorns." (Foulweather hailed from the Wabash flats.) And so it resulted that he did not send for Hamlin at all,—Hamlin who was happily sleeping,—or for his comrade squadron commander, who was gladly doing likewise, for Foulweather had come to a perplexing point in his despatches, and there was only one person to whom Foulweather would ever confess his ignorance, and that was himself.

Tired with his long ride and the events of the past three days, yet too worried to sleep, he had his darky cook set to work on a substantial dinner for Wilson and himself, took a sizable nip from his canteen, threw himself on his blankets, and scowled through his mail a second time. Treacy, his second in command, an ex-sergeant like himself and a good fighting soldier, had bivouacked the wearied detachment close to the banks of the brook and within pistol-shot of a farm enclosure, now as empty of its former occupants, pigs, cows, and chickens, as the fields were of fence-rails. The smoke curled lazily from the chimney of the farm-house itself, which lay close to the roadside some two hundred yards away, but only the upright posts, deep planted, remained to tell where stood the barrier between pasture and public thoroughfare. Close to the stream the picket ropes were stretched, and there the horses were tethered, drowsing in the noonday sun, some lazily switching at the late autumn flies, some sprawled luxuriously on the close-nibbled turf. A brace of travel-stained wagons, with their scarred and battered mules, had come up from Conrad's Ferry earlier in the day, bringing grain and rations, and horse and man were filled and happy. Tents there were none nearer than the wagon-train, awaiting orders east of the Gap, but tents the sun-tanned troopers had little use for. They were sprawling everywhere under the trees, or even on the open, with a blanket propped to ward off the rays of the sun, sleeping the sleep of the just and content. Foulweather was perhaps the only really unhappy man in the lot. The loss of a splendid opportunity was his fault alone, and men bear other men's sorrows much more resignedly than they do their own. Twice the major arose from his blankets and scowled at the scene about him, bold, beautiful, and picturesque as it was. Twice he looked from the hastily written page in his hand to the rock-seamed scarp of the Loudoun and the blue outline of the South Mountain across the Potomac. Twice he turned and gazed along the wooded slopes running away to the northeast. Then back to the puzzling paper went his tired, deep-set eyes, and then the major reached for his canteen and swore and drank afresh. Both performances seemed to do him good, for he turned with renewed energy to the letter and read:

DEAR F.,—The General gets it on excellent authority that Captain Fairfax is no longer anywhere in Loudoun County, that he managed somehow to cross into Maryland two nights ago, and will doubtless try to visit the Heatherwood place despite Mrs. Heatherwood's prohibition. Warning has been sent to Colonel Clark at the Monocacy, and he has been instructed to make search in the neighborhood of Poolesville, where Fairfax was seen and recognized.

"Now we want to capture that fellow, if a possible thing, and not lose the credit to a lot of doughboys. There is a place in the Catoctin Valley not two miles from the river where they say Fairfax has twice been in hiding. It is owned by a Mr. Hutton, who is away in the army, and is cared for by his sister and some servants. I've never seen it, but according to description it is an old, two-story stone house among a lot of rose-bushes and trees about twenty yards back from the road, with chimneys at each gable end, built out like buttresses from the wall. I believe it would pay to keep an eye on it. Let me know how things are going.

"Yours as ever,
"B. J. LORING,
"A. A. G."

This letter bore date which showed it to be forty-eight hours old. Fairfax, therefore, had managed to cross the river before his friends rode down to the rescue, and, failing to find him as expected at Leesburg, had followed on to the very bank of the Potomac opposite Heatherwood. Why had they so confidently gone thither? That was far above his crossing place, provided he had gone to Poolesville. Some point between Edward's Ferry and Ball's Bluff would have been far more logical an objective. But his troop had fairly galloped, so said the darkies, from Leesburg, straight as the winding road could take them, along the eastward slope of the Virginia Catoctins, and were actually hidden in the woods and signalling to Heatherwood when their wary flankers and pickets reported Bob Hamlin's squadron coming back at the trot, and they had to drop any other matter they had in view to receive him with all soldierly honors. Then where could they have expected to find Fairfax if not close to Heatherwood? Mrs. Heatherwood's prohibition might or might not have had the effect of keeping the Virginian captain off her premises. Foulweather was a sceptic as to the prohibition anyway. Despite Presidential safeguards and the endorsement of the War Secretary himself, the veteran of the frontier believed Mrs. Heatherwood quite capable of concealing rebel spies about her house, of using Union troopers as couriers, of involving Union surgeons in treasonable correspondence, and of tempting Union officers from the paths of honor. The more he thought, and in the course of his cogitation another drink became necessary, the more Foulweather became convinced that the much-lauded Captain Belden had more than once visited Heatherwood, though possibly under an assumed name.

And now from the adjutant-general of the cavalry brigade he had received a hint that warranted further search for the lurking Virginian, and might enable him to investigate Belden's movements, Clark or no Clark. Weary as he was, there was inspiration in the thought. He sprang to his feet again, and looked eagerly about him. Wilson, his callow adjutant, was already drooping and dozing over a letter he was trying to write to his mother. The boy was fairly worn out. His older officers were sleeping soundly; so were half the men and many of the horses. The cavalry instinct in him told him they must have rest before he could again set forth, especially as he purposed to ride, with half a troop at least, over into Maryland. So, reluctantly enough he decided that he must wait until after dusk before he could begin, and all the time he never dreamed that not a mile away vigilant eyes kept track of every goer or comer about his camp, and that his movement, the instant it was made, would be signalled up and across the river, even to where stately Heatherwood gleamed white among the autumn foliage, and stood sentinel at the great bend. Before two o'clock that afternoon it was known to certain of the inmates at Heatherwood that Major Foulweather's detachment was dozing through the afternoon and no move might be expected before night. But an hour later came a different story.

Out in the orchard, wandering among the fast turning trees, the plump and rounded form and saucy face of Miss Laura Waddell could be seen when all the mansion seemed wrapped in slumber, so still and reposeful was the homestead, and Miss Waddell, for reasons best known to herself, had refrained from singing. Yet she looked for some one, was impatient of his delay, but dare not call him to her. Every now and then she would step to a point at the west end of the orchard, whence, through a rift in the trees, she could see the Virginia shore, the forest-covered heights beyond, and here and there a house or cottage. Westward over the Monocacy Valley towards Point of Rocks all was open and unbroken, and the rugged scarp of the Catoctins frowned against the autumn skies. North of the grand river the girl found nothing to claim her attention, outside the grounds of Heatherwood. Once in a while, very cautiously, she would glance towards the house, and her black eyes would take quick, furtive peeps at the westernmost of the three dormer-windows that faced the south. It was open to the afternoon sunshine; a white curtain floated in the breeze, but not a soul was visible. Down on the old towpath the sound of drowsy voices could be heard from time to time, and twice a drum had clattered impatiently in the camp of Clark's men. Some unusual ceremony was taking place, for the girl could see the heavy double lines ployed in mass and standing near the colonel's tent. Twice the girl fancied she could hear the deep tones of the colonel himself as though addressing his men. Forbidden to laugh or sing or torment Pettingill, Miss Waddell found time hanging heavily on her hands, and interest had given way to yawning and drowsiness. "I don't care, I don't believe that fella's ever comin'," she said to herself, with that joyous disregard of terminal letters that was so large a characteristic of certain sections of the South a quarter-century ago; "and I don't care if he never comes," she added, when suddenly recalled to herself by the sound of her own name, clearly yet not too loudly called, floating down as it were from the house-top, and, turning quickly, the girl saw a hand waving at that open dormer-window, an eager, beautiful face peering forth, gazing across the Potomac towards the distant slopes of the Loudoun, then quickly down in search of her. There was no mistaking either face or hand, or the slender form now shrinking back from the window,—Miss Heatherwood beyond a doubt; and now right beside her, but keeping back from the open casement, sallow, pallid, bearded, was another face that was itself hidden the next instant behind a pair of field-glasses and thin white hands. Captain Ralph Heatherwood, C.S.A., was then sufficiently recovered to leave his bed and clamber to the garret. "Laura, quick!" was called again, in cautious tone, and the girl sped away like a fawn until she stood beneath the window.

"What is it?" she hailed, curbing her shrill young voice to cautious tone. "I haven't seen a thing."

"We have," was the answer, "and he must know—quick. You must get word to him that the cavalry has broken camp and is coming this way,—coming fast."

Not fifteen minutes later, mounted on an astonished, reluctant, but docile old reminiscence of former days of equine style and spirit, the Virginia girl, her black eyes sparkling, her cheeks aflame with excitement, was jogging down the winding roadway, urging Dobbin into semblance of a trot. Turning from the "S" at the second bend, she followed the grass-grown, leafy track that led southward towards the canal, and as she cast one backward glance over her rounded shoulder for a survey of the rolling fields, the wooded slopes of Sugar Loaf loomed between her and the northern sky,—the lofty watch-tower of the Union army,—and on its very summit, almost among the clouds, a little patch of white and scarlet was swinging furiously, signalling to Maryland Heights full thirty miles away.

CHAPTER VII.

OLD Foulweather had stretched himself out for a "think." Dinner had done him good and sent Wilson sound asleep, but the major was uneasy in mind and only a light sleeper at any time. He was vexed at the tone of official inquiries into his failure to accomplish the object of his Virginia scouting, especially as no clearly defined object existed. In compliance with his own urgent pleading, he had been allowed to run up into Loudoun County for a few days, and, in general terms, had been told to make the neighborhood of Leesburg his exploring ground, to "observe matters in its vicinity, to patrol the roads, watch the passes, break up the enemy's means of obtaining information, and arrest all rebel officers or soldiers whose whereabouts he could learn." This made Hamlin laugh. "There's fifty thousand of them right over around Winchester, if McClellan really wants 'em," said he. But except the ill-starred attempt of some of Porter's corps to snap at the heels of the foe as they crossed the Potomac from Antietam, the sorely depleted, but still savagely fighting, force of Lee had been left alone. Foulweather's instructions further required him to keep vigilant eye on the movements of the enemy, and give prompt notice when he began his retreat, and this, too, made

Hamlin laugh, and Treacy swear. "Retreat be damned!" said the latter. "He's no more idea of retreatin' than Little Mac has of advancin', and as to keepin' vigilant eye through them peep-holes in the Blue Ridge, we never put an eye to wan of em' but somebody blacks it. Them fellers has generals that knows how to use cavalry, bedad, and our generals that knows how—ain't permitted. That's all there is to it. Faix, it's wan thing to name a saddle and another to know how to use it."

And the Irish ex-sergeant was not alone in his way of thinking. The little force of regular troopers had been split up into detachments, a troop here, a squadron there, acting as provost guards, quartermaster's guards, generals' escorts, doing orderly duty, and the like, while the new, undrilled, unseasoned regiments of cavalry volunteers were brigaded under officers who, in several cases at least, certainly knew their trade, but were all hampered more or less by holding reins that kept them dry-rotting about the camps, where there was not room for even riding-lessons, when they should have been afield. One command of nearly six strong regiments was far up the Potomac near Cumberland, another was scattered on the Maryland shore of the river, watching fords and ferries above Antietam Creek. Some regiments with Stoneman were hovering about Poolesville and Darnestown, others with Stahel were out in front of Washington, and Foulweather had been temporarily attached to that command. Dick

Rush's picturesque regiment of Pennsylvania Lancers was picketing the roads about Frederick, while Allen, with the First Maine, garrisoned the town. But most important of all, gallant John Buford, relieved for the time of active command, was chafing under the title of Chief of Cavalry at the head-quarters of the army, where even his vigorous influence seemed powerless to compel proper recognition of cavalry needs. The battling at Antietam had been terrific, but when it was over and Lee gathered up his hosts and slowly re-crossed the Potomac, he had fought so superbly that McClellan dared not follow. Like some sorely wounded but still dreaded lion, the Southern army limped away southward and lay down to rest and recuperate in the open fields between Winchester and Bunker Hill, while McClellan, slow, cautious, "feeling his way," sent his war-dogs warily creeping after them, and on the neighboring heights they crouched and watched, yet drew no nearer, for at the slightest forward movement the foe uplifted a threatening front, and the first growl of warning scattered the pack. Spanning the Potomac and the Shenandoah with his pontoons, manning the heights of Bolivar, Loudoun, and Maryland with his chosen corps, the Union leader halted and waited and clamored for men and shoes, clothing, food, and wagons, and behind him a nation rose up impatient, and at last there came a day, after full three weeks of utter inaction, when something had to be done, for the rebel battle-flags were sweeping into Pennsylvania, the plumes of Stuart at the head of column.

It must have been somewhere towards two o'clock on this October afternoon that Foulweather, sprawled on his blankets under a spreading tree, was roused from his rumination by sudden excitement among the men. Two veteran sergeants on duty with the horses were in lively discussion with a young non-commissioned officer who had just come in (from a "personally conducted" scout through some neighboring farm-yard) with a hat full of apples and a head full of news.

"I tell you I seen it," he was saying, "right up there on the range not three miles north of us. There's a cabin of some kind there, and I could count the flashes. They're signalling to some people down here about the old Hutton place, where the smoke is rising from the chimney yonder. It's looking-glass signalling. You've seen it among the Comanches, sergeant. You'd know it again. Come out with me and I'll prove it."

Foulweather sat up at the instant and rubbed his eyes. He was drowsy, he knew he needed sleep, but he could lose no chance. If there was signalling from the heights to Confederates close at hand, it behooved him to look out. Snicker's Gap wasn't so far away to the west that Stuart's people might not jump through at any minute and swoop down upon him. He had sent Sergeant Almy with a brace of reliable troopers full two miles out in that direction beyond his vedettes, and others still had gone southward, but up to this moment no word had come from either, yet the air seemed heavy with portent. Short Mountain, the easternmost of the Loudoun clump at the Potomac, shut off his view of Maryland Heights, and the Kittoctan hid from him the more distant peak of Sugar Loaf in Maryland. Otherwise, with his glasses he might have made out the signal-towers at these points. He was feeling a trifle sluggish and heavy now. Dinner, whiskey, and lack of sleep were all beginning to tell, but the excited talk had caused a stir among the men, several of whom were sitting up, rubbing their eyes, and beginning to take part in the conference, and then the major's bleary eyes lighted suddenly on Bob Hamlin, strolling up from the brook in his shirt sleeves, alert and refreshed after a souse in the clear, cold water, and the major hailed him at once.

"Hamlin," said he, "what possessed you to let that fellow Bell go over into Maryland?"

Hamlin waited until he had reached a point within three yards of his chief before he answered, and then replied, calmly and respectfully, "Because I believed what he told me,—that you wouldn't find Fairfax on this side, and might on that. If any one can find out his lair, I believe Bell can."

"Well, instead of hunting for Fairfax he's been playing messenger for that rebel rookery at Heatherwood, carrying notes to and fro, and God knows what all. I found that he had spent the night at Heatherwood,—where you had no business to let him go,—and I have turned him over to the provost-marshal."

Hamlin's frank face clouded. He began to speak, then suddenly checked himself, and Foulweather went on.

"And now our men are talking about signals going on up the range there. I'll bet a hat they're flashing, or flagging, or waving something to those Heatherwood people this very minute, and that like as not it's about that very fellow Bell, or perhaps Fairfax. What do you know about Bell, anyhow? What makes you trust him? I'm half ready to bet he was doing some rebel trick with those Heatherwood people when I was lucky enough to nab him."

"I'm wholly ready to take you, major," was the placid reply. "And now to cut this short, I'll bet you that that fellow is as loyal a trooper as you'll find in the cavalry, and, unless he's got to drinking again, I know of no reason why he should be arrested. He was authorized by me to go over and prosecute a line of search. I gave him a note to Colonel Allen at Frederick, to tell him what I knew of Fairfax, and further gave Bell authority that if need be he could go as far as Darnestown. It is my belief that he knows Fairfax by sight, though he will not admit it, and that he can recognize him through any disguise; therefore, I said go. It's my belief, further, that he would have found something valuable concerning Fairfax if it hadn't been for this arrest. Now it's useless to hope for anything on that score. But I protest against the arrest while acting under my orders, and I urge you, major, to send immediate withdrawal of any charges against him." Hamlin was turning away, but suddenly returned and confronted his angry chief. "Furthermore, I will tell you this, sir, you'll wish you had Bell back again before you're twelve hours older. Look what's coming now."

And as Hamlin spoke, he pointed towards the gap through the Kittoctan, beyond which lay Loesburg, Ball's Bluff, and the lower ferries. Riding post haste down the rocky road came a little squad of horsemen, a young officer in advance, two orderlies spurring at his heels. So still was the October afternoon, now becoming overcast, that the sound of the hoofs clattering on the stony way and the hoarse panting of the foaming steeds were already audible. There were rush and excitement in the very sight and sound, and all over the bivouac the troopers were springing to their feet and gazing eagerly towards the coming couriers. Many a time, night or day, had they been roused from their stolen slumbers by just such arrivals, harbingers of battle, and never yet had Foulweather's little detachment, pretty much all that was left of the old regiment, failed to respond. It seemed as though the eager, onward, daring spirit of the rough old trooper at their head permeated the entire force, mounts and men, and that, night or day, Foulweather's fellows were ready for work. "Say what you will of him," said beloved "Uncle

John," a cavalry leader the troopers of the army of the Potomac loved and trusted as Tommy Atkins of to-day swears by the gallant soldier known to the army list as Lord Roberts, but to fighting men the world over as "Bobs,"—"say what you will of Foulweather, he's no fairweather soldier." And now the major stood at gaze, his sturdy legs planted well apart, his fists digging into his hips, his arms akimbo, and his tired eyes lighting up with eager fire, and Bob Hamlin, vexed and more than half disposed to mutiny but a moment before, found his heart warming to the commander who, right or wrong, neck or nothing, was ever ready for fight.

A moment more and the officer in the lead had reached the bend in the road nearest the stream, and, leaping his reeking horse over a shallow ditch, came laboring across the open field. "Where's the major?" he shouted, waving as he did so a despatch he tore from the pocket of his blouse, and a dozen voices and hands uplifted directed him to the tree beneath which stood old Foulweather and his junior squadron commander.

"What's up, Skinny?" hailed the veteran, as he recognized in the coming man the lightest rider in the old cavalry brigade. But for answer the officer tossed him the letter, rolled out of saddle and panted:

"Have your men had their dinner?"

"Lord, yes, long ago. What's the matter?" repeated Foulweather, tearing away at the stout envelope, but seeking quicker tidings in the haggard eyes of the courier.

"Then sound 'To Horse,' for God's sake! I've been hunting for you since morning,—been 'way around beyond Leesburg, and nearly got nabbed."

By this time the major had ripped open the paper and was glaring at the contents. Before he had read three lines his eyes seemed popping from his head. Hamlin felt his nerves tingling, but "Skinny," leaving his exhausted horse to his own devices, reached for the major's ready canteen, shook it, drew the stopper, sniffed at the contents, then applying the spout to his lips, tilted his head back and shut his dust-rimmed eyes. Roused from his slumbers by the sound of subdued, but excited talk, the unusual stir and action, Captain Treacy came hurrying over to join his chief, buttoning his blue coat on the run. Foulweather's eyes were blazing by this time and his thin lips were tight compressed. Here, there, and everywhere among the trees little knots of troopers in their worn jackets or coarse gray shirts were gazing fixedly at the group at head-quarters. Some men sat silently on their blankets, but were pulling on their boots or buckling the shabby old brass spurs. Contrary to expectation, the major did not break out with order or expletive until he had read every word of the missive. Then came the announcement in unexpected form:

"Gentlemen, you may remember my telling Captain Belden I considered Jeb Stuart, whom he so praised as a cavalry leader, as mad-brained a crank as ever rode a charge, and Jeb Stuart has proved my words this day of days."

"What d'ye mane?" growled Treacy, impatient of circumlocution. "What's he doin' now?"

"Crossed the Potomac into Maryland with only two thousand sabres, right in the face of our whole force, and riding for the rear of the army. Good-by to you, Jeb! You laughed at my tactics three years ago at Riley, but we'll have the laugh on you this night, or there's neither brains nor bottom left in the old army. Oh, if we only had the regulars together for twenty-four hours instead of split up all over the land. Listen to this, gentlemen:

"POINT OF ROCKS, MARYLAND,
"October 11, 1862, 10 A.M.

"MAJOR —— F——,

"Commanding Detachment Cavalry, in the Field, near Leesburg:

"Sir,—General Burnside directs me to notify you at once that the rebel general Stuart crossed the Potomac at McCoy's Ferry at daybreak yesterday, covered by a heavy fog, with a force estimated by the signal-officers at two thousand sabres and four guns, and has pushed northward to Pennsylvania. It is probable that he is aiming again to make the circuit of the army and to raid the field hospitals and quartermasters' depots. General Pleasonton, with all available cavalry, will doubtless pursue at once, and it will be impossible for Stuart to return the way he came.

"The general hesitates to give orders to you, as you are not directly under his command, but, it being impracticable to communicate with your brigade commander, it is suggested that you march to the Monocacy by way of White's Ford in order that a force of cavalry may be concentrated to meet and overthrow Stuart should he come this way, as he probably will. The signal-officer reports that Stuart is out of sight, far to the north, and that troops are now marching in pursuit.

"Our cavalry at Frederick are ordered out already. General Stoneman has a big force around Poolesville. We have men enough to block every ford, and Stuart ought to be captured within twelve hours. At all events, you are warned in time, and must not be caught all by yourself over in Loudoun County.

"Very respectfully, your obedient servant,
"J. D. HASTINGS,
"A. D. C."

And as the major finished the paper, he turned, with kindling eyes, and ordered, "Sound to horse!"

And then, indeed, was there a stirring scene along the banks of the little branch of the Kittoctan. Ordinarily a field column strikes its tents and forms for the march with some ceremony and precision, at the bugle sound "The General." Frequently when cavalry are in bivouac and are to pack their traps and start away, and there is no especial hurry, "Boots and Saddles" is the signal, and the troopers take it leisurely. But like the "To Arms!" of the infantry, there is a call to action for the mounted corps that sends each man to his station on the jump, a call at sound of which the chargers stamp and snort, and switch about with ears erect and eyes aflash, and troopers spring for their saddles and arms, for not a moment must be lost. No time is wasted on roll-calls or inspection. Quick as men can jump into their own rigs, fold their blankets, strap saddles, and lead into line, the sergeants order "Mount!" and the squadron is ready.

Foulweather had no tents to strike, no *impedimenta* except the few pots, pans, and kettles to be dumped into the wagon and rattled after them. In ten minutes from the stirring peal the three compact little squadrons were forming line, and in less than fifteen were moving, first at quiet walk, filing out upon the valley road in silent sets of fours, diminishing front to column of twos as they struck the winding ascent to the Pass, and then, following old Foulweather and the fluttering guidon, with jingling spur and clanking sabre and clattering hoofs, away they squirmed and twisted up the westward slope, turned to the northward as they cleared the range, struck the trot as their stocky leader signalled "head of column to the left" when they reached the old, familiar, dusty highway on the eastward slopes, and, with every signal-tower within a radius of fifty miles of Harper's Ferry flagging question and answer, orders and news, rumors and facts from far and near, and regiments marching hither and yon, and brigades and battalions heading northward in search of the daring invader, batteries and squadrons jogging through the country lanes, with wary leaders far ahead, and the afternoon sunshine glinting on Heatherwood towers and glancing from Heatherwood's dormer-windows, and causing strange, blinding, vivid flashes to dart at intervals through a leafy gap towards the silent heights across the placid, plashing waters, on came old Foulweather, with Treacy and Drummond and bold Bob Hamlin, each at the head of his own little band, riding post haste to join an army in its effort to hem in and surround, overthrow or capture, the rash Virginians who, pinning their faith on the gold-laced gray sleeve at the head of their jaunty column, dared to follow him through the lines of the enemy and run the gauntlet of a scattered force of forty thousand men. "Goodby to you and yours, Jeb Stuart!" said old Foulweather, as, forgetful of fatigue or food, or even whiskey, he plashed through the limpid waters of the Potomac at the ford, squashed through the mud in the empty bed of the canal beyond, and was lost in the shades of night on the route to Frederick, ready to bet the last cent in his pocket, the last drop of blood in his veins, that he and "the old regiment" would have it out with Jeb now and for all time, and turn the laugh on him at last.

But as the long column swung its tail clear of the canal, the rearmost troopers exchanging a volley of chaff with the pickets along the bank, a regiment of infantry in bright blue uniforms, with overcoats rolled and bayonets unfixed, came marching by fours along the towpath, a stalwart, bearded soldier riding at their head, who turned in saddle and ordered "Halt!" that the troopers might pass by; then nodded cool recognition to the red-faced old dragoon, who, leading the horsemen as they issued from the ford, reined out to the left to meet him.

"Which way, colonel?" asked Foulweather, personal differences forgotten in the absorbing nature of the work in hand. "I thought you were on guard at the Monocacy aqueduct?"

"Maine relieves us there," was the answer. "We are ordered to report to General Ward near Conrad's."

"Any news of Stuart?"

"Signal-towers haven't seen a thing of him. They say there was rain in the Cumberland Valley last night, and the dust was laid this morning. They can't track him, but he's destroyed all public property in Chambersburg, and cut the wires, and the last heard of him was striking for Gettysburg. It's thought now he aims to get back to the east of us,—Edward's Ferry, perhaps."

"By God!" cried Foulweather, with impatient slap of his broad palm on a burly thigh; "if I can find a guide that knows the roads up there to the northeast, he'll never get back to the river without a fight." And the major looked anxiously northward.

"Keep the road to Heatherwood, Treacy," he called

out, "till I join you," then turned again to the bearded colonel. "I suppose they're filling the whole Monocacy against his coming that way?" he inquired.

"So our despatches say. Burnside sent two brigades into the valley from beyond Point of Rocks. Pleasonton is ordered east through the ridge to head him off, and ought to be north of Frederick now. The Lancers and the First Maine are out already. Stuart will never be fool enough to try to fight his way through such heavy force. That's why I say he's likely to come down through Hyattstown, perhaps,—away to the east of Frederick, anyhow. You've had a guide that knows that country thoroughly, so Homans tells me, but he's out with another party now."

"I had? Who do you mean?" growled the major, a sudden suspicion dawning upon him, as Bob Hamlin came riding up at the head of his squadron.

"The man you ordered turned over to the guard at Heatherwood,—Bell, they say his name is. He's guiding a squadron of regulars from Point of Rocks that passed my pickets two hours ago. My officers recognized him at once."

"D'ye hear that, Hamlin?" roared Foulweather. "That damned man McIntosh is out with his squadron to clip our wings and get our glory, by God! and has had the infernal brass to take my own trooper, the man that I ordered under guard, to show him the way."

"Yes," answered Bob, reflectively, as he reined up a moment to reply to his chief. "I think I remember saying a while ago, that it wouldn't be twelve hours before you'd wish you had Bell back again."

CHAPTER VIII.

There was, indeed, mounting in hot haste all over the army of the Potomac that eventful October Saturday, mad eagerness for the chase, wild rage for battle, and blind ignorance of the movements of the foe. Not two months before had that cavalier leader, Stuart, spurred completely around the halted hosts of General Pope, raiding his very head-quarters train, looting the general's personal baggage, donning, some said, the general's personal uniform, though ardent Southerners denied with indignation the story that their hero knight could ever again stoop to wear the Yankee blue, "but he might have dressed some nigguh in it." Not two months before, Stuart and his merry men had ridden laughing away from the smoking ruins of the Union camp. Barely six weeks agone they had repeated, to our even greater cost, the best part of the same trooper pleasantry: swooped down on the trains and stores at Manassas Junction, filled their stomachs with all they could eat, clothed their wiry selves in all they could wear, turned over huge supplies, still unappropriated, to Old Jack's "foot cavalry" when they came trudging after, and now, having vainly waited an anxious fortnight for McClellan to follow up the advantage gained at so much cost at Antietam, here he was again: "Three raids in less than three months!" It was enough to make a Union trooper rabid.

And what a wonderful raid was this! what daring! what consummate "cheek!" Even the bald official reports read like the pages of romance. Noting McClellan's falter at the Potomac; knowing full well how scattered was the Union cavalry; studying the reports unerringly forwarded by Southern friends at court, and the Union commander's excuses for delay and pleas for supplies; reasoning right well that he need dread no forward movement of his adversary, and that he might be able to fall upon and break up his trains and depots of supplies, the calm leader of the Southern lines called again on his ready cavalry. No matter how great the disappointment that Maryland failed to welcome him with open arms the month before, Lee would leave no stone unturned to win the admiration of the wavering State and strike terror to his foes. "Now is our time," he cautioned Stuart. "Ride for Pennsylvania. Harm no soul in Maryland. Disturb no property there. Wait till you get beyond the line, then hit hard. Blow up the bridges of the Conococheague. Strike Chambersburg; seize all horses and supplies you can use; burn everything in the way of public property that you cannot. Parole all soldiers you can capture, and bring away all civil officials you can carry, to be held as hostages for our own. Then hark back the best way you can,—either westward towards Cumberland, where the foe are scattered and the country is rough and where Imboden will demonstrate and keep them busy in the mean time, or else eastward across the Blue Ridge, where the country lies open as a book but is swarming with enemies on every side. Take only fifteen hundred picked men and horses, then use your own discretion and dash."

Oh, what a thrilling moment for a soldier! Five thousand horsemen has he to choose from, and he chooses well. Six regiments of Virginia cavalry send forward their choicest men and steeds. Wade Hampton's North and South Carolinians contribute their quota. Then from the artillery young Pelham, prince of gunners, picks four flawless pieces, overhauls every axle, pole, and spoke. The iron arms are freshly greased till the new wheels spin like glistening tops. Brand-new tugs and traces are tackled to the harness, collars are carefully fitted to the necks of draught-horses, chosen from the best in the brigade, and, with Wade Hampton and "Roony" Lee for sub-commanders, waving silent good-by to the envious friends in the thronging camps, away rides Stuart, no man in all his daredevil array can prophesy whither. "Soldiers," he says to them in a bulletin that rings like those of Napoleon, "you are about to engage in an enterprise which, to insure success, imperatively demands at your hands coolness, decision, and bravery, implicit obedience to orders without question or cavil, and the strictest order and sobriety on the march and in bivouac. The destination and extent of this expedition had better be kept to myself than known to you. Suffice it to say that with the hearty co-operation of officers and men I have not a doubt of its success,— a success which will reflect credit in the highest degree upon your arms. The orders which are herewith published for your government are absolutely necessary, and must be rigidly enforced."

And with these few words to his shadowy command, read just before they approach the Potomac, Stuart leads his little column into the dusk on Thursday evening, the 9th of October, halts, and bivouacs about the village of Hedgesville for the night, with vedettes well out in every direction. Wade Hampton commands the advance, and from his detachment, six hundred strong, he chooses an enthusiastic young officer,—Phillips, of the Tenth Virginia,— and with him creeps forward under the shadows of the night and posts him with twenty-five troopers, dismounted, at the river's brink. There in the darkness these devoted fellows keep watch and ward through the midnight hours, undisturbed by hostile sight or sound. The plash of the unseen waters, drifting by in the impenetrable gloom, lulls them to security and repose, but sleep, except in cat-naps, half a squad at a time, is not for them. One, two o'clock, the hours glide away. Three approaches, and the young lieutenant calls up his men, for a big squadron has almost noiselessly moved forward from the village and formed, one hundred and eighty berland, where the foe are scattered and the country is rough and where Imboden will demonstrate and keep them busy in the mean time, or else eastward across the Blue Ridge, where the country lies open as a book but is swarming with enemies on every side. Take only fifteen hundred picked men and horses, then use your own discretion and dash."

Oh, what a thrilling moment for a soldier! Five thousand horsemen has he to choose from, and he chooses well. Six regiments of Virginia cavalry send forward their choicest men and steeds. Wade Hampton's North and South Carolinians contribute their quota. Then from the artillery young Pelham, prince of gunners, picks four flawless pieces, overhauls every axle, pole, and spoke. The iron arms are freshly greased till the new wheels spin like glistening tops. Brand-new tugs and traces are tackled to the harness, collars are carefully fitted to the necks of draught-horses, chosen from the best in the brigade, and, with Wade Hampton and "Roony" Lee for sub-commanders, waving silent good-by to the envious friends in the thronging camps, away rides Stuart, no man in all his daredevil array can prophesy whither. "Soldiers," he says to them in a bulletin that rings like those of Napoleon, "you are about to engage in an enterprise which, to insure success, imperatively demands at your hands coolness, decision, and bravery, implicit obedience to orders without question or cavil, and the strictest order and sobriety on the march and in bivouac. The destination and extent of this expedition had better be kept to myself than known to you. Suffice it to say that with the hearty co-operation of officers and men I have not a doubt of its success,— a success which will reflect credit in the highest degree upon your arms. The orders which are herewith published for your government are absolutely necessary, and must be rigidly enforced."

And with these few words to his shadowy command, read just before they approach the Potomac, Stuart leads his little column into the dusk on Thursday evening, the 9th of October, halts, and bivouacs about the village of Hedgesville for the night, with vedettes well out in every direction. Wade Hampton commands the advance, and from his detachment, six hundred strong, he chooses an enthusiastic young officer,—Phillips, of the Tenth Virginia,— and with him creeps forward under the shadows of the night and posts him with twenty-five troopers, dismounted, at the river's brink. There in the darkness these devoted fellows keep watch and ward through the midnight hours, undisturbed by hostile sight or sound. The plash of the unseen waters, drifting by in the impenetrable gloom, lulls them to security and repose, but sleep, except in cat-naps, half a squad at a time, is not for them. One, two o'clock, the hours glide away. Three approaches, and the young lieutenant calls up his men, for a big squadron has almost noiselessly moved forward from the village and formed, one hundred and eighty strong, close to the river bank. It is the Second South Carolina, under Colonel Butler, and his orders are clear. Phillips, with his little party, is to wade the shallow river just above McCoy's, steal noiselessly out upon the northward bank, and seize and secure sufficient ground for their mounted comrades to form as they issue from the ford. If discovered by the Union pickets, who are sure to be watching the ferry landing at McCoy's, they must dash upon them instantly, capture them if possible, or drive them back. If resistance be stubborn, Butler will lead his horsemen into the foaming waters and follow to the rescue. So in they go, knee-deep, waist-deep, maybe breast-deep before they reach the other shore, but who cares? Phillips knows the way, and who would miss the chance of being foremost on this glorious raid! Holding high their carbines and cartridge-boxes, the daring Virginians plough their way, slowly, carefully, until at last the lieutenant issues dripping on the farther shore, and one after another with him group his men.

Meantime, in breathless silence,—eager riders, accustomed steeds,—Butler's little battalion waits the signal. Fifteen minutes pass away, and their venturesome comrades have disappeared from view. The Maryland shore looms dim and shadowy through the mists just curling from the surface of the waters and partially obscuring the stars that here and there are peeping from the cloudy heavens. Stuart, too, and "Roony" Lee have ridden down to the water's edge to watch the crossing, and a long gray column is curling snake-like from the distant village towards the deserted ferry. Will the signal never come? It lacks but a few minutes of four, and not a sight or sound has reached them from the northern bank. With Stuart rides a young Virginia trooper who knows every wood road over in Washington county, who is to guide the advance on the rush through Maryland into Pennsylvania. And even as the impatient leader turns to whisper inquiry, two faint flashes split the mists of the morning. Two, three, quickly follow. Then come the muffled reports of half a dozen carbines. Then all sounds from the farther shore are drowned in the dash and scurry on the Virginia bank. Into the stream splash the leaders, followed by the South Carolinians in long column of twos, and, guiding on the occasional gleams of musketry, they press boldly through the foaming flood, and so, before the faint, gray light of dawn is peering over the Blue Ridge, thirty miles away, Stuart's advance has pounced on the astonished pickets of the Twelfth Illinois. Then as the dawn appears over the dim range at the east, the fog rolls thicker from the stream, and, gray as the morning mists, and well-nigh as silent, the long column comes dripping up the heights, forms line in places along the crest, then pushes sharp-eyed skirmishers out to the front on every lane or open field; and presently these exploring parties stir up other pickets, and more shots are exchanged, and the neighborhood begins to wake up with the day, and the rear-guard of a long column of infantry, marching westward on the old national pike a mile or so north of the river, halts to find out what all that popping of pistols means down there along the misty banks, and presently they find out indeed, for east, west, and south, right, left, and front, there come galloping out on them exultant parties of horsemen in gray jackets and plumed hats and the blithest of spirits,—gentlemen who bid the amazed infantry, burdened with curiosity and baggage, to gratify all they wish of the one and surrender all they've got of the other. Then Major Hairston, division provost-marshal, rides up and receives the prisoners and arranges for their parole,—Stuart has no room for prisoners martial,—and it is broad daylight when Pelham's guns come clinking up the stony path and the advance has split the pickets asunder, captured some horses, and the guide points out the Union signal-station on Fairview Heights, and Hampton sends a platoon of horse to nab the occupants, catching them almost unawares, for the pickets, being so busy looking out for themselves, have forgotten all about these lofty parties whose business it is to look out for others, and only in the nick of time and by the skin of their teeth do Lieutenants Roe and Rowley make their escape and dash madly away to Clear Spring, three miles to the east, and tell their tale to Maryland cavalrymen, who send couriers darting away to warn General Kenly at Williamsport.

Meantime, the laughing rebs have made mincemeat of anything left at Fairview station, and the direful news of their coming, instead of being flagged or signalled to Hagerstown (where are Generals Brooks and Franklin of the Union army, with a whole corps of Union troops within hail) has to be sent at a trot or gallop, and never reaches Hagerstown until noon; and, indeed, not until Roe and Rowley arrive there well-nigh exhausted, at two o'clock, do the Union generals get full information that Jeb Stuart, the redoubtable, is up to his old tricks again and more than half-way up to Pennsylvania.

Just what is being done in McClellan's army along the Antietam and thereabouts all this blessed October Friday, while Stuart, barely twenty miles away, is trotting northward to Mercersburg, no one seems to know. General Kenly, at Williamsport, as early as eight o'clock gets news of the crossing from his pickets, and declares he sends it at once to Brooks at Hagerstown, but it has to go by courier. Close by Sharpsburg camps Major-General Pleasonton, commander of the whole Union cavalry division, but his troops are scattered hither and yon. Close to the Potomac at Knoxville, midway between Point of Rocks and Harper's Ferry, camps Major-General George B. McClellan, commanding the Army of the Potomac, and though Kenly has the news of this important dash through our lines at eight in the day, and all Hagerstown knows the truth soon after meridian, sundown comes without a sign from head-quarters of the army. Indeed, not until nine at night, when Stuart's gleeful men are helping themselves to everything in the line of public property worth having in the Pennsylvania town, is an order of any kind issued for pursuit. Incredible as it may seem to-day, not until four o'clock on Saturday morning, twenty-four hours after Stuart strikes the Maryland shore, does Pleasonton get orders to start. Then he sends reply that he doesn't know where McCoy's Ferry is, that his command is very small because so many horses are unshod, but he'll do the best he can under the circumstances, which sounds anything but inspiring, somehow. And then having started for Hagerstown, not very many miles away, it takes him all the morning to get there, for it is eleven o'clock when he passes through. Then, the enemy by that time having gone east from Chambersburg towards Gettysburg, the leader of the Union horse goes west from Hagerstown towards the point where Stuart crossed, and so doubles the distance between him and the foe.

Yes, all this while, unmolested, unpursued, Stuart and his merry men went raiding. At four P.M. on Saturday they had possessed themselves of the post-office and all government valuables in Mercersburg. Their horses were fed and watered, then on they go at five o'clock in a thin drizzling rain that soon soaks through the worn gray jackets, but never damps their spirits, raiding every farm and barn and stable on the way, leading forth every horse worth having as they speed along, and just before eight o'clock, Hampton, riding in the lead, comes in view of the twinkling lights of Chambersburg, over forty miles from the Potomac by the way they came, and right in the heart of the rich, populous Cumberland Valley; and here, in a downpour, the silent column rides front into line and Hart unlimbers a brace of guns to command the ungarrisoned town, and Lieutenant Lee, of South Carolina, with a score of troopers at his back, waving on high a flag of truce, rides forward into the bewildered little municipality, only to find that every official has fled and Chambersburg is at the mercy of the South. Away goes a battalion up the Conococheague to burn the railway bridge and bar the coming of McClellan's supplies or Curtin's Home Guards, but that bridge is iron, and their efforts are vain in the limited time at their disposal. Hampton is appointed military governor, and, officers and men, the Southern troopers are billeted about the various buildings for the night, while vigilant pickets cover the approaches from every side. The barns and granaries are ransacked for food for the hundreds of horses they have brought along, —men in mid-column have been leading two and three apiece all the way from Mercersburg. Stores and groceries drive a thriving business until all the stock in trade is trafficked off for jovial promises to pay. Every piano in the burgh is "requisitioned" for the time, and many a parlor visited by gentlemen with muddy boots and polished manners. Dames and damsels who had no time to flee rejoice in secret over those who had to go, and lost thereby the most delightful evening some of them have ever known. Mirth, music, and soldier song reign for hours through the erstwhile sombre streets of the sober old town, and the Union sick and wounded, nabbed in hospital to the number of nearly three hundred and paroled on the spot, sit or lie and listen to the fun, and wonder, as well they may, where on earth the Union cavalry are spending the night, and when in realms unmentionable they propose to come and settle this.

It was early in the October evening that a little group of cavaliers sat drying their steaming garments about the great wide fireplace of an old-fashioned Pennsylvania mansion, and sipping a most seductive apple toddy from the supplies produced from the owner's cellar. Virginia toasted the Carolinas; Stuart's own statesmen pledged the health of Hampton's men, and when some one proposed a song, and the old hound, sprawling in the corner, defrauded of his bed before the blazing fire, stirred uneasily at the mournful strains of that sentimental lay, "Lorena," one young gallant threw back a curly head and shouted, "Oh, take a drink, Monty, and give us a fighting song. Floyd Fairfax is the only fellow we had could sing 'Lorena.'"

Whereat the officer addressed as Monty sent his plumed hat spinning at the critic's head and went on with his ditty:

"Since last I held that ha-and in mine."

"Shut up, Monty. The only hand you've had worth holding for a year was an ace full that night at Manassas, and you were too full to know it when Fairfax raised you."

And this time Monty stopped short, turned on his tormentor, and looked vexed.

"See hyuh, gentlemen," said he, "no man knows better'n I do that singin' ain't my strong point, but just let me tell you one thing, if any of you want to hear Floyd Fairfax sing again, the best thing you can do is to fetch him back to duty with his troop. The general don't talk much, perhaps, but you ask Price or Fitzhugh what he said when he agreed to let that troop go off to hunt Floyd Fairfax up at Leesburg."

In a moment the merriment was stilled. The chat and laughter came to sudden stop. It was not good among those that followed Stuart that imputation of any kind should attach to the name of officer and gentleman. For a moment there was a silence almost as of dismay, then, with a simulated yawn, out spoke young Garnett, him of the curling black locks.

"Give us more 'Lorena,' Monty," said he, sweetly. "It's bad, but we'd rather listen to that. Floyd Fairfax is—all right."

CHAPTER IX.

But to see the anxious faces at that dormer-window of the Heatherwood place the afternoon that followed this conversation, no one who could hear one word of the talk between brother and sister, or heard the instructions given Laura Waddell before she rode away, would be apt to believe that Floyd Fairfax was "all right." But where Lieutenant Garnett of the Virginia Horse meant by "all right" that the absence of Captain Fairfax from his command at this time was a matter thoroughly understood by most of his friends to reflect in no wise on his character or reputation, "all right" with Belle Heatherwood and her wounded and supposed to be bedridden brother would have referred more particularly to his physical condition and surroundings. In the one case it was known that he had been quite seriously wounded and had to be left behind at Leesburg a month previous, and that even if he could have rejoined his troop by way of the gaps through the Blue Ridge, he was not yet well enough for cavalry duty. What Fitzhugh and others dreaded was that the Yankees would raid Loudoun County again and carry him off, and if carrying was to be done, therefore, it were better done by his own people. Hence the dash of the Fairfax troop to Leesburg only to find their bird had flown, and that, so far from slipping back to his colors, he had limped away under cover of night to the Potomac, and, said a Leesburg cousin, " 'Fyou want to find Floyd you'll have to ask Belle Heatherwood,"—a bit of feminine acrimony or spite that was destined to harm Floyd Fairfax far more than the speaker imagined possible. The troop had taken advantage of the departure of the Union cavalry to gallop to the point opposite Heatherwood Towers in hopes of finding their friend the captain, but Hamlin, after all, had proved too quick for them. They had ridden back discomfited and yet rather well pleased at their exploit, and reached the camps around Winchester only to learn that they had lost the chance of a far more exciting and important raid, —that Stuart was gone with two thousand picked men, and not a word had been heard from him since he disappeared in the mists of the morning at McCoy's ford.

"Here's a letter from Fairfax marked personal," said one of the staff-officers left behind, "brought in yesterday by some of our patrols who got it from an old nigger. It's addressed to Fitzhugh; explains where he is, probably, and what he's doing. We'll know as soon as the general gets back."

But Captain Fairfax had taken the responsibility of a raid into Maryland all on his own account, all in ignorance of that commanded by his daring leader, and though he, too, might find out a good deal about the position and force and possible intentions of the enemy, and had a certain military purpose in his visit, there was to him, indeed, a greater object, and that was to see the lady of his love, his distant cousin, Belle Heatherwood, and this was a matter difficult of accomplishment.

In her sterling honesty, Madam Heatherwood had accepted the guard tendered for the preservation of her property and the favors extended her wounded son and nephew as things to be scrupulously regarded and even repaid. The fact that she had long and tenderly and successfully nursed certain Union wounded after Bull Run and Ball's Bluff in no wise released her, she held, from the debt of gratitude she now owed the general government. Not only did she observe strict neutrality herself, but she demanded it of the inmates of her household. Her son being flat on his back, as she declared and believed, no disobedience was to be apprehended from him. Young Tighlman, high-spirited and impatient, proved less tractable, but Belle, "my beauty daughter," as her fond father had called her in her girl days, and as the proud mother so often thought of her now, was Southern in temperament as she was in sympathy, and Ralph's descriptive fully covered the case when he referred to her as a "red-hot rebel."

Baltimore associations had much to do with this, but by no means all. Even in school-days, excepting one or two friends like Florence Lowndes, all her chums were Southern girls. Many of her vacations were spent visiting charming old Southern homes.

It was not until a year or so before the outbreak of the war that she saw anything whatever of Northern society, and she found it, as compared with that she had known so well and loved so much, somewhat stiff, if not indeed humdrum. She was a girl with innate love of truth, honor, and courage in man or woman. She had pride of birth and name and beauty. The men her father had best known and loved were of the old cavalier stock, and from her baby days, almost, she had most admired such as he, men of grave, courteous, chivalric dignity of manner. Years of her life, it seems, she had known General Lee. Three years ago this very month, she remembered it well, he and his young associate, Lieutenant Stuart, were entertained at Heatherwood, both in the uniform of the old army, for there had been stirring events at Harper's Ferry. A Northern fanatic, an abolitionist, backed by men misguided and fanatical like himself, had hidden in the fastnesses of the grand range to the west, and begun a secret and wicked crusade that was to array the blacks against their masters, to promote insurrection and rebellion, to place in negro hands the sword and the torch, and bid them kill, burn, and destroy to win their freedom. She had never forgotten the dread and horror with which they heard of Ossawattomie Brown's mad attempt at Harper's Ferry, followed by the uprising, not of the blacks, but of the whites against him,—the bloody fight at the old engine-house, United States troops against the rash invaders.

Then came the capture of the wounded old man, his trial at Charlestown, the mustering of the Virginia militia, far and near, to attend his execution. "Bloody miscreant," she heard him called by every woman except her gentle mother, as the sad, dreamy, friendless old soul was led to the scaffold. But there were men even then who looked grave and thoughtful, who read in that first feeble kindling of the flame the unerring preface to the great proclamation that, springing from the blood of battling hosts that reddened the tide lapping the base of those very heights, should soon sweep the land like a tornado, driving slavery before it. Three years before, the arms of the United States were turned on him who drove the entering wedge of abolition through the mighty rocks here within sight of her ancestral home, and now ten thousand freemen in the Union blue were risen up for every soldier there employed. Obedient to the laws, as then interpreted, the disciplined strength of that little party of regulars had been hurled against that improvised fort, and John Brown's worn old body was sent to moulder in the grave. Yet here, day after day, in that same uniform, thousands of soldiery, lusty lunged, tramped by their very gates proclaiming to the world his soul was marching on. John Brown struck the spark from the rocks at Harper's Ferry, and Abraham Lincoln loosed a whirlwind of cleansing fires, a thank-offering from the bluffs of the Antietam. Here within hail of Heatherwood the initial shot of an immortal struggle echoed from shore to shore of an inland river. Here within hail of Heatherwood was fought the tremendous battle whose issue was the immortal proclamation now echoing from shore to shore of the fathomless sea.

There were no grave, courteous, cavalier soldiers of Virginia now to stand in stately pose on the old portico, as Lee and Stuart had stood in days gone by. Ralph and Cousin Tighlman looked far from stately when lifted out of the ambulance that September afternoon and borne aloft to comfortable beds. The Union officers who called to see her mother on business, or to inquire for the welfare of the household of a long-loved comrade, Belle rarely saw. Belle's heart was hot against that uniform, ever since the spring of '61, until circumstances occurred to render it bearable within the week gone by. Colonel Clark and Lieutenant Homans she had seen only when she chose to peer through the blinds. All her attentions and devotions had been given, since the battle of South Mountain, to those two wounded, but most importunate and dissatisfied heroes in the second story, both wild to get well, get exchanged, and back to their regiments. Both had to be entertained and, harder still, to be kept in subjection. Both were doing well, thanks to tough constitutions and unimpaired digestion, and both demanded items of food and drink either forbidden or beyond their reach. Mrs. Heatherwood, of course, spent much time with both, but she was neither strong nor well. Her daughter was her mainstay about the house, backed by two old family servants, and now within the month Laura had been added to her cares when Laura was quite able, so she said, to take care of herself.

That child's spirits seemed irrepressible. She had not been at Heatherwood a day before she renewed her acquaintance with every feature, taking especial comfort in the barn, wherein she had had so many a frolic as a child, and in the orchard, which, despite its denuded condition as to fruit, proved full of entertainment for her from the day of her arrival, mainly because it seemed to attract every Yankee straggler who could elude the vigilance of the guards. Just when she first met and captured Pettingill the household never knew, but he never forgot. He became her devotee from the start, and she knew it. She cajoled, tormented, snubbed, and wheedled him by turns, but in simple faith he never wavered. Him she questioned when she wanted information, and, if he could not give it, hectored him until he went and found out what she demanded to know. Speedily discovering that Madam Heatherwood was averse to anything that might prejudice her observance of a strict neutrality, Laura carried all she learned to her city-bred cousin, whom she admired and looked up to as a woman without a peer. To Belle she was fidelity itself. Her will was law. Her wishes went unchallenged, even when it presently developed that something was agog to which

Aunty Heatherwood was not a party, and the full nature of which Laura herself was not permitted to know.

Letters came a few days after her arrival, one of which caused Cousin Belle an access of excitement. That night Laura was excluded from her cousin's room, and, wandering into the orchard for refuge, she was startled by the appearance of a light in a window where no light was known to be before, the west dormer on the south front. Who on earth would be in the garret now? Then the light suddenly went out, or disappeared, then as suddenly flamed again, and that was odder still. Half a dozen times it gleamed a moment, then disappeared, and Laura was keen-witted enough to know that some one must be signalling over to the Virginia shore. Later, on sunshiny afternoons, she had twice seen Belle there at that window, and finally had openly charged her cousin with carrying on communication with somebody.

"Not that I object," said Miss Waddell. "I just love it; only you needn't try to hide it from me."

So they did not, thereafter. Belle frankly told her cousin, binding her to secrecy, that Captain Floyd Fairfax, who had been left wounded at Leesburg, was now so far recovered that he had written by a trusty hand to say that before he rejoined his troop he was going to make an effort to cross, as he must see Ralph and Tighlman, if only for half an hour, and must visit some friends at Poolesville. He would be disguised, and the experiment was hazardous, said Belle, but Fairfax had ever been a daredevil. They could not write to dissuade him,—it was unsafe. Yet they had managed to send a message to him, verbally, but all to no purpose. He had devised a system of signals which he wished to teach them, and already was able to warn them what night to expect him. Just two nights before this stirring and eventful Saturday, now drawing to a close, a Maryland farmer appeared at the kitchen door and asked for Miss Heatherwood, and the moment she entered and caught sight of the shaggy-haired, heavy-bearded, rough-looking rustic standing there so awkwardly, she asked if he had brought her a message or letter, then suddenly burst into hysterical laughter that ended in a sort of cry as she sat down on a bench, "shaking all over," said Laura, when, long afterwards, she could dispassionately describe the events of that October week at Heatherwood, and her version may safely be adopted now. "The farmer," said she, "began to chuckle," and Laura was on the point of snapping at him for want of manners, when the whole situation dawned upon her. That farmer was Floyd Fairfax, and she was much *de trop*. They dared not let Madam Heatherwood know of his presence. She liked him well, but would have no unauthorized communication with the enemies of the United States, and not until after she had kissed her son and nephew good-night and retired to her own room dare they pilot the visitor up to Ralph's bedside, where, said Laura, "he, too, nearly died laughing at the queer figure Fairfax made." But what the captain wanted of Ralph and Tighlman could not amount to much, thought she, for he only spent twenty minutes talking to them, while for hours he was hanging around for a chance to whisper to Belle, who seemed none too eager to give him opportunity, for that same night there came to the house that Yankee soldier, covered with dust and dirt, "a soldier who knew the ways of the place, if he didn't know how to be polite to ladies," said Miss Waddell, airily, in referring to the matter later. He rode to the barn by the back way and watered and fed his horse and then brought his saddle and saddle-bags straight to the kitchen door and asked Aunt Chloe, who was cooking, please to take a note to Miss Belle, which he scribbled on a piece of paper, and Chloe said Miss Belle jumped up and turned four kinds of colors inside a minute and ran down the back stairs ahead of her, and Chloe could have sworn Belle was crying and "all trembling like" when she reached the kitchen. (All which was just what Aunt Chloe told her, rather than let Laura believe her cousin awaiting, as she was, that Yankee's coming.) And then the Yankee was shown to a room on the first floor, a room that had been kept locked ever since, and there Aunty Heatherwood went and had a long talk with him, and there he stayed all that night and all the next day and night (so Laura believed), and had his meals taken in to him by Aunt Heatherwood herself, Chloe said so, because he was worn out and dead tired, poor soul, and in some trouble, too, because first thing Saturday morning they had sentries round the house and Yankee officers came there and arrested this same soldier just as he was sneaking away with his saddle-bags, never saying good-by, and Belle wouldn't tell Laura anything about "that fella," and only blushed and laughed when Laura asked her who was the handsome Yankee officer who called on her the previous afternoon, and rode away with Mr. Homans just before the fighting began. Laura was devoured with curiosity about that cavalry officer, but all Belle would tell her was that he was an old friend who had rendered her mother great service in the past, and that she should know all about him soon, but not just now, not until they had got Floyd Fairfax out of his scrape, for scrape he was surely in.

He had come to the house Thursday night in his farmer's garb, and had declared his intention of coming Friday night, too, and Belle was fearfully nervous and anxious, doubly so, because she dared not let her mother know of his purpose. Once before, when Floyd had sent word to the mistress of Heatherwood that he should call whenever the fortunes of war brought him to Maryland, she urged him to refrain, and after Ralph was brought home wounded she sent a letter to Leesburg, warning Fairfax that her doors would not be open to him. But Ralph refused to be guided by his mother in the matter and secretly rebelled. He urged Floyd to come on that Friday night, promising to have certain letters ready for him then, and Floyd had eagerly agreed. But that afternoon, as we know, there came the Fairfax troop and the spirited fight with Hamlin's men, and later old Foulweather. And over towards Poolesville the lurking soldier got word that Heatherwood was surrounded by searching parties and suspicious officers. His presence in the neighborhood was reported, and the sooner he got back to Virginia the better. He planned to go this very Saturday night, taking Heatherwood on his way, but long before the October gloaming came, chill and cheerless, there reached him a farmer's boy, who whispered that Laura Waddell rode out as far as the White's Ford road to tell him the Yankee cavalry were hurrying north from Clark's Gap, hard as they could come, and he must "lay low," and half an hour later there came tidings that thrilled him to the marrow with exultation, envy, and anxiety all in one, tidings that Jeb Stuart had dashed through the Union lines away up to Pennsylvania, had "burned the stores in Chambersburg and Gettysburg," and now was coming south for all he was worth, and every Yankee from Washington to Cumberland was in saddle or under arms in hopes of catching him. Before the sun went down behind the Loudoun the roads to White's Ford and to the Monocacy were thronged with guns and infantry, hurrying west. The northward lanes were alive with patrols of horse, all hastening forth to meet and check the daring raider, and no sooner had night spread her wings over the lovely rural landscape east of the Catoctins than from every signal-tower along the range and from Sugar Loaf, far over northeast of Heatherwood, the flaring torches began to wave and circle through the darkness, and concealment in a country barn became torment. Win or lose, Floyd Fairfax swore he'd meet and join his beloved chief and comrades, as back they came, boring their way through the meshes of the Yankee net,—or would die in trying it.

CHAPTER X.

But Heatherwood was destined to know more than one excitement that never-to-be-forgotten Saturday. It was barely three o'clock when old Dobbin went straddling and stumbling down the drive, an eager-eyed Virginia girl urging him on, and the clouds that earlier had hung over the Catoctins to the northwest, and had laid the dust in lower Pennsylvania for the benefit of Stuart's men, now began to obscure the face of the declining sun and put an end to the occasional flashes at the dormer-window. As a system of signalling it was crude and uncertain at best, pursued by Belle Heatherwood and her convalescing brother more for the sake of doing that which might "worry the Yankees" than to convey information of value to their foes. Indeed, it was only occasionally that the flash thrown from Belle's little hand-mirror went with such accuracy as to assure its being seen by the occupant of the cabin on the distant crest of the Virginia Kittoctans. From that point, however, when the sun was dropping to the Loudoun, flashes could be thrown into the westward valley with much ease, and lively spirits at Leesburg, where were still some ten score wounded, conceived the idea of opening signal communication with Heatherwood, and it was this that

Floyd Fairfax was striving to develop into something of value. Thus far, however, the only information conveyed from Heatherwood was that some of its occupants were actually in that west dormer-window and on watch,—Belle's flashes, though brilliant at times, being too erratic to be valuable. But Floyd had left with her now an ordinary school copy-book filled through several pages with a system by which they of Virginia could convey tidings to the Maryland shore,—principally with candles or lanterns at night and the rising or falling of a white window-curtain by day. The night lights that Laura had noted were largely experimental, for not until Floyd's coming had they possessed anything like a signal-code. Now Miss Heatherwood had one, and the question was, could Ralph, a paroled and wounded prisoner, be justified in using it?

Together they had translated the meaning of the wavings that came to the window from the little cabin on the Kittoctan top earlier that afternoon, though repetitions were necessary, and the ultimate translation was much facilitated by the sudden appearance of dust clouds issuing from Clark's Gap. The rain that had favored Stuart a hundred miles northward had not yet begun to soften the roads across the Potomac.

But that they should know that the Union cavalry was coming, and coming fast, long before any cavalry could be seen, had in itself a mysterious and powerful fascination for Belle. She clung there to the window-ledge after sending Laura on her mission, and with eager eyes studied the distant wooded heights and prayed fervently for more news, good news. Oh, if that sudden withdrawal of the Union squadrons could only mean that Stuart was at their heels, driving them into the Potomac!

Wearied in his weak condition, Ralph had stolen back to his own room, urging Belle to report to him should anything further be signalled requiring his interpretation. It was the hour at which, ordinarily, Mrs. Heatherwood took her siesta, the only hour during the day in which he could leave his room without every probability of her knowing it at once. From morning until noon, and again from four until ten at night, the devoted woman was almost constantly at his side or that of Tighlman in the adjoining and communicating room. There had been a time in the not very distant past when this young Marylander was looking with eyes of more than cousinly love on the beautiful face of his kinswoman, but tidings of Jack Lowndes's devotions, and later of the presence of Floyd Fairfax, had precipitated an avowal, and more sieges are lost in love by striking too quick than too slow. Belle had refused him, kindly and affectionately, had consoled him with the customary offer to be a sister to him, which he declined with thanks, being already overburdened with such near relatives, and had gone off to Europe in a Cunarder and a huff, only to be recalled by the uprising of the South, whose cause he eagerly embraced, was appointed an aide-de-camp on Ewell's staff the first winter of the war, and rode with that grim fighter until the Maryland campaign, when Ewell, minus the leg he lost tackling the Yankees along the Warrenton Pike the evening of the 28th of August, was left behind to repair damages. Tighlman came on with the division, was assigned to other staff duty, and as luck would have it met his cousin Heatherwood and a hostile bullet almost at the same moment in the defense of the Gaps before Antietam. Now he was once more under Heatherwood's roof, his nearest kin having all gone South, and was feeling very sore in spirit, very much aggrieved indeed, all because Belle had told him the year before that he would soon get over his fancy and would fall in love with a girl who could thoroughly appreciate all his good qualities. Tighlman had sworn in December he could never do either, and by April had done both. So there he was at Heatherwood, wounded in body and in spirit. At no time does a man feel much more like an ass than when he has to spend hour after hour in the presence of the woman who, with perfect good humor, has prophesied that he would speedily forget his infatuation for her, and whom he finds to have prophesied exactly right. There lay Captain Tighlman, forced to look lugubrious and sigh whenever Belle came fluttering into the room in order to convince her she had done him injustice in declaring him so light-minded, when all the time he knew his heart was irrevocably bound up in a dear little Georgia girl near whom he had spent long weeks abroad. What would Captain Tighlman say had he seen Belle Heatherwood kissing a Yankee officer? Miss Waddell had indignantly asked; and while Miss Heatherwood had done nothing of the kind, but had only tremblingly inclined her forehead towards the pleading lips of that handsome unknown, it may be safely said that Captain Tighlman would have felt no jealousy other than that aroused by the question of uniform.

He was in a peevish and fretful mood, however, and disposed to sympathize with his comrade's eagerness to be up and away, even on this gloomy October afternoon, when the rain began to patter about the old house and strike the frost-bitten leaves from their feeble hold on the stiffening branches. But he started up in bed, leaned on his elbow, and gazed eagerly as Heatherwood came limping in, whispering,—

"There's fun ahead, Brad. Something's up! I'm blessed if I can tell what, but they're waving like mad up on Sugar Loaf. The troops down by the aqueduct are all under arms. The Yanks are mustering on every road,—guns, cavalry, and infantry. They're all coming this way."

"My God! Can they have found out about Fairfax?" asked Tighlman.

"That wouldn't stir up all the troops in Maryland," was the answer. "With my glasses you can see away over towards Poolesville. There are three or four regiments moving out on the road, and a dozen squadrons. Others are coming now from Point of Rocks, and the old regiment, by gad, is coming up the Kittoctan at a trot, heading for White's Ford. What can have happened, do you think? Can it be Stuart again?"

And just as he spoke, clear and shrill the voice of Laura Waddell was heard from underneath the windows:

"Cousin Ralph! Cousin Ralph! Can you hear me? Such wonderful news! I heard all the Yanks talking about it. Stuart's rode all around them again and is up in Pennsylvania now, and he's going to burn Baltimore and Washington, and they're all out there to catch him,—the whole pack. Ain't it splendid?"

"Sh-sh, Laura. Be quiet, child. You'll wake mother," was the loud stage whisper with which Captain Heatherwood greeted this thrilling announcement, as his haggard face, quivering with excitement, appeared at the window. "Come up here, quick, and tell us all about it.—My God, Brad! Think of it. Stuart raiding through Pennsylvania and we here crippled and paroled!"

"Parole be damned!" was the mad reply, as Tighlman straightened up in bed. "They'll come back this way, like as not, and no parole counts in case of recapture. All we've got to do is to be up and ready to ride. Shut that door!" he cried, as the sound of quick, light footsteps was heard in the hall without, and Heatherwood hobbled to the threshold all too late. There, her face aflame with excitement, stood Belle, and it was plain to see that she had heard her cousin's words.

"Ralph," she pleaded, laying her hands on her brother's arm, and speaking low, hurriedly, "you surely cannot think of such a thing as attempting to leave this house until you are thoroughly well. You're weak as a child yet,—both of you. You're not fit to stir. It would bring on fever again, or re-open your wound."

He placed his hand upon her lips and strove to check her. "Hush! Mother must not hear. She must not be wakened," he whispered, but already Laura was pattering up the stairs, dancing with joy and excitement. She rushed upon them, clapping her hands.

"It's true! it's true!" she cried, hugging Belle in her delight. "Pettingill's out there in the orchard now; says he had to come up and see me—just think of it—before he marched to battle. Just as if I cared. He's got on all his fixings, knapsack and things, and looks like he wanted to cry; says they're ordered to be ready to march just as soon as the relief guard comes, and they are coming over the Monocacy now. He says they're going to cover the whole country with Yankees, and I told him he needn't trouble himself, Jeb Stuart 'd cover the ground with 'em three deep wherever he goes." It was impossible to check the wild exuberance of the girl's outbreak. She danced about the hall, a buxom imp, until Heatherwood seized her and clapped his thin hand over the rosy mouth.

"Quiet, child! Mother must not hear this yet," he ordered. But she shook herself free in an instant, her rustic health and strength far outmatching his enfeebled muscles.

"Aunty? Why, she's heard it! She's out there on the gallery now, talking with Colonel Clark. He's just ridden up with that stiffy Homans, comin' to tell her there's to be another guard. Guess we can take care of ourselves now, and I just wanted a chance to tell him he'd better look out for his own crowd." And shaking the rain out of her shining hair, the girl went dancing and springing and gamboling up and down the wide hall in wild exultation and delight, just as there appeared, coming slowly up the stairs, her sad, placid, beautiful face clouded with new care and trouble, the beloved mistress of Heatherwood. At sight of her and the gentle rebuke in her eyes, the girl almost instantly checked her mad whirling and ran to aid her. Heatherwood, hearing Tighlman's voice, had for the moment turned to look within the room, and did not see her. When he reappeared it was to be confronted by his mother, amaze, distress, and deep anxiety in her gaze, all giving way to utter dismay as the door swung open and there, leaning feebly against the casement for support, pale with exhaustion, yet with excitement and resolution firing his eyes, there in his Confederate uniform, stood Bradley Tighlman.

Mrs. Heatherwood was first to speak.

"In God's name, my boy, what does this mean?"

"It means that Stuart is coming, aunty," faltered Tighlman, almost gasping for breath. "It means that he is sure to come this way, that we can be recaptured, and, well or wounded, every soldier of the South must be ready to follow."

"Not from this roof," she answered, solemnly. "Not so long as that parole lasts. You pledged your soldier honor never to take up arms or render any service against the United States until properly exchanged, and every soldier, North or South, must stand by his soldier word.—Help him off with that uniform, Ralph. Then back to your beds, both of you," she ordered, almost as though it were ten years gone by and in their boyish days again, "and stay there until you're dragged out by Stuart's men, for if by word, sign, or deed you attempt to communicate with Stuart's command, as God is my judge, I'll surrender you both to the Federal guards."

CHAPTER XI.

The sun was still an hour high, invisible through the rain-clouds that hung dripping along the crest of the Catoctins and the opposite heights of Loudoun, when the New Hampshire men were relieved of the care of the aqueduct and the empty ditch of the canal by the arrival of a brace of battalions from the Pine-Tree State, and Clark, pursuant to his orders, left his tents standing in the grove and marched away with his long blue column, gathering up the guard under Heatherwood Towers, the solemn-faced Homans and the reluctant Pettingill with the rest.

"Remember," said he, to the commander of the Maine contingent, "we leave our heavy baggage with our tents under your charge. This thing will be settled, probably, within twelve hours. If Stuart comes this way we may reasonably expect to beat him back until the cavalry surround him. If he goes far to the east or turns to the west, we won't be needed and will be back again to-morrow. Here are the written orders about protecting Heatherwood, on the height yonder." And the precious paper was handed over.

"I don't know about that place," was the doubtful answer. "There was a soldier arrested there and sent up to the provost-marshal at Point of Rocks this morning. What had he been doing?"

"Arrested by a cavalry major of regulars who said he was a straggler from his command. I could not interfere, though I believe him to be the same man that galloped away from my camp a night or two ago, refusing to have his pass examined. There's something about him that's wrong. I don't know what."

"Well, they didn't keep him in limbo ten minutes," said the Maine officer. "He asked to see Captain McIntosh, and when Mac was sent out to scout towards Sugar Loaf this morning, he had that fellow riding with him. They say he knows the country like a book."

"Very likely," said Clark. "One thing you can be sure of, and that is this, Mrs. Heatherwood will knowingly allow no man to enter her doors who is not there by authority of the War Department. She is nursing her son and nephew, both of whom are still in bed, and they are the only men about the place, unless you count the old darky."

"And you've had no reason to suspect anything wrong? No attempt to communicate with rebels at Leesburg or elsewhere?"

"Certainly not," was the prompt reply. "Why do you ask?"

"Because the provost-marshal at Point of Rocks tells me the signal-officers on Sugar Loaf say there is signalling going on over there in Loudoun County to some point here. Now, what could it be but Heatherwood? He has word that that Virginian captain, Fairfax, was over here somewhere, and that your people yesterday were imposed upon by a stranger claiming to be Captain Belden, of Hooker's staff. Why, you ought to know, or they ought to know, that General Hooker was wounded at Antietam and went into Washington, and Belden with him. Belden hasn't come back yet."

"I've heard that story. Old Foulweather, of the cavalry, asked Madam Heatherwood in my presence, and she declared that she never knew such an officer as Captain Belden. There has been some masquerading going on, perhaps, but she knows nothing of it. You'll find no people there she cannot account for."

And so saying, Clark, the bearded, who believed solemnly in women, rode rapidly away, and placed himself at the head of his column as they struck the road to Conrad's Ferry, meeting, oddly enough, the column of regulars just as they came dripping up from the ford. The New Hampshire men retook their silent tramp down the towpath, as the muddy tail of the cavalry column swung out over the steep ascent. The infantry were marching away from the expected foe in order to occupy the heights overlooking the lower ferry. Foulweather, however, profiting by the field orders which turned him loose in Loudoun County for a week's scout, was now pushing northward into Maryland, a free lance, practically, with glorious possibilities ahead, Burnside, of course, having to accept the responsibility for his change of base.

And Foulweather had reason to be hopeful and elate. Both in Stuart's cavalry, south of the Potomac, and among the widely dispersed camps of the Union horse, from Cumberland to Washington on the north of the river, their mounts were suffering with equine maladies known as "greasy heel" and sore tongue. In addition there were hundreds of horses in Pleasonton's camp in need of shoes. Just why this should have been the quartermaster could not say. But most of the Union commanders reported their horses in poor condition. Foulweather, however, serving east of the mountains and nearer Washington, had been able to supply himself as to forage and shoes, while the epidemics that so affected the chargers in the Shenandoah and upper Potomac valleys had made no inroads on his stock. He was, except for fatigue, in tip-top condition for sharp cavalry service. He reasoned that Stuart's column, both men and horses, would be worn out by the time they met, and, though he had barely two hundred and fifty sabres at his back, the stout old plainsman meant that they should make their mark on the gray squadrons if he could possibly reach them.

And why should he not reach them? Here he was, far from the grasp of any brigade commander, his own master for the time being. Now was the chance for independent action, now the golden opportunity to win those long coveted silver stars, now the time to distance all competitors in the race for recommendation for the brigadier-generalship to come from the cavalry. So far as he could hear, there was only one rival in the field,—McIntosh, he of the provost-guard at Point of Rocks, already out there somewhere to the north of him, and scouting the roads down which Stuart might come. True, Stoneman was throwing forward cavalry from Poolesville, but who were they? said Foulweather, disdainfully. Stoneman had no regulars to speak of, and even Rush's Lancers up at Frederick had not served to modify the old major's disdain or to change his dictum that "a volunteer trooper was only a dummy on a cart-horse." McIntosh, however, was a man to dread, guided as he was by a trooper who knew every bridle-path in that part of Maryland. How dare he release Bell from durance vile? How dare he utilize him instead of sending him back to Foulweather,— now that his services were so sorely needed? The major was hot with jealous wrath as the darkness slowly settled down, and riding straight for Sugar Loaf, he saw the red torch waving at its lofty summit.

And now the men had slept through hours of the earlier day, had feasted on soldier fare at noon, and could be counted on for all-night work if need be, even though the sun had given place to shower and the night wore on chill and wet. At seven o'clock he was pushing northward, following some old country road that meandered among the groves and fields. He relied on reaching the broad pike before eight, the main road that led from Frederick through

Hyattstown and Rockville to Washington, and there surely he would intercept couriers with tidings of the foe; surely by that time it would be known which way the fox had turned. Off to the eastward faint lights were gleaming here and there in little villages or farm-houses. Foulweather left Barnesville well to his right, for there, though news might have been had, he feared that at this moment he might find some officer superior in rank who would take it upon himself to order him to join some detachment of volunteer horse and act in concert with amateurs, and so spoil all the old major's plans of action. Foulweather would take no chance of losing his autonomy, and, like many another cavalryman, good or bad, he would rather be his own commander in a wilderness than ride as second or subordinate in Elysium.

And the farther north they pushed through the shadowy lane, moving slowly and cautiously for fear of running into unseen ditch or obstruction, the more to their left had loomed the rugged height of Sugar Loaf, where, slowly waving, the torches could still be seen at intervals, and the major would have given six months' pay to know what tidings were passing to and fro. Where was Stuart? Oh, where was Stuart?

By this time, too, so much rain had fallen that the road was squashy under hoof. The lane was so narrow that they had been compelled to reduce front, and were riding by twos instead of fours, his long column thereby stringing out to more than twice its normal length. Halting at dusk to shift saddles and tighten girths, he had ordered forward a little advance guard consisting of a veteran sergeant and some twenty troopers,—he had no officers to spare,—and now felt confident that no sudden dash could double him up; and just about half-past seven, as he was jogging along at brisk walk, Wilson on his left and the orderlies and trumpeter following at his heels, a dark form appeared just in front and a voice was heard:

"Sergeant Walsh sends me back to tell the major the road forks about a hundred yards ahead, sir. Which shall we take?"

"Has he sent men out on both?"

"Yes, sir; a quarter of a mile or so. There are farm lights on the right, and it's all dark on the other."

Old Treacy had sputtered alongside from the head of his squadron to listen to the reports. There was not an instant's halt. The column moved steadily on and the messenger had reined about and was riding by the major's side.

Foulweather hesitated a minute. The lights were too near for Hyattstown. He might find information there, and he might just as likely run across the head-quarters of some of Stoneman's cavalry commands, thrown, fan-like, forward from Poolesville.

Treacy impulsively put in his oar and decided matters. "Tell him to go to the right, major."

"Tell him to go to the left," was Foulweather's

characteristic reply, and, swearing through his grinding teeth, Treacy fell back to his place.

And so it happened that when, a little after eight, a trooper came trotting back to say the advance had reached the pike in the broad valley to the front, and that torches were still waving at Sugar Loaf to their left rear, and far away to the northwest other signal-lights, faint and dim, could be made out by sharp-sighted men in the lead, the whole column had passed within a dozen rods of one who wore their own uniform, and who, dismounted and firmly gripping the nostrils of his wearied horse to prevent his neighing, was crouching beside a hedge on the other fork of the road, shrinking from possibility of discovery. Not until the rearmost trooper had gone jogging by the fork, not, indeed, until five minutes more had passed without the sound of other horsemen coming from the south, did the solitary shadow lead forth to the narrow roadway, mount, and ride on and on with the unerring confidence of one to whom every bend of the bridle-path was familiar, on until Sugar Loaf bore straight to his right, the west, on to a point where faint lights could be seen gleaming away over to the southwest, down by the shores of the Potomac, and here, at the foot of a steep slope, a lane still narrower led away southwest, through open fields, and this he took unhesitatingly, and, pressing on at rapid trot, ever bending forward and with ears attent, ever encouraging and urging his tired horse, rarely spurring now, for the gallant fellow was doing his best, and no true horseman spurs a willing beast, mile after mile he rode until half a dozen were left between him and the point where Foulweather's ghostly train had passed him by, and then there rose before him, dim and vague, a lone height, forest-covered, with every line of which he was familiar, though hardly a trace of it could be seen. Overhead the heavens were shrouded in their veil of cloud. Under foot the earth lay dripping. To right and left the autumn leaves came fluttering down, pelted mercilessly by the unseen rain, and the patter of the myriad globules fell on the ear like soothing, drowsing melody. And all this distance had the rider traversed without sign of friend or foe, yet now, at a sharp turn in the narrow lane, he reined in his horse and listened. Not a sound beyond the ceaseless plash. Slowly he moved forward again until he could feel, rather than see, that the road had opened out, and that it had joined a broader, better-travelled thoroughfare. Another gentle bend, and then, not two hundred yards away, underneath a clump of trees, some camp-fires smouldered and the shadowy forms of men and horses, half a dozen, could be dimly seen. And presently he came to where a big stone, once whitewashed or painted, so that now it could be faintly discerned, stood at the roadside, and here he flung himself from his horse, led confidently through a shallow, muddy trench, his horse as confidently following, then forced his way through a gap in the dripping hedge, and the next minute he had remounted and was moving slowly and cautiously up a winding path among the fruit-trees, steering for another gap in the foliage near the crest, through which a dim light was throwing feeble yet sufficient beam, a light that was to guide him back unchallenged, though unbidden, once more to stable his tired horse in the comfortable old barn, and then, cautious, noiseless, dripping wet, but bearing with him his arms and saddle-bags, the same trooper that issued from that door at dawn, came to claim once more the hospitality of Heatherwood.

A light was burning dimly in the room. He could see it gleam through a crevice. Cautiously he tapped, quick and low, then listened for coming footsteps.

Utter silence and no other response. Yet he could have sworn some one was moving about within the old wing as he approached. Again he tapped, quick and low, three rapid knocks, a pause, then one, as though he would have signalled thirty-one, and this time there was instant result. There were hurried whisperings, a scurry of footfalls. A bench was overturned and something tin came clattering to the floor. Then at last the swish of skirts, a cautious approach to the door. The latch clattered hesitatingly, a voice, tremulous, whispered, "Who is it?"

"It is I. Don't you recognize the number? Open, quick."

But only slowly would that door open, and at last the face of Belle Heatherwood appeared, white as that of the dead, as she stood there looking first one instant over her shoulder, the next glancing in surprise, pity, and compassion, all in one, at the impatient soldier. He saw the consternation in her eyes.

"Some one has frightened you," he exclaimed, as now he strode within the door and dropped his saddle to the floor, while his right hand threw back the flap of the holster at his waist-belt and grasped the butt of the ready Colt. "No one of our men dare molest you here. Who was it? Where is he?"

The color flew back to her cheek at the abrupt demand, and fire to her eyes. She would have spoken impetuously, but something in his worn face deterred her. She read there suffering, anxiety, distress, far more than command. Whatever his present mood, he had come a suppliant. Quick-witted, the girl saw her advantage and seized it.

"After the scene this morning you need not wonder that we take alarm," she answered, bravely, though her breath came quick, her bosom rose and fell like troubled sea. She pressed her hand to her heart, too, as she spoke. "We were in misery over your arrest. What does it mean? You've escaped, or what?"

"Never mind that *now*," he answered, shortly, as his eyes flitted suspiciously about the kitchen, glancing warily at the door-way leading into the house itself, and the flight of stairs down to the cellar. On a table was a basket containing eggs and vegetables, and on that she had rested a trembling hand.

"Why, I never saw you show such fear before! Some one was here with you. Was it——"

"Hush," she whispered. "Some one is here— without. It's a patrol," she continued, her cheek blanching again, for the sound of hoofs and clanking steel could be distinctly heard. "Is it you they seek again?"

For answer the soldier sprang to his saddle, knelt, tore open the nearest bag, and with eager hands drew forth a flat tin case, firmly strapped.

"It may be," he murmured, desperately. "And now, whatever happens, they must not get this. Hide it, quick. I'll answer them. Only guard this for me, and I'm in no danger."

Then, as, seizing the packet, the girl sped swiftly away, the trooper turned and blew out the candle. Low voices were heard without. Spurred boots and clanking sabres were already at the door. Then came an imperative knock. Bell drew himself to his full height and, deliberately closing the holster and adjusting his belt, was about to step forward, when a hand was laid on his arm.

"To your room, quick, for mother's sake. She was kneeling, praying for you when I left her," whispered an eager voice. He thrilled as the warm lips almost touched his ear. "Oh, for God's sake," she added, as he hesitated, "for—my sake, quick!"

And on tiptoe he hurried into the dark hall beyond just as Chloe, lamp in hand, came shuffling into the old wing, and the clamor at the door redoubled. At a sign from her young mistress, who stood leaning against the table, her hand on her fluttering heart, Chloe, setting her lamp down, stepped to the door and threw it open. There stood two soldiers of the Union cavalry,—an officer, backed by a sergeant. Dimly seen beyond them, still in saddle, huddled possibly half a dozen escorting troopers.

"Can I see Mrs. Heatherwood?" demanded the foremost; then, gazing beyond the negro face, he caught sight of the young lady's and the basket. At sight of the first he had whipped off his wet forage-cap, at sight of the second he clapped it on again, and with kindling eyes strode straight into the room.

"By heaven, he's here! At least,"—and here he turned quickly to the lady and lifted his cap once more,—"at least, that is the basket of the man we're looking for. Pardon me,—Miss Heatherwood, I presume,—but my men must enter at once and search."

"They shall not!" she cried. "We have orders from the President himself, protecting us from such outrage. I deny your right—I forbid. I——"

But in spite of her indignant protestation, three or four troopers had sprung from saddle and, carbines in hand, came surging into the old kitchen. "Search,—search everywhere," were the brief orders of the young officer. "Look for the dress of an old farmer, with beard and wig." And despite Miss Heatherwood's impulsive move to check them, a corporal and trooper darted by. Others, without, as promptly surrounded the house. The first door to the right led to the cellar, and down the stairway, lantern in hand, leaped a non-commissioned officer, followed by a single soldier. Again Miss Heatherwood spoke, her voice broken, pleading, now that angry menace had proved unavailing.

"Oh, I implore you, do not, do not. It will rouse my mother. She must not be frightened." And now in her terror the girl sprang back to the hallway and stood at the door, desperately barring the entrance.

"Not there, sir," bluntly reported the corporal, as he came trotting up the cellar stairs. "In the house, most like," and, turning as though to enter, recoiled before the quivering face of the brave girl.

"I deplore this, Miss Heatherwood," said the officer, sorrowfully, "but we have no choice. Search we must, or stand court-martial. Pray step aside," and the gauntleted hand closed on her white wrist.

And then a door was heard to open overhead, and quick footsteps followed, and presently these latter were heard bounding down the stairs, and along the dimly lighted passage there came the tall figure of an officer, an officer in Confederate uniform, at sight of which Belle Heatherwood gave one cry of anguish and fell heavily forward. The Union soldier caught and raised her ere she struck the floor. The Confederate took the senseless form from his arms and laid it flat upon a lounge within the hall-way.

"Water, quick!" he whispered. "Let us restore her first; then I—am the man you want."

And on this picture gazed sternly, yet almost in stupefaction, the tall trooper, who had stepped forth from an adjoining room just as Mrs. Heatherwood's wan, white face came slowly within the zone of the lamplight.

CHAPTER XII.

For the first few moments no one seemed to think of anything but the unconscious girl. Kneeling by her side was Fairfax sprinkling water on her white face and slapping her nerveless hands, striving piteously to recall her from the almost deadly swoon, losing himself utterly in his anxiety for her. Awkwardly, as men will, yet in eager sympathy, the Union officer essayed to aid him, while poor old Chloe ran to the support of her invalid mistress, who, leaning heavily against the balustrade of the back stairway, stood for a moment with blanched face, as though dazed and unable to realize the sight before her eyes. A moment only she stood there, then, leaning on the arm of the old negress, came slowly forward, and at her approach the officer again removed his cap and laid a warning hand on the shoulder of his prisoner. Fairfax looked up, and for the first time saw the mistress of Heatherwood, and the eyes of the Maryland dame and the Virginia soldier met. A faint sigh, a slight movement, told that consciousness was returning to the daughter of the house, but Mrs. Heatherwood's eyes were fixed on those of the man, who slowly raised himself from his knees and stood almost humbly, yet with the unconscious dignity of deep misfortune, in the presence of the honored mother of the girl he loved,—the gentlewoman who, loving him from early boyhood, had yet forbidden him her doors. Out in the kitchen, clustering near the door, gazing in with mingled sympathy and curiosity in their war-worn faces, stood the few troopers. Peering over the balusters halfway up to the second story was the pretty face of Laura Waddell, bathed in indignant tears, and for a moment not one word was uttered. Hardly a sound but that fluttering sigh was heard, until at last Mrs. Heatherwood slowly spoke:

"Floyd Fairfax! You here in my house—after all!"

And the soldier bowed his pale face and stood silent and defenceless before her.

Another sigh from the couch, a tossing of the white hand, and quickly, but without a word, Laura sped down the stairway, turned, and, brushing past old Chloe, threw herself upon her knees beside her cousin, who was slowly opening her eyes.

Then again Mrs. Heatherwood spoke, gravely, slowly, and this time to the Union officer. "Were you sent here—in search of—this gentleman?"

"My orders are to arrest," was the solemn answer, "Captain Floyd Fairfax, of the Virginia cavalry, reported to be lurking in disguise, a spy within our lines."

"A spy!" exclaimed Fairfax, hotly. "I'm no spy! This uniform——" But even in the mortal peril of his position the Virginia gentleman could not stoop to lie.

"The dress in which Captain Fairfax succeeded in passing our patrols and entering these grounds was that of a farmer, and with it the additional disguise of beard and wig," said the officer, almost sadly.

Mrs. Heatherwood looked from one to the other in silent dismay. "Do you mean that within these doors—you had this uniform concealed—awaiting you?" she demanded, in tones so sad and stern they thrilled the hearers.

"Mrs. Heatherwood," impetuously spoke the Virginian, "I implore you to blame no one but me. Ask no questions now. Do you not realize—do you not see—my life depends——"

But before he could finish his statement Laura sprang to her feet.

"'Fanybody wants to know how this gentleman happens to be 't Heatherwood to-night," she cried, her fists clinching, her eyes flashing, "just tell 'em *I* did it. I told him to come. I rode out and tried to find him, and sent him word that made him come," she stormed. "'Twasn't his fault, or Belle's or aunty's, or anybody's but mine," she cried. "I sent for him, and he's a Virginia gentleman, and he had to come."

"Hush, child!" interposed Madam Heatherwood; "hush! You don't know what you're saying."

"I do know, and they can 'rest me for a spy or anything they like. I'm not afraid. Captain Fairfax came because I made him believe that aunty wanted him here and wanted to see him, and he just couldn't refuse,—no gentleman could,—and no gentleman would think of taking advantage, *mean* advantage, of another gentleman under such circumstances." How her black eyes flashed at the Union officer as she spoke! "You can do anything you like to me, but don't you blame anybody else," said she.

"Ah, my dear young lady," interrupted the officer, smiling sorrowfully——

"I'm *not* your dear young lady, or anybody's like you——"

"Pardon my presumption," said he, bowing with the utmost gravity; "that was indeed unwarrantable. What I was about to say was that I feared even your imperious orders will not warrant the captain's coming, in the sight of our Secretary of War; and now I shall have to ask that he accompany me at once. The ladies can attend to Miss Heatherwood far better than we can."

"At your service, sir," said Fairfax, gravely. "But, have we far to go? I'm hardly fit to walk."

"You shall ride, sir, and it is only to the nearest camp, for this night at least."

"Yes," shouted the irrepressible Laura, despite the efforts of Mrs. Heatherwood to silence her, despite the picture of Miss Heatherwood, now glancing dumbly about from face to face, in piteous appeal, "you'd better not try to go too far, for if you run into Jeb Stuart hereabouts I wouldn't give much for your chances, Mr. Yankee. I don't care where you lock

Captain Fairfax up, we'll get him out just as soon as General Stuart comes, and put you in—see if we don't." But Fairfax himself was interposing now.

"Laura, Laura!" he warned. "You must control that unruly tongue of yours. These gentlemen have their orders, and soldiers can only obey. Go up to your cousin's room and get my overcoat for me.—Forgive me, Mrs. Heatherwood," he murmured, "I must get rid of this child a moment." Then as the girl swung saucily away, totally unable, apparently, to realize the gravity of the situation, and casting annihilating glances at the Union lieutenant as she sped up the stairs,—glances which made his lips twitch and his eyes twinkle, despite the solemn nature of his duty,—Fairfax again turned to his captor.

"One thing I beg leave to assure you, sir, and that is that Mrs. Heatherwood had no idea of my presence within her gates until she came upon me here to-night."

"That I understand," was the courteous reply. "No one will accuse Mrs. Heatherwood of harboring the enemy.—What is it, sergeant?" he asked, as a trooper entered hurriedly from the rear and seemed impatient to speak.

"There's firing up to the northeast, sir. There's a patrol coming up the road."

The officer's eyes blazed with excitement, but his voice was firm and quiet. "Then I shall have to hurry you, captain. You really need no overcoat to go to the Monocacy. There you'll be comfortably housed for the night."

Fairfax turned. Belle, covering her face in her hands, was shuddering and almost hysterical, and the mother bent to soothe her.

"Give me one minute's conversation with these ladies," said the Virginian, almost imploringly. "What I have to say concerns us alone. There shall be no effort to escape you. I give you my word."

For a moment there was hesitation in the young officer's face, then he turned and motioned with his hand. The silent troopers fell back to the kitchen, whither their officer followed, halted at the door, turned and took one more earnest look at his prisoner; then his hand went up to the cap in military salute, which Fairfax gravely returned. The door closed behind the cavalryman. Mother, daughter, and the Virginia captain were alone. Trooper Bell had stood for a moment gazing fixedly at the group about the sofa on which lay the stricken girl, then had disappeared within his room. Aunt Chloe had drifted up the hall, and was rocking to and fro on a settee, wringing her black hands in distress. Aloft, Laura's shrill voice could be distinctly heard behind closed doors in lively altercation with somebody. Presently back she came, bounding, with Ralph Heatherwood's coat upon her arm. A smell of burning hair came floating down after her, and now her face was white with anxiety. "What do they mean, telling me you can be tried for a spy? as if a man hasn't a right to wear a wig in a free country," she prattled, as she threw herself upon Fairfax and seemed striving to envelop the new gray uniform in sheltering folds of heavy cloth. "The Yankees can't get that old wig and beard, anyhow,—Ralph's burned 'em,—but," and now at last she lowered her voice, fearful lest her words might reach the kitchen, "there's no place to hide those farmer clothes. Ralph says we must get rid of them before the search is made."

Outside the trampling of hoofs and the eager voices of men, though only faintly heard in this sheltered hall, told of the coming of additional troops. There was stir and excitement among the soldiers in the kitchen. Belle Heatherwood, weeping silently, had buried her face in her gentle mother's breast, and Mrs. Heatherwood, kneeling beside her, was whispering soothing words. Fairfax stepped to the door as though to bolt it against intrusion, but Mrs. Heatherwood looked up into his pale face, and, though she spoke no word, he seemed to read disapprobation of the move, and dropped his hand dejectedly.

"Blame no one but me, Mrs. Heatherwood," he began, so low and sad his voice that her heart welled over with pity.

"My poor boy! My poor boy!" she cried. "How could you be so rash? Floyd, Floyd, what would your mother have said? Is it true you came here—disguised? Didn't you know what that would mean if you were taken?"

Sadly he bowed his head. "It is true. It was the only way. But they have not yet found it. They cannot prove I wore it. You see how we arranged it the moment we realized that search was to be made. I ran to Ralph's room and changed from farmer clothes to his uniform and came down in that. No one of their number has seen me in anything else. 'Prisoner of war until exchanged' is the worst I need fear, unless they discover those things. And now," —his eyes turned with sad entreaty to the weeping girl,—"have you no word for me, Belle? Go I must at once, but," and again the fire flashed in his eyes and he drew himself to his full height, "if it be true that Stuart is coming,—Stuart,—I'll be with my own within another day."

Mrs. Heatherwood had risen to her feet, listening eagerly to his words, yet with straining ear seemed catching some far-away sound borne on the night wind. The soldiers in the kitchen but a moment before had also apparently heard some sound without, and had swarmed over to the lawn to the east of the old house. Footsteps, halting, were heard overhead; Ralph was stealthily hurrying to the head of the stairs. His mother hastened to the balustrade and gazed up at him, but Chloe, whom he first caught sight of, had lifted her head, and he tossed to her a bundle of clothing, tightly knotted.

"Burn it, Chloe, in the big fireplace, quick as you can," he cried. "Mother, have you heard firing? Brad swears he can hear shots off beyond Sugar Loaf." The old negress mechanically gathered up the bundle as it rolled to her feet.

"They ain't been a spark of fire in the old chimney-place this fall," she moaned, "and I can't stuff this yeah in the kitchen stove."

And at that instant there came heavy footsteps and clanking sabre in the kitchen again—an imperative rap at the heavy door. Impulsively Mrs. Heatherwood seized and thrust the trembling old darky into the door of the little room at which, only a moment or two before, Trooper Bell had stood and gazed so strangely at the group. Then the hall door was thrown open, and there in the light of the lamps stood a burly officer in blue, splashed with mud from top to toe, the taller and younger soldier, Fairfax's captor, gazing anxiously over his shoulder.

"Captain Fairfax," said the former, with hardly an instant's notice of the ladies, "you are my prisoner. It is my duty to tell you that you were recognized in disguise near Poolesville to-day; that you came here in the garb of a farmer. In Confederate uniform you could never have reached this house, and your disguise must be here. It will save these ladies the distress of having our men searching about the house. Where shall we find it?"

Out came old Aunt Chloe, wringing her black hands about her head and rocking back and forth, the picture of Ethiopian misery. Behind her the door was softly closed. Fairfax faced his accuser haughtily. There was no strain of sorrow or half sympathy in the new arrival's tone as there was in that of the junior officer.

"I am your prisoner, sir, and in the uniform of my rank," was the slow reply, as, leaning on her mother's arm and Laura's, Belle Heatherwood painfully lifted herself from the sofa and stood facing the new-comer, her tear-wet face white as the wall behind her. It seemed almost as though she had ranged herself by the side of her kinsman lover to share his danger and confront his foes. Speechless with grief, Mrs. Heatherwood, too, could only gaze at the intruder, as though imploring him to spare their guest.

"I have no time to argue," were the officer's next words. "If you do not choose to tell where those garments are, it will be my duty to search, and my men are ready."

"The laws of war, sir, do not compel a prisoner to produce evidence on which to hang himself, but I hope you will refrain from anything that may be distressing to these ladies."

"Step in here, three of you," was the curt and instant order, and the officer, uniformed as a major of cavalry, followed by three troopers, muddy as himself, strode clanking into the hall-way. Instinctively Laura sprang and stood at the door of the nearest room, and the burly soldier saw it at a glance.

"In there," he said, almost shouldering his way past the silent, trembling, tearful women, and still there stood Laura, both cheeks and eyes aflame now, stretching her arms across the space and glaring defiance at the coming foe.

"Laura, child," expostulated Mrs. Heatherwood, "you'll only make matters worse. Step aside." But in the heart of Miss Waddell the spirit of rampant rebellion had smouldered long and now burst into flame.

"Don't you dare lay hand on me, you—you Yankee villain!" she cried, as the officer coolly stretched forth a burly arm and not too gently grasped her rounded wrist. "Oh, you'd, you'd pay for this if we were in Virginia," she panted, fiercely struggling now, for he was calmly drawing her away, and a private soldier, bounding past them, thrust open the door. Both Fairfax and Mrs. Heatherwood had stepped forward as though to relieve the strange officer of his struggling spitfire of a combatant, but as the soldier disappeared within the darkness of the room, a gust of cold night air set the lamps to flaring and smoking, and the door swung to with a slam. A second trooper reopened it and followed the first. Again the night wind blew fresh and strong into the open hall, and, borne on the breeze, came floating the sound of a cavalry trumpet, some brisk, merry signal from the northward lane.

"They're sounding forward, sir," sang out one of the men, "and this window's wide open, like as though some one had jumped out. The curtain's twisted——" But, seizing the lantern borne by the younger officer, the major hastened into the room, and looked about him. The bed, somewhat rumpled, stood at the left of the door. There was an old-fashioned clothes-press, and then a bureau and dressing-table combined, a stand, and some chairs. There were some pictures on the walls, pretty curtains at the window floating in the breeze on one side and twisted into a sort of rope on the other, hanging outward. It was a drop of seven or eight feet to the ground, and the major called for instant search below. A trooper or two, lantern bearing, ran around from the rear and gave one look. There in the soft wet soil was the print of shapely boots. Some one had leaped from the window and darted off into the shrubbery within the minute or two that the men had clustered on the eastward lawn, listening to the sharp firing that burst upon the night away out over the fields towards Hyattstown. When the major came forth from the little room his face was very grave.

"Mrs. Heatherwood," said he, "my colonel received instructions at Washington not forty-eight hours ago requiring that every protection should be accorded you and your property, with the assurances that you were a loyal woman. Yet at Poolesville to-day we are warned that a spy was harbored in your house, and now that I am sent here to arrest him, I find indications that there has been more than one."

"This lady, sir," interrupted Fairfax, hotly, "was utterly ignorant of my coming. Your colonel heard the truth. I came against her express wish and without her knowledge, but except her son and nephew, wounded and paroled, who are in their beds up-stairs, no one else is here or has been here. Am I not right, madam?"

"Not another soul!" was her low, firm answer, and Mrs. Heatherwood's wan face was uplifted proudly as she spoke.

Then of a sudden there came from without the muffled sound of excited challenge, and then, loud and sharp, the ring of a cavalry carbine from the shrubbery on the northwestward side, a rush and sputter of hoofs, and the major sprang through the little room to the window.

"What is it? What's happened?" he shouted to a soldier who was darting by.

"A spy, sir, or something,—a feller that was sneaking away a-horseback from the barn, takin' a short cut down among the trees there. The moment they challenged he clapped spurs to his horse and rode like the devil. They fired at him, but it's too dark, sir. He's probably got away."

And now a second time Belle Heatherwood sank nerveless to the sofa and Fairfax turned upon her with wonderment and inquiry in his dark-brown eyes. She was trembling with dread. She hid her face in her hands and seemed to shrink from his gaze, and again Mrs. Heatherwood bent to soothe her. Two minutes' search showed that there was nothing in the little room even faintly resembling farmer's garb, and at this announcement Fairfax looked at Mrs. Heatherwood and she at him, incredulous.

"Go on to the next room then," ordered the major, half angrily, as he turned once more into the hall. Then hurriedly there entered the lieutenant who was the first to reach them that strange evening.

"Major," said he, "Colonel Belden sends word that he desires your squadron to follow at once," and it sounded as though the junior delivered the message with no little comfort.

"Then I leave you in charge of the prisoner and to continue the search, sir," was the sharp reply. "Ladies, I hope I may never have another duty like this." With that he turned abruptly and went clanking from the door.

"Colonel Belden!" exclaimed Fairfax, in surprise. "May I ask what Belden, and what regiment?"

"Colonel Grosvenor Belden, sir, —th Pennsylvania. He has been our colonel less than a week."

"And he is here—near us?"

"Not two miles away when I came forward. We are marching to the Monocacy, where we expect orders to meet us. The whole country knows by this time that Stuart's up there somewhere, and we hope to find him at daybreak."

CHAPTER XIII.

MIDNIGHT came and Heatherwood was still as the grave. Even the plash and patter of rain-drops had ceased, though once in a while the night wind, sighing by, would stir the trees and shower the place beneath. The sounds of distant battle that were wafted on the breeze an hour earlier had ceased as suddenly as they began. Up on Sugar Loaf the signal-men seemed keeping ceaseless vigil, and from time to time their torches swung some message to distant towers on the Catoctin. Ralph Heatherwood, sleepless with excitement, had been moved to a room at the northeast corner, from whose windows he could gaze out over the black void before him, broken only by the occasional flare of that signal-torch. With his glasses he searched in vain for tiny ground lights that might tell of the movement of troops, but northward and northeastward not a spark could be seen. From Tighlman's windows on the south side, through rifts in the thinning foliage, they could make out bivouac fires down along the towpath to the southwest towards Conrad's Ferry, and over the rolling fields towards Poolesville. But the Virginia shores beyond were invisible in one general pall, neither star above nor spark below relieving the black monotony. Tighlman, too, half dressed, was hobbling fretfully about his room, a prey to a dozen hopes, fears, and perturbations. He had looked on Fairfax not a year agone with jealous hate, and had even taken to the New Yorker, Lowndes, because he, too, seemed rejected and wearing the willow, and together they had gloomily spent several days at Frederick, and then had gone into Baltimore for a whirl at the club, but there Tighlman found the Gothamite set a pace too fast for his untutored head and stomach, and he, falling early by the way-side, repented of his folly, while his more seasoned associate kept at his cups until prostrated by illness that so alarmed his friends as to lead to their notifying the woman who seemed a saint to all men, North or South, who knew her,— Madam Heatherwood; and she had come and nursed Lowndes as a mother might have done had mother been spared to him. Tighlman saw no more of him. He went back to Heatherwood to reopen the siege, but found Belle intractable and far more disturbed about his New York friend than about himself. She plied her cousin with questions about Lowndes, refusing to answer as to Fairfax, who had gone back to Leesburg for a few days before the expiration of his leave, and Tighlman left the Towers with jealous heart and went abroad, as we have seen, and then— forgot all about it.

Now here he was again at Heatherwood, and Floyd Fairfax was again beneath its roof, lured thither by his love for Belle, no doubt, despite the project for a signal-system, and that visit had cost him his liberty and might cost him his life.

Yielding to Mrs. Heatherwood's appeal, the lieutenant left in charge of the prisoner had consented to pass the night with his guard under her roof rather than expose a still enfeebled man to the pelting of the rain. The camp at the Monocacy would be damp at best, and would he not be just as safe here? she argued. Lieutenant Wardner was a gentleman who believed in square fight in the field and no unnecessary friction at other times. He couldn't hit a man who was down. He was ordered to continue the search for that farmer's suit, so, while some of his men rummaged in room after room,—no one of course daring to inform him that the important bundle had most mysteriously been spirited away from the very first room opened,—Wardner, with armed troopers in the hall and at the window, sat in the parlor with his captive, chatting, as soldiers will, as though no thought of enmity had ever existed. Before midnight Mrs. Heatherwood with Belle had retired to a room where they were urged to try to sleep, but not an eyelid closed save those of the drowsy negroes up to the time the old Dutch clock, ticking solemnly in the hall-way, trolled in prolonged, mellow notes the hour of two. Despite the fact that Stuart with his bold raiders was somewhere there to the dripping north, that war to the knife was waging between the sections, North and South, the silence of utter solitude had fallen on the heart of Maryland.

"Where on earth do you suppose Stuart is to-night?" was the question Tighlman asked his cousin, as the latter came limping over a little after twelve, and Heatherwood shook his head.

"God knows," said he. "They've got men enough gathering about us to swallow him alive. I don't see how he can come this way. I don't see how he can get back, anyway."

And, indeed, the Union men were gathering in desperate earnest as well as in urgent haste. Down in the valley to the west two Maine regiments of infantry were guarding the aqueduct and the Monocacy crossing. Down the towpath to the southwest near Conrad's were Clark and his New Hampshire men, in close touch with other infantry from Stoneman's force at Poolesville. Up the valley of the Monocacy, crossing to the west bank at midnight, rode a tall, athletic, most soldierly looking young colonel at the head of four strong squadrons of Pennsylvanians, the silver eagles of his shoulder-straps apparently brand-new. Over on the pike near Hyattstown old Foulweather was swearing like the pirate his men declared him to be, for with his fatal propensity to butt his head against a stone wall, he had succeeded in bringing on a sharp fight in the dark, crippling some of his own men and knocking spots out of a squadron that, knowing nothing of his being in that neighborhood, had opened fire on a scouting party that came jingling in towards Hyattstown from the northwest. The squadron commander had the not unreasonable supposition that here was

Stuart himself, since all Union cavalry was marching the opposite way, and challenged sharply. Foulweather when challenged had instantly ordered the troop to charge and clear the road, which Treacy did in tremendous style, only to fetch up standing in a whole circle of fire flashes and the midst of blasphemous men in muddy blue.

"You fired on us furrest!" howled Treacy.

"You ran down our advance," yelled the opposing commander. "Who in paradise are you, anyhow?"

"—th Regulars and be dashed to you! You've shot three of my best harrses. Hwat were ye before we broke the backs av ye?" demanded Treacy, for Foulweather was picking himself out of the wreck of a cart his horse had tripped over.

"—th Pennsylvania. Dash, dash, double dash you for a gang of blear-eyed, butt-headed idiots! Get out of our way and let us straighten out!"

And so between execrations and exertions the officers gradually got their men into column again, and then Foulweather damned a trooper off his horse and climbed into saddle and bade Treacy gather up the débris and let the Keystone cavalry by.

"Wait till we finish this business," said he, shaking a brawny fist at the opposing major, "and I'll give your colonel a lesson he'll not forget in a hurry. Where is he, and what's his name?"

"Half-way to Frederick by this time and waiting for us at the Monocacy, where we might have been but for your infernal blundering. You talk to our colonel, if you think it wise, dash, dash you. He's a regular of the right sort, which you're not. Grosvenor Belden's his name, and I'll warrant you he'll meet you more than half-way."

Foulweather's jaw dropped like lead. "Grosvenor Belden!" he cried. "Since when has *he* been a colonel, I'd like to know?"

"Since the first of the week, sir. And who shall I tell him charged his fourth squadron without answering challenge?" demanded the Pennsylvanian, wrathful to the core.

"Tell him, by God! you tell him you were ridden down, your whole damned squadron, by a platoon of his old regiment, that he ought to be with this night instead of tin soldiering with a lot of yahoos that don't know a horse from a hospital. Go your way," he raved, furiously, "and thank God there was only thirty of us in it, and be damned civil to those of ours that you pass along the pike, or you'll get into more trouble."

Pleasant talk did troopers deal in during those halcyon days that tried men's souls—and tempers, and neither leader felt the better for that hapless clash in the darkness. Stirring up the inmates of a neighboring farm-house, who were scared half out of their wits already, the regulars bore within their door the half-dozen shot or sabred men of both parties, gave the *coup de grace* to the wounded and suffering horses, and then came the question, "What next?"

Up to the moment of the catastrophe, Foulweather had been full of hope, pluck, and fire. Confident that he would get farther out to the front than anybody else, even McIntosh, and be the first to tackle Stuart in the morning, he had pursued his northward way unhesitatingly, but now, as the squadron stood horse in the dark and empty fields, he gazed miserably to the northwest, the direction of the pike, and was at a loss what to do or say. It had just dawned upon him that, in his eagerness to keep his own counsel and command, he had separated himself from the men who might know something of Stuart's movements, and here was Belden, colonel of volunteers after all, the position that the young captain so eagerly had sought before, and the chances were, two to one, that that hated Belden had the "tip" as to Stuart's route, and had been hurried towards Frederick purposely to meet him.

And this meant that, of all men in the world, Belden, Grosvenor Belden, was now between him and Stuart, with every chance of being first to strike the foe in the morning.

"Mount! Sound the mount!" ordered Foulweather, as with savage oath he sprang into saddle. "By fours, Treacy, and come lively."

An hour later, despite weariness and hunger, the squadrons were jogging away northwestward, following the pike to the crossing of the Monocacy and on up towards Frederick, meeting now and then belated and bewildered orderlies and couriers, whom Foulweather would eagerly question, and who could only tell that Belden's squadrons were still in the lead, and that Stuart was raising merry hades far beyond him. And so it happened that when the cold gray dawn crept into the eastward sky, and slowly, reluctantly lifted the pall of night from the sodden fields and muddy lanes and dripping copses, most of the Union cavalry in that part of Maryland had been drawn away far up the west bank of the Monocacy to head off Stuart, who, laughing in his gray sleeve, was trotting swiftly far down the east bank; and just at sunrise, after a twisting, tortuous, but most hilarious all-night march, mostly at the trot, with about a thousand fresh horses from Southern Pennsylvania, with new clothes and boots and weapons for many of his men, with only two or three troopers missing, and Pelham's guns clinking merrily as ever in the column, Stuart burst out upon the pike just where Foulweather crashed into the Pennsylvanians eight hours before, and there wasn't a single squadron to oppose him.

A wonderful march had he had. Yet when Stuart left Chambersburg on Saturday morning, after burning the railway shops and trains, and destroying such public property and stores and arms as he could not carry away, he well knew that an eventful day was before him, and that only by most adroit, rapid and daring movement could he hope to dodge his way through to the Potomac. By this time he felt assured the valley of the Antietam was swarming with troops, assembled there, and along the Conococheague to the west, to head him off should he return that way. By this time Averill, with all the force at his disposal, and Cox, with his division of infantry, would be lining the upper river towards Cumberland. Southward, however, east of the Blue Ridge, the broad, beautiful valley of the Monocacy was comparatively open, and Frederick, crammed with wounded and convalescents, filled with stores and supplies, and guarded only by a little force of cavalry and infantry, was a tempting bait to lure him down the right bank of that storied stream. Eastward, however, he headed his columns, leaving Hampton to bring up the rear and beat back pursuers should any appear,—eastward as though he meant to burst through the South Mountain and swoop down on Gettysburg, lying there defenceless in the heart of the beautiful farming country beyond. And that was how the cry went up that Gettysburg, too, was to be sacked and burned, but even while the governor of Pennsylvania was urging that troops be ordered thither by rail, Stuart dodged to the right. No sooner was the gray column (headed, so they say, by certain squadrons all tricked out, spick and span, in Yankee blue) safely through the range, than it turned southward, marching leisurely yet, for Stuart's object was to delude and deceive; then, back by the road to the southwest, again he pierces the range, and scouts and citizens, who watch him from afar, give tongue that the fox has doubled and is coming back to Hagerstown, where, too, are huge stores and supplies and heavy battalions of infantry ready to receive him. Six or eight miles, until the sun is high, does he march for all the world as though he meant to dare the whole Union force to the west of the mountains, and then, after long hours of easy jog, gathering in horses from every side as he rides along, the wary leader once more turns abruptly towards the east and darts for Emmittsburg, close to the boundary line, and here the Southern sympathizers cheer him to the echo, so he says, and here, while rejoicing in their joy, he misses one splendid chance, for a big scouting party of Dick Rush's swell lancers had only just passed northeastward up the pike towards Gettysburg, looking for him in that quarter, but never intending, we may be assured, to jeopard their own safety by running far into those clutches. They are to be the eyes of the army, to peer about the valley towards the old seminary town and send word back what Stuart is doing and whither he is going. Yet here comes Stuart from the westward, not the north, slips in between this venturesome party and its main body down towards Frederick, captures within the hour the colonel's couriers galloping after its commander with despatches which Stuart joyously reads to his staff, and laughs over the perplexity he is causing. Then away he goes again as the night wears on, this time straight for Frederick, and every soul in its rapidly augmenting garrison believes him still far up in Pennsylvania; otherwise, the lancers on the lookout would surely have sent warning. There is actually nothing now to prevent his dashing down and sabring the outposts of the beautiful old Maryland town, nothing but the realization that, just as skilfully as he has slipped in between the detachments of the enemy, "all ascout" for him, so may he slip out, and all their traps be unavailing. Darkness comes to aid him, and even while Pleasonton, with eight hundred cavalry and Pennington's light guns, after struggling through the rocky passes of Harmony Gap in the Catoctins, reaches Mechanicstown at half-past eight and halts, wearied with his long, long day of marching to and fro, Stuart's light-heeled column, moving at the trot,—with daring fellows far in the advance and out on either flank wherever there is road or byway, riding as though they had known each lane from boyhood, halting at times to feed, water, and care for their stock, to drink their coffee or sample Maryland cider,—crosses the Monocacy away above Frederick and passes through the little village of Middletown just at midnight, only five miles from where Pleasonton's jaded column waits expectant of his coming from the north, instead of which he is slipping around the easternmost pickets and patrols.

And now, leaving nearly all the Union horse, regular or volunteer, west of the Monocacy, away rides Stuart, free and untrammelled, bequeathing to Pleasonton after all only the galling fortunes of a stern chase. Thanks to their ill condition at the start, thanks to long delay in getting news or orders, thanks to having gone far west of Hagerstown at the very moment when the foe was far to the northeast, thanks to rough and rocky roads and unseasoned horses, the little Union column is well-nigh spent when it halts at Mechanicstown and sends patrols out scouting north and east, only to learn an hour after midnight that instead of interposing between Stuart and the Virginia shore, as Pleasonton intended, he has been outridden by the nimble Virginian, who, giving him the slip, is already far ahead. Disheartened, but determined, Pleasonton calls up his men and, by two o'clock this still and should-be-peaceful Sunday morning, takes the shortest route to the mouth of the Monocacy, and just as the first faint streaks of dawn are lighting the eastern skies he rides through Frederick, even as the advance of Stuart, ten miles away to the southeast, dashes boldly out upon the Washington Pike at Hyattstown.

Sunday morning, and over farm and hamlet eastward the angel of peace seems still to have folded her wings, yet all through these erstwhile quiet old Maryland towns, Monrovia, Liberty, Woodsborough, the lights have been flitting for hours, and honest burghers jabbering excitedly. Such a night they had never known before. Two thousand rebel cavalry have been passing through since midnight, and it seemed like twenty thousand, and as though they could never cease, and all this time, with all this trouble, only once does a Union force, big or little, come within pistol range of the main body. Away over towards Gettysburg a little knot of gray-jackets, thrown well out to cover Stuart's flank, is charged by some mounted horse-guards, who claim five prisoners as the result. But the column itself was miles away to the westward at the moment, apparently moving back towards Hagerstown. But this midnight betwixt Saturday and Sunday one of Rush's troops, scouting into Woodsborough, finds the town agog with excitement and squadron after squadron of Stuart's cavaliers trotting through, and wisely the lancers do not make their presence known. Just one straggler does the column leave behind,—young Scott, of the First Virginia, whom the lancers had nabbed far in rear of his comrades and led before their colonel. "A most intelligent young man," said Rush,—a young man who entertains him with full description of the composition of the command, and how it came and how it proposed to return; and, furthermore, Scott entertains no fear for either Stuart's safety or his own. Sunday morning, and already in Frederick there are bells a-chiming, summoning the faithful to arise and worship, while mud-bespattered troopers and black-mouthed cannon are hurrying southward through the stony streets. Away down the Monocacy the Maine regiments have thrown out companies on every road, and there they stand and shiver, so many spectres in light-blue overcoats, wondering which way that bewildering Stuart will really come. And far to the northeast, McIntosh, with his squadron, has crossed the Baltimore and Ohio track during the night and found the line and wires all right, yet when he sends back orderlies with despatches to be forwarded by telegraph at dawn, the operator shakes his head and looks fearfully westward. No trains are moving, and the lines have all been cut within the hour. Somewhere towards dawn, old Foulweather, bivouacking in the fields southeast of Frederick and close to the Monocacy, is electrified by the news brought in by a farmer from near Monrovia over to the east of them, —that the rebels were actually riding into Liberty two hours before; and, though men and horses have had hardly two hours' sleep, the veteran routs them out again, and noiselessly, so as to give no information to Belden, whose detested squadrons are resting half a mile above, away he leads northeastward, with the unwilling farmer as his guide, bound to recross the stream and be the first to challenge and bait the coming foe. But Liberty is much farther than he thought. Not until long after daylight does he reach the excited village, to find nothing of the rebel column but its muddy trail. Stuart, said the villagers, had gone south hours before, and must be crossing the Potomac now. Foulweather could have turned in pursuit at once, but here was grain in abundance; his horses had had no mouthful since noon the day before, had been marching almost constantly, and so he ordered dismount, unsaddle, water, feed, and feast, as best they could, threw himself upon a bench at the village tavern, and opened the Sabbath-day services with a string of bitter execration, just as the flags on Sugar Loaf began to swing in mad earnest, for away down in the open fields about Hyattstown the lookouts could faintly distinguish dense masses of moving objects that, as the light grew stronger, proved to be cavalry with led horses and wagons galore,—cavalry mainly in gray uniform.

Sunday morning at Heatherwood, and hour after hour while some of the inmates slept others kept watch and ward, and just at daybreak, at least as soon as it grew light enough to see, Tighlman, limping from his bed to the adjoining room, heard his name called in eager and excited tone, and found his fellow-captain crouching by the open casement gazing with eager eyes through his binocular.

"Look, Brad," cried Heatherwood. "Look, and thank God! Oh, if Fairfax, too, could only see it. By heaven, I must tell him!" And forgetful of pain, wounds, or peril, the young officer hobbled to the head of the stairs, and the halls of the old homestead rang and re-echoed to his joyous cry: "Fairfax! Fairfax, old boy! Take heart, man! Here we are, not five miles away. Stuart in force, by all that's glorious!"

And out on the lawn there was instant response, and men in blue took up the cry with variations of their own, and horses, tethered to the trees by the winding roadside, snorted in sympathy with the stir and excitement, and down in the timber by the river bank a hoarse thunder of drum began, and then, shrill, blaring, and insistent, the bugles struck up the thrilling call, "To arms!"

CHAPTER XIV.

Sunday morning, and, apparently unconscious of coming battle, the farm and village people on the broad plateau southeast of Heatherwood are donning their Sunday best, and many a stout father of the family has hitched in the farm team to drive the good wife and brood to Monocacy church at the cross-roads north of Poolesville. Sunday morning, and over on the Virginia Kittoctans eager, anxious eyes are gazing across the Potomac, studying the distant fields of Southern Maryland, while throbbing hearts are praying for the safety of their hero Stuart. Sunday morning, and the signal-towers on the loftiest summits are flagging thrilling messages to and fro, and here at Sugar Loaf the occupants watch with keen anxiety every movement of the massing foe so close at hand. Thirteen hundred feet in air their eyrie towers over the plain, but less than forty-eight hours ago some of these same indefatigable riders galloped up the twisting road to Fairview, sixty miles to the west, and played havoc with the signal-station there. Suppose it should occur to Stuart to detach a troop or two to clamber Sugar Loaf and raid their lofty rookery. Suppose it should occur to Pelham, trotting out yonder with a brace of those light guns he sights as a Kentuckian would sight a squirrel rifle,

to unlimber one of his pets, sink the trail into the
ditch beyond the road, and risk an axle tossing high
a few shells, just to try the range to Sugar Loaf's
summit. Lieutenant Carey can be excused for thinking how Roe and Rowley were chased from their
station the misty morning of two days gone by, but
Carey sticks to his post and watches like a cat. Sunday morning, and the companies sent out to picket
the roads are peeping through snake fences and
hedgerows at those far-away gray squadrons, and
wondering will Stuart come their way (in which case
the quicker they scurry back to supports the safer it
will be), or will he take some other road and leave
them undisturbed? Sunday morning, with the sun
an hour high, and there is thrill and excitement and
swift riding to and fro everywhere along the river
from Point of Rocks to Edward's Ferry, and all
along the Monocacy, for has not the Iron Secretary
wired from Washington that not a man of that in-
vading host must be allowed to escape back to Virginia? Stoneman commanding at Poolesville, and
Ward at Conrad's Ferry, and Pleasonton, with his
exhausted command strung out in long column
northward from the bank of the Monocacy, which he
reaches with his advance at eight o'clock, and Burnside's brigades over to the west, are all striving to
throw a force across the path of the dim gray squadrons coming swiftly southward now, covered by their
veil of skirmishers, making straight for Poolesville,—
so straight that Stoneman's outposts, falling back to

avoid capture, spread the tale that Poolesville will be attacked within an hour, and that Edward's Ferry, or possibly—barely possibly—Conrad's, is Stuart's objective point. Burdened with led horses and with the persons of civil officials whom he cannot parole and is ordered to bring with him to be held as hostages, the blond-bearded leader rides with more deliberation now, and it is beautiful to see the style and skill and finish with which his advance and flankers do their trooper work. The masses of the main body issue from Hyattstown about as the sun is rising. No stop for breakfast this time, gentlemen. We'll lunch in Loudoun County in comfort later on, say the aides. But while these masses, with the prisoners and the led horses, are moved steadily southward on the Poolesville road, other squadrons, with two of Pelham's light guns, are far to the front. Other platoons and sections are spurring out on every lane, south, east, and west. Every little ridge and hillock is held and occupied, every roadway picketed against the coming of formidable force. Before their dash the scattered fragments of Union cavalry, still in the neighborhood, recoil upon their slim reserves, and the word goes flying right and left, "Look out for Poolesville; Stuart's heading there!" Far to the north still Hampton, who led the advance, now covers the rear, and it is late as seven o'clock when his rearmost troop lets go at Liberty and trots away to Monrovia, turning from time to time to show its fangs to the few pursuing scouts. Away up the

Monocacy the lancers and the Maine cavalry are rubbing their eyes and wondering how it was possible for Stuart to go so fast and clear around them, and Belden, with his newly recruited but enthusiastic Pennsylvanians, is raging over the orders that sent him far to the west of the river when his own instincts warned him to keep to the east. And away up at Liberty poor Foulweather is grinding his teeth in bitter wrath and dismay, for Stuart has tricked them one and all, has ridden one hundred miles in twenty-four hours, and, still alert, jaunty, and debonair, comes trotting out upon the open fields to the east of Heatherwood to choose his homeward path across the broad Potomac.

Sunday morning, and the hour has come at Heatherwood when for all the years of her occupancy it was the custom of the gentle mistress to summon her household about her in the southeast parlor for family prayers. Here lies the sacred volume on its accustomed table, but no worshippers kneel at the quaint old-fashioned chairs and sofa or on the matting-covered floor. A fire has been started during the night in the wide fireplace, but is smouldering now. The shades and blinds are tightly drawn, and only a dim, ghostly light penetrates an empty room, silent and neglected in the midst of stir and bustle and excitement and sound of scurrying feet and straining voices such as Heatherwood had never known before.

In Ralph's room overhead are his mother, with

Belle and Laura, the former pale and silent, the latter flushed and radiant, and the three Confederate officers, Fairfax, Heatherwood, and Tighlman, with their embarrassed guardian, the young officer of the cavalry guard. Aunt Chloe and her husband have prepared breakfast, and the table is spread and ready, but no one heeds. To the scandal of these old-time domestics, the hall doors, front and rear, are open, and soldiers in muddy boots clank through and through without so much as "by your leave." Indeed, nothing but the presence of the sentry at the drawing-room door prevents the hungry intruders from helping themselves, as most of them have done in the kitchen, where Aunt Chloe has been making coffee and corn-bread since earliest dawn. Tighlman, trembling with weakness and excitement, has had to lie down again. Fairfax and Ralph, with their glasses, crouch at the eastern window. The Union lieutenant, placed in the most embarrassing position he has ever known, conceives it to be his duty to keep Fairfax constantly within reach, yet will not curb or hamper him in any way. Mrs. Heatherwood, in whose gentle eyes the tears are welling, is seated close by Tighlman's couch, with Belle sometimes crouching at her feet, sometimes starting up in irrepressible eagerness and excitement, and running to the window to gaze over her brother's shoulder. Only here and there in little patches can the eastward fields be seen, for the rain has beaten but few of the fading leaves to earth, and the autumn foliage still hangs thick and clustering. But southeastward a broader vista can be obtained, and yonder, nearly eight miles off, lies Poolesville, and the intervening roads and farms and fields are spread out like a map. From the lawn below the voices of the men come drifting up, eager and excited. Some of the more agile have clambered into the trees, and all of a sudden from one of their number comes the shout:

"I see 'em, boys, not a mile away. Cracky! a whole regiment of 'em, and artillery. Oh, if we only had a couple of guns up here, we could sweep the whole line!"

Mrs. Heatherwood bows her head in her hands, something like a groan forcing itself through her quivering lips. Ralph, gritting his teeth, springs to his feet and strives to find some point from which he, too, can penetrate the thick veil and see the fields beyond, and, even as they are clustering at the windows, there comes the sound of crunching gravel under horse's feet, the well-known sputter and crash, as, up through the bowered gate-way, on reeking steeds splashed with mud and mire, three horsemen come spurring along the worn old drive and out upon the once stately lawn of Heatherwood. The foremost, in glazed cap and poncho, a powerful, bearded man, is evidently an officer of high rank. The bedraggled housing of his horse still shows the edging of gold and the gleam of silver star.

"What do you see? Where do you see?" he demands, impetuously, of the soldier in the tree, and whips out his own field-glass.

"Rebel cavalry, sir, and guns, right out here across the fields. You could rake 'em if you had a gun here."

"Here, general, here!" cries another blue-coat, peering through the eastward hedge; "here you can see." And the stalwart officer spurs to the gap and takes one quick glance.

"By the Lord, he's right! Back with you, captain! Ride like mad. Tell Pennington to get a gun up here if he has to double up half a dozen teams. Tell him there isn't an instant to lose."

"God of Battles! It's Pleasonton!" cries Fairfax, springing to his feet. Then, his face blanching at the thought, "If guns are planted here they'll make this house the target for every piece in Stuart's column. For heaven's sake, lieutenant, tell your general there are defenceless women here. Tell him whose house this is." Then, as the officer seems to hesitate, mindful of his orders to hold his prisoner, the Virginian draws himself up and speaks proudly and deliberately. "Surely you have my word, sir. I shall take no advantage of your absence."

It is humanity that is pleading. It is for the sake of helpless women for whom there can be no shelter from the crash of shell, the deadly spatter of case-shot, if once the rebel gunners open on that height. Down goes the Union officer, three stairs at a jump, and reaches the broad portico, where at the moment an orderly is with difficulty holding an eager, spirited horse, the young lieutenant's, and this fresh and

"Back with you, captain! Ride like mad."

beautiful mount has caught the general's eye in an instant. "Whose horse?" he is repeating, as booted and spurred the young officer comes bounding from the hall.

"Lieutenant Wardner's, sir. Here he comes now."

"What is your regiment, and where is it, and who commands?"

"—th Pennsylvania, general. Somewhere up around Fredrick, I suppose. Colonel Belden," is the concise answer.

"I know," cries the cavalry commander, his eyes aflame. "We passed their bivouac in the dim light, though they were too far from the road to be seen. Your horse is fresh, sir. Ours have come over eighty miles since yesterday morning. Mount, gallop every inch of the way till you meet Pennington's second section. Tell them to flog their horses every inch of the road till they reach us. Then go on till you find your colonel. Tell him everything depends on his supporting me at once, and to come at the gallop. Here's Stuart's whole force not two miles away, and I haven't two hundred men to meet him!"

"I have a prisoner, sir,—Captain Fairfax,—and there are ladies here,—three,—who'll be in peril if artillery——"

"Never mind that. You'll have a thousand prisoners if you get Belden here in time. No, sir. I'll take all responsibility," answers the chief, impatient of expostulation or remark. "Mount instantly and ride. Yours is the only horse that's fit to gallop five miles. Go, sir, at once." And the general's mandate ends all further delay. Springing into saddle, the young officer rides straight for the leafy gate-way, then takes the gallop as he strikes the winding road. Aloft in the east room Ralph and Fairfax still remain at the windows, enthralled and eager. Tighlman covers his eyes and groans with impatience and anxiety combined. Somewhere down along the towpath a cavalry trumpet is sounding a thrilling call, at sound of which there is quickening of the pace of some unseen column, and, followed by his single orderly, the general rides round to the southwest, through the old orchard, and out beyond its westernmost tree, where he can see the Monocacy and the roads beyond, and there, crawling southward, more than a mile away, comes a jaded little command with somewhere in its depths a section of light guns, lugged all this distance, and towards them, as though riding for life, a solitary courier is speeding. But Pleasonton knows the leaders of his column are closer at hand. That trumpet call is from the head of a squadron of the Eighth Illinois, escorting the foremost section of Pennington's guns, and the general spurs for a gap in the fence and finds his way down a cow-track towards the canal, catching the little column as it rounds the front of the heights under which stood Homans's camp only a few days gone by. The guns have disappeared, led by his aide back to the north so as to climb the winding but more gradual ascent from that side. "Send one troop forward on the Barnesville road!" he orders. "Take the route to Poolesville with the rest. Stuart's out there on the plateau somewhere. Seems to be heading straight for Poolesville."

"And now, indeed, does it begin to look desperate for Stuart. South of him, at Poolesville, Stoneman has deployed his men, infantry and guns, to bar the way. Southwestward, towards Conrad's Ferry, are three regiments of infantry under General Ward. Westward, with several hundred soldiers of the Third and Fourth Maine to back him, Pleasonton is deploying his advance. Eastward the daring Southerners cannot turn, for there lie the deep river, Washington, and enemies by the thousands. Just one chance remains of squirming through without severe fight and having perhaps to lose his captured civil list and Pennsylvania horses. Three miles below the Monocacy and as many above Conrad's is White's Ford. Beyond that the bold heights of Loudoun County and perfect safety. Ward's men are still below it, Pleasonton's still above; but, should the head of Stuart's column turn that way, his purpose would be apparent in an instant. Stuart knows a trick worth two of that.

Brushing out of Barnesville the few vedettes and outlying pickets that dare to hang on his advance, his foremost squadrons push boldly out towards Poolesville, Stoneman's scattered cavalry slipping away from their front with warrantable agility, and now at last they have reached a belt of the beautiful farming country, rolling and fertile, wooded here and there and traversed by winding roads and lanes, that lies in full view of the thrilled occupants of Heatherwood's eastward rooms and windows.

"Yonder they go!" cries Fairfax, fairly ablaze with eagerness to join his comrades of the Virginia Horse. "See! See! Watch those fellows scooting away down that lane. Our men must be close behind them. Great God! they cannot see those heavy lines of infantry over beyond, and there's no way— no way—to warn them."

Belle and Laura, trembling with excitement and clinging to each other, are both now leaning over the captive captain and striving with their unaided eyes to make out the objects he can only distinguish with the glass. Ralph, at the adjoining window, has less sweep of the land before them, and can only see the Poolesville lines. He, too, springs over to the now crowded casement, and soldiers, glancing up from the lawn, look at each other in no little wonderment. That gray uniform within their lines seems out of place somehow. But suddenly an exclamation from below calls every blue-coat to the hedge, and a shout goes up from Fairfax:

"A charge! A charge! By all that's glorious! Look! Look! See them sweep that field! Good God! I cannot stand it—I cannot!" And springing away in uncontrollable excitement, he turns, throws his arms against the casement, and hides his face in them, quivering from head to foot. Only for an instant thus he stands, Belle's soft eyes filled with that dangerous pity that is so akin to love, for the next thing there is a chorus of half-startled "Ah!'s" from the blue-jackets, a jet of white smoke shoots across the distant fields, and a few seconds later the window shakes and a sharp bang—the angry bark of field-piece—rends the air, and Fairfax springs with uplifted, clinching fists. "Pelham!" he cries, exultant. Ralph, too, struggles to his feet, forgetful of his wounds, and yet turns, thoughtful for his mother, and finds her slowly sinking to her knees by Tighlman's bed, just as a second shot, sharper and clearer than the first, rings on the autumn air. It is church time, and morning service has begun in earnest.

Then, listen! From the north side now there comes the sound of violent motion, the thunder of hoofs, the rumble of wheels, the crash and sputter of gravel, the fierce cracking of whips and loud shouts of exultation and encouragement. "The guns! the guns!" cries Fairfax; "actually here. By heaven! It must not be." And, bare-headed, with his gray uniform hanging loosely about his enfeebled frame, the Virginian captain totters towards the door just as, drawn by panting, sweating, straining horses, six to the carriage, lashed and spurred to mad effort, there comes rushing through the bowered gate the foremost of Pennington's light guns, and, spurning flower beds and flowering plants, around it swings on the grassy lawn; scattering mud and shattered plaster of Paris, it is whirled into battery, unlimbered like a flash, and run by hand to the hedge. Furiously three or four cannoneers hack away at the bushes with their short curved swords. A gap is torn in the twinkling of an eye. The drivers spring from saddle and busy themselves about the harness of their teams, one and all looking just as though they had swam through miles of liquid mud. A dashing sergeant leaps from his horse, followed by several of his mounted gun detachment, tossing their reins to the horse holders, who quickly swing their half-dozen reeking chargers over to the side of the house, tearing huge rents in the once well-trimmed flower-beds. A tall, lanky cannoneer has gripped a sponge-staff and sent it whirling through the gap. A cartridge is rammed home, while a corporal casts his eye over the field a mile away and chisels a section of his paper fuse. A shell is sent home, and, with the rammer high above his head, the foremost cannoneer springs back from the muzzle. There is an instant grouping about the breech of the gun,—a group of grimy men in dirty blue.

"They're going to fire!" screams Laura, stopping her ears with her fingers and rushing to bury her head in the pillows. There is a moment's squinting through the slit of the brass pendulum hausse, then, lifting the instrument from its socket, the gunner springs back, both arms uplifted in signal "all clear," and orders "Ready!" A stocky little fellow jumps in to the breech and drives the priming wire home in the vent. Another drops the friction primer in, and is back in a second at the end of his taut lanyard. "Fire!" rings the hoarse order, and with a resonant bang that shakes the house and shivers a parlor window on the floor beneath, echoed by shrieks, half stifled, from the girls, the saucy rifle bellows its challenge to Pelham's guns nearly a mile out over the fields, and then, as they spring in to reload, the cannoneers look up in amaze, for a tall, hatless officer, in Confederate gray, leaps among them, with uplifted, imploring hands.

CHAPTER XV.

For a moment the members of the little detachment seemed stunned or stupefied. The sight of the Confederate uniform in their midst, of a soldier of evident rank and distinction, pallid from recent wounds and confinement, was in itself a thing to cause amaze, but that he should presume to interfere,—to speak to them in tones that, despite the appeal of his words, yet rang with the resonance of accustomed command,—was still another. The swarthy gunner at the trail was the first to recover himself, and his eyes flashed angrily.

"Who in hell——" began he, in the battle fury that had seized him, but the sergeant interposed.

"This is my business, corporal. Out of the way, sir," he ordered, sternly, as he turned to Fairfax. "You're a prisoner, or you couldn't be here. Take charge of that man, some of you," he cried, to the open-mouthed troopers who were grouping about them. "Load, lively there! Shave her half a second, Con. She bust ten yards beyond 'em." Then, as he straightened up in his mud-besplashed stirrups, his eyes dilating with fire, he swung his sabre towards the gap in the shrubbery and fairly yelled with joy. "Yonder comes a gun now. Look, Con! They'll be in your line of fire in half a shake. See?"

And leaping on the trail, the gunner peered through the gap. Three or four cavalrymen had, half reluctantly, laid hands on the Virginia captain and, despite his earnest words of explanation, insisted on his falling back from the gun. Corporal Con threw up his hat with a yell of delight. "It's Pelham's," he cried. "They're heading for the knoll beyond. It's there they'll unlimber. Shall we give 'em one now, sergeant?"

"Aye, sock it to 'em, quick, Con!" was the answer, as the chief of piece reined his snorting horse back from the gun, and the cannoneers sprang out from the wheels. A groan burst from the lips of Fairfax, a wail of anguish from the window above, and some men, glancing an instant over their shoulders, beheld Miss Heatherwood leaning from the open casement, wringing her hands, a wild-eyed, black-haired girl clinging to her side. Then all eyes were riveted on the spirited scene out on the rolling slopes half a mile away. A light gun-carriage, followed by its prancing detachment, drawn by six spirited horses, whose gray-jacketed drivers sat jauntily in saddle, came lunging through a little lane, turned square at a gap in the snake fence that bounded the slopes of an open field, and, following a dashing leader, went plunging and swaying up the ascent. Pennington's war-worn gunners knew them at a glance. Something in the dash and abandon with which they swung through the gap stamped them at once. "Pelham's Own!" was the cry. "Let 'em have it, Con."

The corporal, quivering with excitement, was astride of the trail, tapping gently its mud-stained side, while two stout cannoneers, panting and eager-eyed, gripped a handspike and swung the black muzzle into line. Squinting through the peep hole in the brass hausse, Con was spinning the elevating screw with one hand as he tapped the trail with the other, getting range and line at once, sighting square at the crest of the knoll. An instant more and the leaders of the distant gun came trotting up against the sky, then the "swing" team, then the wheel-horses, then one could almost hear the command, "Action rear!" as the team fairly settled back on their haunches and the following horsemen threw themselves out of saddle and scampered to the gun.

"Now, Con!" cried the sergeant, and a stifled shriek went up from the window, and Fairfax wiped the sweat of agony from his brow and called aloud,—

"Away from that window, Belle! Run to the cellar, quick! Away, I say!" he repeated, as the girls hung there, fascinated.

"For God's sake let me go to them," he cried. "I am pledged not to escape."

But the stern soldiers seemed deaf to his plea; seemed only alive to the scene at the gun. Again the corporal sprang back, both hands thrown high, again the order, "Ready!" again the lithe young batteryman leaped in, lanyard in hand, then the taut cord slipped through his fingers as he stretched away for the next word, "Fire!" and a jet of flame and smoke burst through the gap, the light gun leaped back a foot or two, the shot went shrieking away southeastward in long curve. A second or two of suspense, and then against the dull hues of the clouded horizon a puff of snowy smoke burst in front of the black objects on the distant field, and in an instant they were hidden from sight. Only for an instant, though; the little cloud went drifting away, a cheer rang out on the Heatherwood lawn, for two horses were seen to be kicking and struggling on the turf beyond the opposing gun. Then as Pennington's men sprang in to reload, the cry went up, "Lay low! Look out, fellows! They're aiming." And here and there a blue-jacket, crouching, went scattering to right or left, and others flattened out on the sodden ground. Again Fairfax cried aloud,—

"Leave that window, Belle, instantly! Down to the cellar, all of you!" But he might as well have ordered the dead. With dilated eyes the two girls hung there, gazing at the distant guns. Then Laura's voice, shrill and exultant, pierced the dripping air:

"Yonder's another gun. O Glory! See it a-jumpin', coming right up by the first!" And she clapped her plump hands in mad delight. "Now, Mr. Yankee, look out for your hide," she cried. "Aw, why don't they fire? What are they waiting for?" She danced impatient, utterly blind to the peril in which she stood if Pelham opened. Again wondering at the unusual delay in the Virginian's answering bark, the cannoneers were driving home their charge, when, far over the fields, furiously waving his hat, a horseman was seen, riding straight for Pelham's foremost gun, whose detachment in wonderment had ceased their skilled loading, and with unwilling ears were listening to words and orders inaudible to all at Heatherwood.

"Let 'em have it, Con!" again cried the sergeant. "We'll drive 'em off that ridge with another shot." And again was the gunner bending over the breech and the cannoneers ramming home, when loud, stern, authoritative, a soldierly voice rang out over the lawn, and, striding forth from the open door-way of Heatherwood, a tall, splendidly built officer in the uniform of a captain of cavalry, a man with flashing blue eyes and clear-cut face and blond moustache and imperial, came straight to the edge of the portico, and there halted and towered above them all.

"Drop that lanyard, men! You wouldn't fire from behind a petticoat. Can't you see those fellows will not answer because they know this house is full of women?"

At sound of the voice the sergeant had whirled in saddle and up went his hand in salute. The cannoneers turned in surprise. The lanyard slackened. One or two troopers who had thrown themselves under the hedge to dodge the expected shower of shrapnel squirmed out and gazed at the soldierly figure; but it was left to Captain Fairfax to exhibit strange and unaccountable emotion. He sprang forward, despite the resistance of two sinewy hands, until he had cleared the little group of captors among whom he stood, then halted in his tracks. Three men threw themselves upon him and seized him in vigorous grasp, but he never seemed to notice. With pallid face and quivering lips,—lips that were turning almost livid,—he hung there, glaring at the form at the edge of the portico, and the rough grasp of the soldiers slackened, for they saw the beads of sweat still starting from his brow and that he was trembling from head to foot. Aloft at the northeast window, as though striving to see the cause of this sudden silence on the lawn, Miss Heatherwood and her impatient cousin were leaning forward and gazing with all their eyes. But the strange officer stood where the projecting roof of the old-fashioned portico hid him from their sight. He had unslung a field-glass, and, applying it to his eyes, had concealed the upper portion of his fine face. He leaned against a heavy column, breathing hard as though he had ridden fast. His boots and breeches were daubed with mud, but the trim-fitting frock coat was innocent of a single splash. The polished scabbard shone like newly minted silver. The sash, though carelessly knotted, was of costly crimson silk. Half of him looked as though he had ridden through miles of mud, the other half as though he were marching on parade.

"Limber to the rear, then," ordered the sergeant,

though his eyes snapped angrily. "We could have knocked that gun off the ridge next shot, sir," he cried, regretfully, "and my orders was to do it, but the officer that gave 'em isn't here. Where'll we go, sir? There's no such spot as this within a mile."

"Down the road to join your battery," was the brief answer. "They've gone already, heading for Poolesville," he added. "Tell your captain you drove 'em off with one shot."

The horses were crunching round with dangling traces on the arc of a small circle as he spoke. The limber whirled about in front of the piece, its right wheel bumping, battery-fashion, over the iron trail-plate. The handspikes and sponge-staff were stowed away. "Halt! Limber up!" was the gunner's order, given in disgusted tone, and bitter disappointment brooded in the gaunt, war-worn faces as they glanced resentfully up at the windows. What business had women there anyhow, spoiling as square a fight as ever they had hoped for?

"I had the range of them fellers," swore Corporal Con, as he climbed to saddle, "and could have blown me shell square into the thick o' them."

"Dry up, Con!" was the sergeant's order. "Sure you wouldn't hit a man that couldn't hit back? Come on at the trot now." And down the winding road he led, his gun and gunners clattering after, just as afar out over the fields there came from the southeast a throb and sputter of distant musketry, and down on the invisible towpath southwest of the orchard a cavalry trumpet sounded, "Trot!" and then, "Bang! Bang!" in quick succession two booming reports told that Stuart's guns had opened on the Union lines, and that the renowned cavalier was making good his word and fighting his way through.

Up at the window, still, Belle and Laura hung, athrill now with excitement and enthusiasm. What mattered it that Captain Fairfax had failed in his mission;—that another, and one in evident authority, had ordered off their unbidden visitors? What mattered it that Fairfax was there a prisoner, and Ralph and Tighlman invalided and paroled? They could see nothing of Fairfax now. His captors, eager to reach a spot whence they could peer through the hedge at the distant fighting lines, had turned him over to two of their number to be taken back to where the horses were picketed about the barn. The cavalry officer, too, had suddenly disappeared within the house and was seen no more. Ralph, gazing through his glasses, still studied the movements out on the distant fields, his features working strangely. It was after nine o'clock. Not a mouthful of breakfast had they touched, for who could tell what phase of battle the next minute might bring forth? Over by Tighlman's couch knelt the gentle mistress of the mansion, her lips still moving in fervent prayer. The powerful fascination that had drawn to the windows most of the occupants of Heatherwood, except the now terrified servants, had attracted most of the soldiery to the eastward gaps in the hedge, or to points in the westward orchard whence they could catch occasional glimpses of Stuart's men. Within the kitchen two of the Maine infantry kept reluctant guard. Chloe and her trembling liege were hiding in the cellar. Officers of every kind had disappeared. Fairfax, under guard, found himself practically alone. A shy country boy, whose corporal's chevrons were new as his face was smooth, seemed to know not what to do with his charge, and readily assented to the captive captain's proposition that they should go to the upper windows of Heatherwood, whence they could see the progress of the fight, and Fairfax was weak and dazed, and the corporal's heart was moved to pity.

"You look sick," said he. "When did—when did you get captured?"

"Only last night," was the reply. "This house is the home of relatives of mine whom I wished to see. I have given my parole. You need fear no attempt to escape, but if you are ordered to stand by me, come up there. Did you see—did you know that cavalry officer?"

"Saw him, yes," said the soldier, awkwardly, lugging his rifle in one hand, as with the other he aided the weakened Virginian up the stairs, "but never saw him before. Those battery fellows knew him. I heard them calling him by name as they rode away."

"You did?" demanded Fairfax, leaning on the balustrade and breathing hard as he clung to it for support. "You did? And what name did they give him?"

"Captain Belden, they said; —th Regulars—cavalry," was the innocent reply, whereat Fairfax stared the harder, gripped even tighter the balcony rail, and the corporal, fearful that his prisoner was collapsing on his hands, called loudly to a trooper in the hall-way to come and help him,—a trooper who was issuing from the door of a little room on the north side, and he glanced hurriedly upward.

"I'll send help," he muttered, in a strange, smothered tone, and hastened into the kitchen, but from the floor above came Mrs. Heatherwood and her daughter. Hurrying and with anxious questioning and troubled looks, they bore down upon the oddly assorted pair. The soldier fell back at sight of them, glad of such relief.

"What is it, my boy? What has happened?" was Mrs. Heatherwood's anxious question, as her arm was thrown about the shrinking form. "Help him, please," she added, turning to the young corporal, and, laying down his rifle, the latter almost lifted Fairfax to a sofa on the floor above. "Bring some wine, quickly, Belle," ordered Mrs. Heatherwood, as she knelt by the sufferer's side. "What is it, Floyd?" she murmured. "You've overtaxed your strength."

"I did not dream how weak I was," he whispered, "or that I could behave like a woman, but," and now his eyes flitted eagerly about until he was assured that Belle had gone, "I saw Jack Lowndes lying dead by the roadside at First Bull Run, and could have sworn it was he——"

"Hush, Floyd! Listen!" appealed Mrs. Heatherwood, laying her fingers on his lips, for Laura was screaming excitedly at the window, and Ralph's voice was adding to the clamor. Far out afield the firing was growing quick and fast, but what Ralph saw was something that thrilled him to the marrow.

"Fairfax! Fairfax!" he cried; "come here, for God's sake, and tell me what it means. There's a squadron of Yankee cavalry right in the midst of Stuart's reserve, and it's coming this way."

With a brimming glass of Madeira in her hand, Belle was hastening down the hall. Fairfax struggled to his feet, drained the glass, and staggered to the eastward window. Ralph handed him the binocular, pointing excitedly through the gap that commanded the fields. Across one of the nearmost the gun detachment so recently at the hedge was now laboring with their heavy charge; across another, coming straight towards them, five hundred yards farther away, a compact little squadron in the Union blue was spurring at rapid trot, their sabres glinting at the "carry," a slender young officer well in the lead; and at this distant array Floyd Fairfax took one rapid glance through the glass and dropped it with a cry:

"*Yankee* cavalry? God of heaven, no! It's Garnett and the First Virginia!"

And as though he heard the cry, and were expecting it, a tall trooper, splendidly mounted, dashed the next instant around the corner of the house, spurred straight for the gap where lately stood the gun, swung high his forage-cap in air, as with magnificent bound his horse carried him through and over and careering on down the orchard slopes beyond; and then over the fields rang a shout, powerful, resonant, that sounded strangely familiar to the straining, startled ears at Heatherwood, and bore with it the same challenge and power of command as that which checked the fire of the gunners not ten minutes before: "Gallop, men! Gallop with that gun! That's rebel cavalry coming! Gallop and follow me!"

CHAPTER XVI.

For five minutes that followed Heatherwood was the vortex of a storm of excitement such as the old mansion had never known in the past and was destined only once to know again. Swiftly spurring over the eastward fields, bending forward in their saddles in the eager pose all troopers know so well,—the crouch of the tiger before the spring,—the little squadron seemed making straight for Heatherwood, and had not yet come in view of the lone detachment of horse artillery down on lower ground, the single gun with its accompanying squad of cannoneers that had followed the winding drive into the ravine and was now jogging and jingling through the lane that led to the Potomac.

Obedient to authority he dare not question,—the orders of a regular officer,—the veteran sergeant was hastening by the shortest line to overtake his battery commander, who with another gun was at this moment hacking his way through the fence of a sloping field to the southeast and striving to reach a low ridge beyond, whereon appeared the well-known form of General Pleasonton, with two of his staff and a brace of orderlies, most of whom were eagerly waving their hats and urging the young artillerist to full speed. A squadron of cavalry spurred wearily behind the gun, and a dozen men, dismounted, were lashing at the nearly exhausted horses or working at the wheels. Another squadron was pushing out on the Barnesville road to the east, all ignorant of this swoop of hostile cavalry across the higher ground to the left. Absorbed in the effort to fasten on the right flank of Stuart's force out in the open ground towards Poolesville, the commander of the pursuing cavalry seemed to think it impossible that any of the raiders should have ventured to dash at Heatherwood, now nearly a mile in his rear.

Still farther out to the southeast a lone skirmish line, stretching from east to west, was faintly indicated by dim dots of horsemen beyond a fringe of woods. Stuart's advance, then, had met the expected resistance, and a squadron or two had been deployed to feel the way. It was on the ridge half a mile out in that direction that Pelham's guns had appeared long enough to draw the fire of Pennington's one rifle; then, forbidden by some old friend to fire at Heatherwood, the Virginians had popped out of sight into the depression beyond. Doubtless they and their supporting cavalry could now be seen from where Pleasonton boldly rode on the bluff-like crest to the southward, but here at Heatherwood only by the sound of distant firing could anything be determined of Stuart's movements. All around about the mansion was scurry and excitement. A knot of country folk on their way to church, frightened by the sound of battle and the sight of hurrying guns and cavalry, had climbed the steep slope at the south, the pathway Homans and Pettingill had known so well, and were gathered with the few lingering troopers about the hedge. The young officer commanding the guard had disappeared, sent, like Wardner, on some errand by the urgent leader of the Union horse, whose own mounts were apparently exhausted. At sight of the coming squadron the sergeant left in charge had looked eagerly about for aid, but the column descending the Monocacy was far beyond supporting distance and on a muddy road, and the infantry at the aqueduct and along the canal could not begin to reach the height as quickly as could the nimble cavalry.

"Gallop to that Maine colonel down there at camp," he ordered a trooper, " and tell him that rebel cavalry is in sight not half a mile away, coming straight at us, and I've only a dozen men." Then, although he ordered his people to mount and await orders in the barn-yard, their eagerness to see what was going on prompted first one, then another, and finally the entire party, to come sputtering around to the front, completing the ruin, with the iron-shod hoofs, of the once trim pathways and flower-beds at the side, as well as the havoc of hoof and wheel upon the lawn, and here beneath the eastward windows, with half a dozen infantrymen detailed as the guard, the troopers clustered, some tossing their reins to comrades and climbing into the trees, others nervously unslinging their carbines and lining the eastward hedge and gap, all impervious to Laura's fine scorn and fierce denunciation.

At the windows, thrilled with excitement at the scene and sounds, the little household gathered, even Tighlman, now unrebuked, having limped from his bed and seated himself where he could peer over Heatherwood's shoulder. With them was Madam Heatherwood, her sweet, wan face pallid with anxiety and distress. At the other window Fairfax knelt, his embarrassed guardian, rifle in hand, close behind him, while Belle and Laura, clinging to each other, gazed from the casement, the former trembling with dread, her beautiful eyes brimming with tears, the latter quivering with excitement, her black orbs fairly snapping with defiance and delight. And now, until it disappeared at a lumbering gallop down behind the shrubbery, all eyes were fixed on that imperilled gun and its shouting, urging guard and drivers, then on the swift advance of that daring little squadron, now not fifty yards beyond the brow of the westward slopes, along the foot of which that dashing trooper who leaped the gap a moment before was now striving to guide the precious gun to safety. Who was he? Who is he? asked each captive officer, confident that form, face, and voice were all familiar. But no answer came from Belle or the trembling lips of her mother.

"Look! look at Garnett!" was the cry, for now, even without the glasses, the waving plumes on the young leader's jaunty head could be plainly seen, and he at least was in the gray, though throughout the bounding rank almost every trooper rode in brand new blouse or jacket of the Union blue. Ten seconds more and they must reach the edge of the gentle slope, must surely see the gun. Although the range now is too great for accurate shooting, the soldiers at the hedge are in eager conference. Some are cocking their rifles and carbines. "Shall we fire, sergeant?" cries a trooper.

"For God's sake, no!" sings out a nervous recruit, who, sitting in saddle, holds the horses of half a dozen men. "You'll bring the whole pack on us." A grin spreads over the pallid face of Fairfax.

"That fellow has sense, at least," he mutters. A jeer bursts from Laura's lips, a groan from Mrs. Heatherwood, and then, an instant later, wild shouts of warning from the hedge, a cheer of exultation from the windows, a distant—a glorious burst of melody like that of the hounds in full cry, the prolonged "Ch-a-a-a-rge" of the leader, a blast of the trumpet, and above all the thrilling chorus of trooper yells, as, never checking at the sight, the squadron commander comes in view of the quarry, and, swinging sabre over his head, in magnificent circling swoop down the grassy slope like darting falcon he heads the rush of his Virginians, and then the air rings with shot and clash of steel, and fierce oaths and imprecations and exultant cries. There is a popping chorus of pistols that accompanies a wild scurry of hoofs away and around the lower edge of the timber to the south, and Fairfax leaps to his feet and cries aloud:

"By heaven! they've got the gun! They're driving 'em into the river!"

Then there is another warning yell, from the hedge this time, as several of the troopers come tumbling out, and running for their horses. A sergeant is shouting, "Mount!" An infantry corporal, red in the face and raging with fight, begs him to order all of his men to occupy the timber and open fire on some troopers now drifting back from the chase after the gun. It is a moment of mad excitement, and no man there knows just what should be done. Then comes another shout, this time from the orchard. That settles it. "Lay low, fellers! Look out! The whole caboodle's coming back, and they'll be on you in a second!" To the very edge of the canal have the Virginians pursued the helpless gunners, to the very teeth of the infantry guards of the aqueduct, for now a fierce sputter of musketry opens at the foot of the westward slope, and the thunder of returning hoofs is heard, mingled with loud laughter and derisive cheers and yells, and then, before the hampered troopers on the lawn can swing into saddle and form for action, a shot rings at the back of the house, another, and another, and up through the old orchard come the nodding plumes and panting, struggling horses, and all the sergeant can find words to say is, "Come on out of this!" and away he goes through the bowered gate-way to the northeast, his fellows clattering after. There's no place there to wheel and fight. They are only a dozen all told, and Stuart's men seem popping out of every lane and hedgerow and shaded aisle. There's nothing else to do but dash out of the trap and gallop to the nearest supports, and there, not half a mile away, wearied, but gamely struggling on, comes Pleasonton's main force along the Monocacy. The sergeant is wise in his generation. Thitherward he gallops with his pack, a dozen sabres swinging at their heels, and there are left only the infantry sentries and that lone corporal in the second story to receive with proper honors the mud-bespattered, but triumphant band of merrymakers who rein up in front of Heatherwood, and the young cavalier at their head bows low over his reeking horse's mane, sweeps his plumed hat groundward in salutation to the ladies at the nearest window, and bids Miss Heatherwood a joyous good-morning.

Fancy the scene as Heatherwood and Tighlman shout greeting to him from their casement, and Laura, springing down the stairs, four and six at a bound, fairly hurls herself upon the mud-besmeared lieutenant and ecstatically hugs him, all maidenly shame forgotten in the delirious joy of the occasion. But wary eyes have seen the dart of the infantry sentries for shelter. Grim, battle-worn troopers are watching at the orchard and at every gap. A veteran sergeant, binding a slashing sabre cut upon his bridle-hand with an old bandana, warns his young chief there is not a moment to spare.

"How are you, Ralph? How are you, Brad?" laughs Garnett. "All ready, you fellows? Got a couple of tip-top horses here for you if you're ready to ride. Run you over to Virginia in less than an hour, but you'll have to be lively, boys. Come right along. Thought I'd find you here; and we've got that gun, too, all right. S'pose you saw Pelham wouldn't answer."

And all this he has to shout, handsome, bareheaded, well-nigh breathless, while Laura, possessed of one hand, is dancing madly on the portico. Down about the canal the sputter of shots has died away as the troopers come scurrying back, but here and there far out over the muddy roads and lanes, bugle speaks to trumpet and rallying calls are sounding, and away to the southeast Pelham's guns are booming challenge at Stoneman's still more distant lines. All around is throb and stir and sound of battle, yet here at Heatherwood, save where Laura dances in elfish triumph, there has fallen sudden silence and gloom. Heatherwood and Tighlman have disappeared from their window, so has Belle. Fairfax has not been seen since the moment of the Southern troopers' coming. With a word to his bewildered guard, who follows him as he would his own captain, he has left his window and stepped across the hall into another room. Astonished at this strange reception, Lieutenant Garnett looks one moment wonderingly at the now vacant windows, then, hearing his name called close at hand, turns and finds himself almost face to face with Madam Heatherwood.

"My son, my nephew thank you, Mr. Garnett, for your daring effort, but—they are my prisoners now. They are bound by their honor until exchanged," she says, with sad and gentle dignity.

"But, Mrs. Heatherwood," he interrupts, impatiently, "no parole holds good in the event of a recapture." And as he speaks, standing there with uncovered head beside his drooping horse, away out over the southward fields the quick crackling of musketry redoubles, and Pelham's guns are barking savagely. The sergeant, bending in saddle, sweeps the gap with anxious eyes.

"We haven't a minute to spare, sir," he mutters.

"I know what you would say," is Mrs. Heatherwood's reply. "Neither of them is fit to ride, but neither of them should ride, even if he could, for the government at Washington has treated us with kindness we can never repay."

"Mrs. Heatherwood," bursts in Garnett, impetuously, "we have counted on this recapture. It was to be my proud duty to bring in your boys from Heatherwood and Fairfax from Leesburg. Here come their horses now."

"Floyd Fairfax!" exclaims Laura, eagerly. "Oh, do take him, quick! The Yankees call him a spy, and say they'll hang him. They got him here, but they didn't get his farmer clothes."

Garnett's face grows yellow-white at the instant.

"Floyd Fairfax here! You cannot mean it!" he cries, turning almost angrily upon her.

"I do. They followed him here,—'rested him here."

"Where is he?" demands Garnett, springing up the steps, as the sergeant leaped from saddle as though to detain him.

"Mount, lieutenant! Mount, for God's sake! They're driving us back. We'll be surrounded here in a second," he cries.

And then Garnett halts with blazing eyes, for at the door-way—a soldier with carried rifle at his back—there stands Fairfax, pale as is the younger soldier whose hand goes up in salute, but the words he speaks are full of sternness, even suspicion.

"Captain Fairfax, only night before last I offended a brother officer in defending your name, but I never thought to find you—here. You, of course, can come—will come with us."

"I of course would come, sir, and if I live will come to answer any imputation, but go you must at once. I cannot; I have pledged my word."

"Floyd—Floyd Fairfax! If you don't go you'll be hanged for a spy!" shrieks Laura Waddell.

"Say to General Stuart," is the solemn answer, "that I pledged my word not to attempt to escape."

And with the words there comes the sound of hurrying hoof-beats through the yards, through the orchard, up the roadway, and the sergeant fairly hurls himself upon his young leader, almost throws him into saddle, and then together they take the leap through the eastward gap in the hedgerow, only just in time to avoid the rush of half a score of Union troopers, two of whose horses drop exhausted, dead, at the doors of Heatherwood.

CHAPTER XVII.

ONE o'clock, and the guns have almost ceased their sullen thunder, for a wonderful thing has happened. Despite Stoneman's opposing lines at the southeast about the fields of Poolesville; despite the hurriedly aligned regiments of Ward facing northward at Conrad's Ferry; despite the utmost efforts of Pleasonton's mud-covered and exhausted little command attacking from underneath the heights of Heatherwood; despite the later coming of Belden's Pennsylvanians on one road and swearing old Foulweather with his gritty regulars on the other; despite the fact that Union batteries, battalions, and squadrons confront him north, east, and south, and a river rolls to his right on the west, Jeb Stuart, the redoubtable, has skilfully slipped through the meshes, and while "the incomparable" Pelham, with two of his guns, sends shot and shell at every approaching column from the low heights at the east of White's Ford, the other two splash through the Potomac with the prisoners and plunder, and reappear in a twinkling on the wooded bluffs of the Virginia shore, covering the ford so that, squadron by squadron, the jaunty invaders trot dripping back to Dixie, leaving their skirmish lines to show their teeth to the slowly enclosing ranks of the pursuers, until Pelham limbers up and lashes his remaining light barkers through the flood, quickly to bellow new challenge from the Loudoun shore. Then away skip the rearmost skirmishers, and at two o'clock, on the very ground where stood the Southern guns the hour before, the commands of Ward, Pleasonton, and Stoneman come butting their heads together, asking each other how the devil this thing was possible, and why the dickens this, that, or the other thing wasn't done by somebody else. It was all simple enough when one came to study it out. Pennington's rifles got stalled in the sodden fields, and even "doubling up" teams didn't help them out. Pelham's guns had the pick of Pennsylvania horses to hitch in the moment a wheeler weakened. Pleasonton's men had ridden night and day since four o'clock Saturday morning, and, not being used to such things, had only covered eighty miles, a dozen of them misdirected. Stuart's fellows, trotting night and day and never minding it, had ridden all around Pleasonton, and seemed to hugely enjoy the trip, for raiding and riding were things they took to as they did their daily bread, and got with greater regularity. Stuart had made Ward and Stoneman believe he meant to push through to Edward's Ferry, below the big bend, so they were hastening to block the goal towards which the gray skirmishers in advance were so steadfastly pushing. Then, when Ward's regiments were all handsomely headed thither and well out of the way, the Virginia leader quickly slipped his main body along a sheltered wood road, screened by his skirmishers, straight westward to White's, and not until their guns unlimbered on the Loudoun side did he draw in the threatening veil, leaving Ward and Stoneman to storm and swear, sole answer they could give at such long range to Pelham's derisive barking on the westward heights. A prettier piece of skill and audacity even Stuart had not yet essayed.

Then when the Union leaders came together and Ward pluckily demanded permission to push across, forgetful of Ball's Bluff, and attack the lion in his lair, he was wroth because Pleasonton would not lend his mired guns and worn-out cavalry, and Pleasonton declared that Stoneman should have covered White's and thereby made escape for Stuart impossible, and Stoneman responded that what Pleasonton said was absurd. And so in such sweet accord they spent the Sunday afternoon, digging their guns out of the mire and damning each other for letting Stuart go. But what they thought and said wasn't a circumstance to what the Iron Secretary remarked in Washington,—he who had thundered, "Not a man of Stuart's command must be allowed to escape back to Virginia." And all this had the Southern leader risked and accomplished without the loss of one man killed. But these were the days before the leaders of the Army of the Potomac learned the use and need of cavalry; before Hooker had organized the fine divisions that with another year had clipped the plumes of Stuart and were destined, so soon after, to lay him low at Yellow Tavern.

One splendid piece of daring had shown like a rift in the clouds through the darkened skies of that hapless day,—Trooper Bell's magnificent attempt to save that isolated gun of Pennington's from the dash of the Southern squadron, and the heroic fight of the little detachment against four times their number. Thrashing the maddened gun horses with their sabres, they had urged them at the gallop to the narrow towpath, while with pistol and blade the devoted fellows fought furiously to beat off Garnett's yelling pack, and, aided by the fact that the road was narrow and hemmed by cliffs on the right and thick shrubbery on the left, they finally landed their precious charge safely under the muzzles of the aqueduct guards, but not without the loss of two gallant fellows, shot from their saddles by Virginia lead, and the severe hacking of Trooper Bell himself, who was turned over to the surgeons, hero of the day perhaps, yet battered for the time being beyond recognition.

"No," said Foulweather, as he bent and gazed into the bandaged face of the sleeper in the improvised hospital tent, late that afternoon, "that isn't Bell of my command. If it was," he added, with savagely grinding teeth, "I'd kill him."

But Bob Hamlin noted how daintily white was the hand that twitched outside the worn gray blanket, and let his wrathful leader remount without gainsaying his word. Foulweather had that he wished to say to Belden of the brand-new Pennsylvanians, and rode off in hot haste to find him, while Bold Bob more leisurely examined the kit of the prostrate trooper, now sleeping under the influence of opiates. The boots settled the matter.

"Take good care of that man, doctor," he whispered, as he pressed the weary surgeon's hand. "There's mettle in every bone of him."

"Take care of him, of course," growled that overworked practitioner, "though you're not the first to bear witness to his worth, by a dozen."

And so as the sun went westering behind his shroud of mist, and the rains came pelting down again, and Pleasonton's bedraggled column sought shelter under their dripping ponchos, and the wearied horses munched at the hay their masters bore from Heatherwood and the adjoining farms, the cavalry general rode off disconsolate to Point of Rocks, in search of army head-quarters, that he might report what they already knew, that Stuart was safe across the Potomac again and laughing at them from the Loudoun bluffs. And Stuart himself, finding that nobody proposed to come across in face of his barkers, ordered "limber up" and rode away to the nearest gap, plunder, prisoners, and all, to tell the marvellous tale of his wanderings to the applauding camps of Lee.

With nightfall the Maine men rejoined their brigade, for Clark and his New Hampshire boys came dripping back to reclaim their camp, bearing half a dozen wounded and leaving two unshrouded dead. Clark could have said true if not temperate things about that morning's work, but he clamped his jaws and only looked black and stern when men inquired what he thought of the mess. Among his wounded, poor boy, was Reuben Pettingill, who, with the foremost of Ward's skirmishers, got near enough to be shot through the leg by one of Stuart's outermost flankers. The first thing the colonel did was to see his men safe once more within his guarded streets and his wounded carefully attended to. Then came the straightening out of the accounts of the day, while the cooks prepared supper over the sputtering fires. And then, as the officers gathered about his tent, and other officers, hunting for lost commands, came in to crave and receive soldier hospitality, there came still others with rumors and reports,—rumors of what they termed a red-hot row between two regulars, Belden and Foulweather, at the camp of the Pennsylvanians, and then all of a sudden a swift courier from the camp of the regulars a mile up stream, a courier who bore a bundle and a note, which Clark examined in his tent, then called for his orderly and horses, and, bidding a guard follow him, took the winding road to Heatherwood. He found the lower floor swarming with stragglers, the riff-raff of every branch of the service, men and boys who swore they hadn't an idea where to look for their regiments, and so had invaded Heatherwood's once sacred precincts until their regiments should look for them. These he sternly ordered forth into the ranks of the guard, bidding the latter search the barn and sheds, then made personal examination, finding every room,—parlor, drawing-room, dining-room, the sleeping-rooms on the lower floor,—all looted and littered, even to that little chamber, usually kept locked, that opened off the rear hall-way close to the kitchen door. Finding no organized guardians, these armed banditti, foul birds of prey, worthless to their own colors, had skulked in hiding while better men were straining every nerve for the cause they served. With battle-lines forming under their very eyes, these wretches could only skulk and sneak and steal. Kitchen, cellar, and closet they had robbed and ransacked. Beautiful old colonial furniture and ornaments, things which they could not carry away, in sheer wantonness they had destroyed. Clark's flattened sabre came down with savage whack on the back of one burly ruffian snoring on the couch in the hall-way, an emptied wine-bottle still clutched in his hand. Short work the colonel made of the tough element sprawled about the house or swarming in the cellar. Full a score thus caught red-handed he sent under guard to the tents of the provost-marshal, a proceeding which Miss Waddell, from the landing at the head of the stairs, hailed with shrill approval and delight. That country boy corporal whom Wardner had left in charge, backed by one or two comrades whom he had called into service, was all that stood between Heatherwood's second story and the throng of stragglers on the floor below, for the Virginia officers would have been powerless.

"Well, I never thought I'd be glad to see a Yankee uniform so much in my life!" exclaimed Laura as the bearded colonel finally came wearily up the stairs to inquire for Madam Heatherwood. "She's better. She bears it better'n any of the rest of us, but Lawd sakes, it was enough to make me wild to see her go down and plead so gently with those thieves and scoundrels. Why, they were just smashing everything. 'Course they stopped while she was there; the man don't live that could be rude to aunty. But the moment her back was turned they began again. Floyd Fairfax, he went down—he took off his uniform—Aunty made him,—but he couldn't whip a hundred of 'em."

"Floyd Fairfax! Yes," responded Clark, "and where is this Captain Fairfax?"

"Oh, I forgot. He wasn't here when you were. He's—you know he's a sort of a cousin of ours—he's —he's a prisoner. He was caught. But," she added, with pouting lip and rush of vivid color, "General Stuart's officers recaptured him to-day, only he wouldn't go, wouldn't——"

"Pardon me, Miss Waddell," said the colonel; "I must see these gentlemen at once; and then will you announce me to Mrs. Heatherwood? Where shall I find the officers?"

For answer the corporal at the landing motioned

to his right, and, leaving the girl, the colonel followed his guide to the front room on the north side of the hall. The doors to the south were closed. A dim light was burning within. A tall officer in shirt sleeves, a man with haggard face, was nervously pacing the floor. Two others, spent and weary with the wild excitement of the day, were lying, one in bed, apparently exhausted, the other on the sofa on the northward side. Silently Clark entered the room, instinctively removing his black felt hat. Silently the tall Confederate halted and faced him. Silently Ralph Heatherwood rose and leaned heavily on a chair. Curious to hear what this officer of rank might have to say to the prisoner left in his charge, the boy corporal followed to the door-way, where he stood respectfully at the threshold, then again drew back as a tall lieutenant in the dress of the Union infantry came hastening after his commander.

For a moment no word was spoken. The New Hampshire colonel, the Virginia captain, stood facing each other, two war-worn men whose years widely differed, yet whose days of active service must have been nearly equal. There was an expression in the calm, stern face of the Northerner that seemed to stir resentfully the current of the Virginian's blood, for his dark cheek flushed and his eyes slowly began to glow, symptoms which Heatherwood was quick to see, for he came hastily, painfully forward.

"Colonel Clark," he said, "I feel sure you have received some impression or information concerning our kinsman, Captain Fairfax, that is unjust to him. If you knew what he has refused to-day you could never suspect him of having come here as a spy."

"Unless Captain Fairfax came here with Stuart's command this day he could never have reached Heatherwood except in disguise," was Clark's cold answer. "And it is my duty to say to Captain Fairfax that an officer with suitable guard from my regiment will be here presently to conduct him to the quarters of the provost-marshal at Point of Rocks. Mr. Homans," he continued, turning to the doorway, "send my orderly for the adjutant."

And then he himself stepped back a pace and bowed gravely and reverently, for, leaning on her daughter's arm, and followed by Laura, Madam Heatherwood, as they loved to call her, came slowly into the room.

"The fortunes of war have gone heavily against poor old Heatherwood to-day, my friend," she said, a sad, sweet smile upon her patient face. "Surely it cannot be that any of my poor boys must be taken away to-night."

The tremulous appeal in her gentle voice, the rising tears in her fading eyes were more than Clark could bear. Quickly he pushed forward an easy-chair, and now, with Miss Heatherwood assisting, seated her and found a footstool for her feet before he could trust himself to reply.

"You do not know how I deplore the havoc these skulkers have played, dear lady," he said at length. "A dozen of them are now under guard, and it shall go hard with them, for it will anger your friends at court to know that in all the confusion of this day your home has been desecrated and you and those you love have been put to distress."

"But—Captain Fairfax?" she interposed, appealingly. What was the desolation over which poor Mammy Chloe was wailing now below to that which might prevail at Leesburg if ill were to befall the gallant boy in whom so many hearts were centred?

"For Captain Fairfax, I regret to say, the government entertains views far different to those which concern your son and nephew. They were brought here wounded and helpless, sent to you in return for all the loving care you gave our wounded after Bull Run and Ball's Bluff. Captain Fairfax,"—and here his deep-set eyes turned full on the accused officer, who, folding his arms, stood erect, his head thrown haughtily back,—"Captain Fairfax, whose absence from his regiment is in itself a matter——"

"A matter between Captain Fairfax and his regiment only, sir," sternly interrupted the Virginian.

"Whose absence from his regiment is in itself a matter that involves him in suspicion," calmly continued the colonel. "He is known to have reached Poolesville and to have lurked there in disguise, and he could have come here when he did only in disguise."

"And didn't your cavalry fellas last night hunt high and low through this house," burst in Miss Waddell, her black eyes snapping, "swearing Floyd Fairfax came dressed like a farmer, as if a Fairfax would dress like a farmer anyhow, and never a stitch of such a thing could they find, 'cept some rags belonging to old Uncle Joe in the cellar?"

"Laura, child, you must not interfere," said Mrs. Heatherwood, reprovingly. "Yet what she says is true, colonel," she continued, turning again to the stalwart New-Englander, while the sound of heavy footsteps could be heard coming hurriedly up the stairs, and silence fell on the group in the room, and all eyes were turned to the door-way, where presently there appeared another officer, two or three soldiers in dripping overcoats at his back. The rain pattering on Heatherwood's roof was for another moment the only sound. Then once again, in wistful appeal, the gentle lady's eyes turned to Colonel Clark. Words were unnecessary. He read the question in her anxious face.

"It would be useless to attempt to deceive you, Mrs. Heatherwood," he said, so simply and sadly. "Some one has tried hard to shield your unfortunate kinsman by making way with the disguise in which Captain Fairfax reached this house," and here Belle Heatherwood's white face was lifted in terror from her mother's lap, and, kneeling, she gazed speechless into the colonel's face. "But he had not time to examine the pockets before he flung it into the Monocacy. This memorandum book—these papers—were found within the bundle not two hours ago."

And then the white face of the girl dropped, inert, sightless, and the pliant, drooping form slid suddenly in dead faint to the floor.

CHAPTER XVIII.

A FORTNIGHT longer, despite impatient proddings from Washington, McClellan clung to the Maryland shore, and allowed his plucky adversary to regain strength and "second wind" across the Potomac. Finer marching weather he could not ask for, but shoes for man and beast he could and did. The army could not move without them. Observant statesmen suggested that Johnny Reb seemed to skip about the country hatless, shoeless, and often breadless, fighting like the very devil with nothing but pluck and parched corn in his wrinkled stomach. Suggestive statesmen observed that perhaps the Northern lads might try a little of Johnny's dress and diet with better results. Whereat McClellan smiled placidly and said that all military authorities agreed that armies moved upon their bellies, and he would be no violator of precedent. The careworn, patient leader of all, scanning the situation from the White House, whimsically remarked that he could stand a few cases of such violation of all military precedent as the tactics of Stuart and Stonewall Jackson were declared to be by the little chieftain at the head of the Army of the Potomac. But neither smiles nor sarcasm could prevail against book-rooted theories so long as a man remained without a hat or a mule without a shoe. Not until the fag-end of October did the pontoons span the river opposite the Catoctin valley, and the long blue columns began the crossing that was to lead them on to the useless sacrifice of Fredericksburg, the snarl and disaster of Chancellorsville. And ere they passed away from under the shadows of the rock-bound heights new sorrows had come to the gentle mistress of Heatherwood, new calamities upon her household. Convened at Point of Rocks, a military commission sat in judgment on Captain Floyd Fairfax, C.S.A., declared to have been caught as a spy within the Union lines. Transferred to Washington as convalescent, Ralph Heatherwood and Bradley Tighlman were impatiently awaiting their exchange and wondering why, when Southern prisons were teeming with Union officers, there should be this delay. Worn with the strain of excitement, anxiety, and distress, Belle Heatherwood had broken down and was lying very ill at the old homestead, nursed by her devoted mother, who, even in all her own cares and physical weakness, had found time to spend an hour, at least, each day in the neighboring field-hospital that Stuart left well provided with patients, and there had she discovered Trooper Bell, there had Laura pounced on Pettingill.

November 1st had come, and all day long the blue columns had been trudging away through Loudoun County, and only the guards along the aqueduct, the now partially restored canal, and the field-hospital remained about Heatherwood to remind Miss Waddell of the bustling days of September. The bees had long since ceased to hum in the orchard. The trees were bare. There was a whiff as of snow in the frosty wind, and winter had come down early on the blue Virginia mountains. All the same, with a shawl thrown over her head, her black eyes snapping and her cheeks aglow, Miss Waddell found her health required frequent exercise at the old tryst, and thither, day after day, a long, lank hero would hobble on crutches up the heights and plead in the unmelodious *patois* of the Connecticut Valley for a promise Miss Waddell scorned to give, but would have hated him had he ceased to importune. Reuben Pettingill, commended in orders and personally congratulated by Colonel Clark for intrepid conduct in face of the enemy, decorated now with the chevrons of a corporal and deluged with letters from home, was after all only a lion in a snare, bewitched by the black eyes of his buxom sweetheart. For five days she had toyed with and tormented him, and now the spirit of the Puritan rose in his breast, and he'd have no more of it. In the inner pocket of his blue coat he bore that day a trump card he had determined to play for all it was worth, but not until he had reconnoitred the ground. Ordinarily he made his way up the path by which Pleasonton had disappeared the day Stuart's squadrons went dancing by. But on this sunshiny, November morning, rejoicing in returning health and strength and in the keen, exhilarating air, he straddled with his crutches the narrow foot-track leading from the spring at the westward base of the Heatherwood height and winding through the leafy woods to the rear of the barn. There to his left as he climbed he could see the familiar cone of Sugar Loaf, the signal-flags waving at the summit, their more languid sweep a marked contrast to the frantic haste with which they swung the morning he and his New Hampshire fellows were double-quicking into line away down there by Harrison's Island and shouting with joy when the word was passed that now Jeb Stuart would find himself confronted by fellows he couldn't sweep aside. He wondered what they were signalling about to-day, and what there was going on that should keep the flags at Maryland Heights and above Point of Rocks and here at Sugar Loaf all swinging away for dear life. He wondered whether there could be any more of that looking-glass foolishness from the dormer-windows of Heatherwood. Hard times had come to the kindly household, certainly, and all through that absurd experiment that Laura so vehemently declared now was only just for fun and "to fool you Yankees," but that at the time she devoutly believed was to compass the overthrow of the Northern arms. Things were going worse still with that Virginia captain, Fairfax, Pettingill had heard. The evidence was all dead against him. A real signal-code, though a crude one, had been found in the pockets of the suit of farmer clothing he was proved to have worn at Poolesville and that was fished out of the Monocacy by some of that old Swearweather's squadron—what awful curse-words that fellow could use, to be sure!—the very night he, Reuben Pettingill, was landed in hospital with a hole through his leg. That was a dreadful find for Fairfax; but for it his neck might have been saved; and somebody had tried hard to save it, as it was, for even Laura could not deny that those clothes had been actually within the walls of Heatherwood. It was a dreadful find for kind Madam Heatherwood, too, for ever since it seemed as though the Washington folk had denied her, and Reuben had heard Colonel Clark mournfully say that when Secretary Stanton once got an idea that people were tricking him or tricking the government, God Almighty couldn't make him change his mind. That was why they had taken her son off to Old Capitol Prison or some such place; that was why the provost-marshal had paid her that solemn visit only a few days ago, the second day he and Laura were sitting together out in the orchard, and Laura said they wanted information about some officer—some staff-officer who wasn't in the army at all; at least, Lieutenant Homans said he was personating an officer who, as it turned out, was nowhere near Heatherwood at the time, a splendid-looking fellow he was,—they had all seen him,—and here at Heatherwood the family must know him. Reuben stopped to breathe and rest awhile as he reached the fence at the back of the barn-yard and sat him down and looked back over the broad valley, hemmed in at the west by those grand ranges. Away to the north the isolated peak of Sugar Loaf rose against the sky, its verdure gone, its rocky sides tinged with crimson and brown. Away beyond it, west of north, the sunlight glinting on distant spire and whitened wall told where Frederick lay,— Frederick, to whose jail they had ordered transferred the prisoner whose earthly home snuggled there to the south among the copper-colored slopes and heights only as far away one side as lay Frederick on the other, yet so far that Floyd Fairfax might never look upon it again, for, despite the fact that there was still one witness to examine, the finding could only be guilty, the sentence could only be death, and in the present temper of the Iron Secretary what hope for mercy could there be?

And yet, he mused, there was that queer, silent fellow they called Bell, that regular that did such magnificent work saving the guns on the day of Stuart's raid, the fellow for whose evidence the court was waiting. Talk about his, Pettingill's, "intrepidity" because he kept going forward at a hot run firing at those skip-acks of Johnnies in saddle until one of them drove a hole in him,—talk about that being intrepid,—why this fellow Bell had fought like a fiend, hand to hand, hilt to hilt, with more'n a dozen of 'em, and got hacked and hewed and battered until he lay like a man with a split skull for nearly a week, and he was to be made sergeant as soon as he was able to rejoin; and his commander,

Lieutenant Hamlin, had come and sat by him when he grew conscious again, and so had Captain McIntosh and other shanghai regulars, and the surgeon had let out that here was a man that could have a commission any day; and if any man ought to be proud and happy it certainly should be Bell, yet no sooner was that fellow able to be up and moving than he became queer. He damned the attendant for a fool when he heard him say Captain Fairfax was a spy who was sure to be hanged, and flew into a regular tantrum about it. Then, when they told him it was true that Fairfax was being tried by a court, and that he, Bell, was going to be called as a witness, and that the clothes that Fairfax had worn and the note-book and other things were found, Bell just suddenly collapsed. That night he was missing from hospital, and the next day, too, until they found him, raving drunk, wandering about Heatherwood and crying like a baby. He was back in the doctor's hands now mad as a hatter, and Madam Heatherwood had implored the doctor to let him be moved to a room in her house, and the doctor had had to refuse. Laura knew something about that fellow, said Pettingill, smiting his thigh, then starting in pain with a yelp of "Mighty Man!" that Laura herself might have heard even at this distance had Laura not been singing.

Weary of waiting for her Yankee adorer, impatient of his coming, the girl was resorting to her old time method of telling him so, and, Lilly Dale having been buried, she had resurrected another heroine of school-girl romance, and high and shrill rose her voice over the withering hedge and floated back to where her lover sat beyond the barn, and he mounted his crutches and heaved himself up to listen.

> "Thou aht gone, a-las! gentle Annie-e-e-,
> Like ah flowah thy spirit did depaht;
> Thou aht gone, a-las! like the man-eee-e
> That have bloomed in the summuh of ma haht.
>
> (Louder) Shall we nevah mo' behold thee?—
> Nevah hee-ah thy winning voice again-n-n
> When the spring time comes, gentle Annie-e-e-e,
> When the wild flowahs blossom o'ah th' plain?"

Corporal Pettingill came seven league booting it through the barn-yard, and was near the hedge and stirring up old Dobbin as the girl reached the end of the first verse of her rural lay. Then he ducked to avoid observation and to listen to any observation she might let fall.

"Ah wish that fella'd be here when he said he would," pouted Miss Waddell, instinctively substituting broad a for i, as she generally did when vexed, and eliding her r's as she did at any time. "Ah'd pay him off good 'f theh was only 'nuthuh fella wuth notc'sin 'round. All the nice ones have gone." Then she stopped to listen. The heavy, languorous days of early fall had disappeared. November had come in wintry and gusty. There was silence as of the grave about Heatherwood, broken only by the voice of the sentry and the few guards chatting on the eastward lawn, for a new guard there was and not too kind a one, and its commander slept in the parlor on the ground floor. Madam Heatherwood and her household, despite her many kindnesses, were objects of suspicion. A general officer left with the Twelfth Corps to guard the line of the Potomac had been ordered to keep an eye wide open and to permit no more nonsense there.

The first apostrophe to gentle Annie having failed to lure her crippled hero to her feet, Miss Waddell tried a second, to which the members of the guard in front seemed to lend appreciative ear, as, indeed, they had bestowed upon the singer appreciative glances. It was possibly in recognition of the fascination of this rural beauty that the general commanding had ordered that the guard should be changed every day. They were a rusty-looking lot, the five boys in blue, chatting there on the bluff, and Miss Waddell would have naught to do with them beyond assuring herself that her presence and song had received due recognition. And still Reuben the Faithful lurked in his lair and refused to be called forth. It was getting late and Laura weary. Belle Brandon was another damsel whose demise was much lamented in the lyrics of the day, and Laura tried a line or two of that young lady's life history:—

> " Belle Brandon was a birdling of the mountain,
> In freedom she spohted o'ah the lea ;
> And they said that the blood of the red man
> Tinged her veins from a fah distant sea."

And this far-fetched statement, or the sight of the corporal of the guard peeping through the trellis, proved too much for Pettingill. He broke cover forthwith and came stilting it into the orchard.

"Guess you thought I never was coming," said he, placably.

"Guess Ah wouldn't 'a' cared if you'd nevuh come," was the mendaciously pert reply.

"Well," said Reuben, bluntly, "that's real good. I didn't know but you might feel bad after all—if I went away."

"Huh!" said Miss Waddell, in deep disdain. "No danger you'h goin'! *You* couldn't march or fight."

Mr. Pettingill had seated himself on the rustic bench close to which his inamorata was standing when his sudden appearance surprised her. He carefully placed the crutches to his right side and then invitingly patted the wooden slab at his left.

"Ain't you going to sit?" he asked.

"It's too late," said Miss Waddell, pouting. "I've got other matters—impo'tant matters—to attend to." And the toss of the head was fine to see, so was the side glance at the supervising corporal at the old garden gate.

"I admire to know," said Reuben, simply, then reached for his crutches. "Well, if you have to go, so must I. Doctor says he wants me to get all the exercise possible without tiring myself. I'll be taking a longer walk later, likely enough," and he slowly adjusted his crutches as he spoke and began lifting himself from his seat.

"I didn't tell you to go," said Miss Waddell. "But you can't see aunty now even if you do go to the house."

"Sure," said Reuben, placidly. "I know she's like to be busy, but I don't want to go away without thanking her for all her goodness to me. She's an angel, she is."

"Well, you needn't be in a hurry," said Miss Waddell, not without an anxious glance, however. "You won't have to follow the regiment for weeks yet, and they'll be retreating back here before you can get away."

"'Tisn't that," said Reuben, sweetly. "You see they're powerful anxious to have me come home a spell,—mother and the girls." And here he slowly produced the all-important paper from the breast of his coat. "They've sent me this from Washington. The doctor thought I might start to-morrow just as well as not."

"'Tain't well as not!" flashed Miss Waddell, taking genuine alarm at once. "You know you're a good deal too weak and sick to ride so far—alone."

"That's it," continued Reuben, thoughtfully, rubbing his chin. "Sis and two of the girls were coming down as far as Albany or Springfield to meet me—perhaps to York. They've never seen the Hudson, you know, and we could all go up to Albany together and home that way."

"Well, I just bet you now you don't go, Reuben Pettingill," flamed Miss Waddell, "not until you're a mighty sight stronger." Then, swift to assume the appealing, now that other means had failed: "Least not if you ca-yuh for what I care." And Miss Waddell's fingers were hopelessly tangled in the cord of her cloak. Her cheeks were flushing, her bosom tossing like a troubled sea, and her downcast eyes were full of reproach, and all the time he had the hardihood to stand there actually trembling with hope, yet unrelenting.

"It's a chance any fellow would give months of his pay to get," said he, reflectively.

"Then go to your—your girls!" exclaimed Miss Waddell, with prodigious flounce, as she whirled indignantly about. "And—and don't bother us any more." But big tears were starting in her great black eyes as she spoke, and Reuben found his heart hammering glory hallelujah! almost as though the New England men had sung it.

"You—never told me there—were any girls," said Miss Waddell, disheartened at his silence.

"I didn't suppose you cared," he answered, humbly.

"I didn't!" this with prompt indignation. "Only —I know you meant to be mean, and—and hide it."

"I swow to gosh!" averred Mr. Pettingill, whose mild blue eyes were twinkling with delight at his success, "I didn't even s'pose they'd interest you. Sis has only two,—eight and ten." And then he hopped two paces nearer, in one spoke-like, semi-revolution of his crutches, only in time to meet her fire-flashing eyes and a burst of wrath.

"You've—you've just been fooling me!" she cried. But further words were stopped, for there came a sound that caused their sudden pause, the sound of crunching hoofs by the score, of clanging scabbards and jingling spur, the sound of the stern command, "Left into line!" and a platoon of cavalry had suddenly occupied the space in front of the old mansion. Two officers, dismounting, were already at the door, and one of them, short, swarthy, straddle-legged,—the girl knew him instantly before she heard his voice,—was already under the colonnade and at the door. Foulweather, for all the world! Foulweather, whose brow was black as thunder.

"Say to the mistress of this place," they heard him boom to some unseen servant or orderly, "that I purpose searching it from garret to cellar at once for the person of the arch rebel and spy, Fairfax, who escaped the guard this morning."

"Glory! Glory! Glory!" screamed Miss Waddell, clapping her hands and dancing in uncontrollable delight. "Glory! Glory! Glory! That's the last chance the Yankees will ever have to hang *him*, anyway!"

CHAPTER XIX.

No wonder the signal-flags were waving. No wonder there was wrath in the breast of Foulweather, stanchest of loyalists. No wonder there was consternation in the camp at Point of Rocks, for treason was lurking in their midst. A state prisoner, a brave, reckless Virginian, captured within the lines, and proved to have ventured thither in disguise, arraigned before the commission ordered, swift and sudden, for his trial, with further orders that an irate War Secretary had given to lose no time in formalities, a prisoner whose case was seen to be hopeless from the very start, despite the fact of one missing link in the chain of evidence against him, had been spirited away from the thick of the guard, and had gone no man knew whither. "One thing was certain," said the chagrined officials charged with his safe-keeping, "there must have been collusion on the part of the sentries, collusion that doubtless involved non-commissioned officers and possibly commissioned officers, for without the aid of the guard no living being could possibly pass their lines."

And why should there not have been collusion, all things considered? Captain Floyd Fairfax was a member of a proud and once wealthy family whose home was near Leesburg barely a dozen miles away.

He had devoted friends and relations at Poolesville and Heatherwood and Frederick, many of whom had visited the camp and vainly besought an interview. Acting under orders from Secretary Stanton, the commanding officer sternly refused. Even the gentle, sorrowing face of Madam Heatherwood had failed to overcome, though it could not fail to move him. He, too, knew her story, and was gentleness and courtesy itself, but sadly he told her his orders were imperative. No wonder the prisoner's Southern relatives could be permitted speech with him only on the written order of the War Department. Even that brief interview nearly cost the Union major his commission. Secret service detectives, eager for reward, commendation, promotion at the hands of the Iron Secretary, reported that the officer had had a long, confidential, and almost tearful interview with the mistress of Heatherwood, and in twenty-four hours flashed the order from Washington relieving him from duty and directing the detail of new guards from Clark's New Hampshire regiment, with Colonel Clark himself placed in charge. There at least, said Washington, was a man whose character was above suspicion, and nothing could have exceeded the care with which Clark stationed and instructed his men. Vigilance personified were the officers and non-commissioned officers, for there came hints to the effect that the friends of Fairfax both in Maryland and Virginia would make concerted effort to effect his rescue and release, and the guard was none too large, covering as it had to do all the space stretching along the canal from the east of Harper's Ferry away down almost to the mouth of Seneca Creek. Of infantry there was only one brigade watching the fords, bridges, and roads and guarding the canal. Clark and the main body of his New Hampshire regiment had been detained at Point of Rocks. Belden's Pennsylvania squadrons were scattered along the Potomac from the now abandoned head-quarters of the army at the mouth of Pleasant Valley away up to where Stuart crossed at McCoy's Ferry, and, to his bitter wrath at first, old Foulweather was held with two of his squadrons at the rear of the long column instead of being at their front where longed his soul to be. There was this compensation: here in Maryland he was his own commanding officer; there at the front he would have to serve under Bayard, Pleasonton, and other cavalrymen he had known in the old days, and he hated to serve under any of them. There was this embarrassment, too, not to Foulweather, but to his superiors: it left him and Belden together, or nearly together, on the north bank of the Potomac, and everybody knew by this time that the bad blood between them had thickened; that Foulweather had called at Belden's camp and said unwarrantable things, and that Belden, disdaining either to draw sword upon him or make the matter official by preferring charges, had simply ordered a file of the guard to escort the raging old regular outside of his lines, and, though foaming with wrath, Foulweather had sense enough left to know that the colonel of volunteers had the upper hand.

"If those two meet on neutral ground," said the men at McClellan's head-quarters, "it will be a fight," and good old John Buford, it was known, looked with keen anxiety to the result. Belden's orders were to scout and cover from the mouth of the Catoctin to the west. Foulweather's jurisdiction, under the orders of the general commanding the division, were to control the north bank of the Potomac from the Catoctin to Conrad's Ferry, with authority to cross to the Virginia side should occasion require. And this made possible a meeting in the Catoctin Valley, and there came a day when that meeting was inevitable.

The court was taking a recess pending the production of a material witness for the prosecution. Foulweather had at last learned that the battered patient in the field-hospital at Heatherwood was really Trooper Bell, but his sanguinary intentions were modified when he learned from McIntosh that Bell had accompanied him as guide only with evident reluctance, and had managed to ride away ostensibly to find his own command early that eventful night when they were scouting for Stuart. All the same, he meant to bring that "cocky" young swell to a strict accounting just so soon as he should be declared convalescent by the surgeon. It was all very well that Pennington and others should praise his gallantry and devotion the day of the fight. Who wouldn't fight under such circumstances? But as to promotion or reward, Trooper Bell would have to explain some very suspicious things before he, Foulweather, would consent to such advancement. What business had Bell to get on a tear the moment he began to recover, and at the time his evidence might be of vital importance before that court. No man on earth, said Foulweather, knew more about that duplicate Captain Belden than did Trooper Bell, and no man in the Union army, probably, could tell more about the inner workings of Heatherwood, the movements of Fairfax, than that same trooper. As to the fatal bundle of farmer clothing dropped in the Monocacy, Foulweather was ready to bet his last dollar that Bell knew all about it and could be forced to tell. With feverish eagerness he had imparted all his suspicions to the court, and with eagerness as fierce he awaited Bell's restoration.

But here there came disappointment. The doctors declared that while Bell's wounds and injuries were rapidly healing, his mental condition was a cause of deep anxiety and perplexity. He seemed rapidly regaining bodily strength, but was clearly out of his head. "He's shamming," said Foulweather, when he rode over and insisted on seeing for himself. "He may be," said the doctor, "but it's the best piece of acting I've ever seen." Foulweather was for having Madam Heatherwood come and talk with the patient. "She's been here twice," said the doctor, "and he doesn't know her from the Goddess of Liberty." The 30th of October came, and the doctor reported that though able to be up and moving about, his patient was daft and utterly irresponsible; but the next day came an order from Washington to send Trooper Bell under safe-conduct to Point of Rocks, that the court might judge of his sanity.

An ambulance was provided, so was the escort,—Foulweather gladly furnished that,—and the entire "outfit" marched away with the dazed and muttering occupant of the vehicle, only to learn on reaching camp at Point of Rocks that the ride was useless after all. The court could not meet because the accused was gone.

And how on earth to account for that escape was the question agitating every man from the commanding officer down to the drum-boys. Clark had been summoned to Harper's Ferry by the general commanding the Twelfth Corps, and went the evening of the 31st, leaving his lieutenant-colonel in command of camp. The night was bustling. Troops were still crossing on the pontoons up-stream. There was a good deal of stir and movement. A light battery that had been parked within two hundred yards of the house in which Fairfax was confined had orders to march at dawn for Leesburg, and the men were up grooming and feeding as early as four o'clock. A thick fog was creeping up the valley, and camp was shrouded in the misty veil, as the reveille was sounding.

The guard fell shivering into ranks to receive the officer of the day, and that gentleman, lantern in hand, strode into the narrow hall-way, followed by the lieutenant in command of the guard, who unlocked the door of the first room to the right and bade his superior enter and see for himself, for Clark had ordered that every time the officer of the day visited his guard he should enter and assure himself of the presence of the prisoner. At one A.M. the officer had found him in bed, slumbering peacefully. At 5.30 the fact that the position of the sleeper was apparently unchanged made both officers suspicious, and they made instant and closer examination. Dressed in a white night-shirt lay one of the pillows. The blankets were skilfully arranged and drawn up to look as though a human form lay beneath. By the bedside lay the shoes Fairfax had worn when captured, also a pair of socks. Folded on a chair near the head of the bed were the gray trousers (Ralph's). Hanging on the back of the chair was the gray uniform coat, also Ralph's, and a handsome drab felt hat, heavily plumed, stood on the table near at hand. All the garments, all the belongings of the prisoner, apparently, were undisturbed, but where was he? There was no trap through which he could have gone. There was but one window, and that was cross-barred outside, and the bars tightly screwed to the wood-work. Only through that or the door could he have gone, but the window bars were still snugly screwed. While one officer ran out to notify the guard and alarm the camp, the other stopped to study the situation, and he found only one significant circumstance, that the dust had been brushed away from the window and window-seat. The shade, a cheap green paper affair, was unrolled from the top so as to cover the entire window and exclude light from without and prevent parties without from peering inquisitively within. He recalled that the prisoner, though accepting uncomplainingly the hardships of his lot, and asking no favors of anybody, had courteously thanked Colonel Clark when that officer called upon him the previous week, and, in answer to the question as to whether there were not something he could do, without violating orders, that would add to the comfort of his prisoner, had said that he would like a shade to the window at night, as the men occasionally came and stared in at him as he sat reading or writing by the light of his solitary candle. It wasn't much to ask, and Clark gave directions accordingly.

The house itself was a little, old-fashioned, two-story affair, with a hall in the middle and four rooms of nearly equal size on the ground floor. The prisoner occupied the back room on the north side. It was lighted by this one window at the back, was entered from the hall, and the old door-way communicating with the front room had been bricked up. There was a fireplace and chimney in the north wall, but nothing bigger than a cat could squeeze up the chimney. There was a sentry in the hall night and day, another on the porch in front, another in the little yard in rear, which was reached by a narrow passage on the north side of the house, so narrow that it was possible for soldiers sitting in the side window of the upper story to prod with their bayonets the walls of the adjoining premises. The back yard opened into a narrow alley at the rear some twenty paces from the remains of the wooden kitchen that was tacked to the house before federal occupancy thereof, and other back yards were adjoining, but tents were pitched in all of them, for here had been the station of the provost-marshal's guard up to the time the army marched away. Soldier culprits by the dozens, stragglers, and mild malefactors had been corralled in these tents, while men accused of more severe offences, deserters or men accused of sleeping on post, had been imprisoned in the house itself. If Fairfax made his exit through the door and hall, he had to pass two sentries and the main body of the guard. If he escaped by that barred window, three at least of the iron slats must have been removed, then replaced, and all the time a sentry stood or walked within six feet of that window unless bribed or drugged to insensibility.

It seemed no time at all before half the officers on duty at the spot came hurrying to the post of the guard. Every man of the four companies of the infantry provost party was under arms at reveille, and within ten minutes searching parties were rummaging through the yards and houses in the village streets. Orderlies were sent for Major Foulweather, and that fiery old dragoon came galloping up the Barnesville road in less than half an hour, his squadron following half a mile behind, and under his energetic leadership despatches were sent or signalled to every neighboring camp. The officers of the court, many of them of high rank, kept back from their regiments until the case should be concluded, were among those aroused, and their grave faces showed how serious a matter they regarded it. "I should hate to be the officer to have to break this news to Stanton," said the president; but Foulweather seemed to share no such dread. So long as none of his command could be blamed, he did not mind. Almost the first thing he did was to send a despatch to the War Department at Washington to this effect:

"The spy, Fairfax, escaped from charge of the infantry guard some time between midnight and reveille. If given immediate authority, I believe I can recapture him with my command. Some of his haunts are known to me."

And while awaiting answer, Foulweather saw that men and horses both had substantial breakfast, and then ransacked his luggage to find that letter of Bayard's aide-de-camp, and once more read the words:

"There is a place in the Catoctin Valley, not two miles from the river, where they say Fairfax has twice been in hiding. It is owned by a Mr. Hunt, who is away in the army, and is cared for by his sister and some servants." Again he went over the description: "An old two-story stone house among a lot of rose-bushes and trees about twenty yards back from the road; chimneys at each gable end, built out like buttresses." Not a soul would he tell of this knowledge. It was too precious. By nine o'clock, to his huge delight, the New Hampshire men declared that they had searched every "scrap" of the neighborhood and could not find hide or hair of Fairfax. He prayed they might have no better luck throughout the livelong day. He waited with eagerness unspeakable the coming of the answer to his despatch, giving him, as he prayed, authority for independent action, and then, without a hint to a soul of where he was going, he would strike for the Catoctin. It would go hard with him if he did not find the Hunt place and Fairfax with it. It would go hard with Fairfax if he did.

And just at ten o'clock, to his almost mad delight, just as he was reading an order from the division commander directing him to search the river towards Conrad's Ferry, there came a wire from Washington that superseded any orders any general might give him, for it bore the august mandate of the Secretary of War:

"You are authorized and directed to take such steps as in your judgment may enable you to recapture the rebel spy Fairfax without delay, using your entire command if need be. Notification sent to commanding general at Harper's Ferry and to commanding officer at Knoxville."

"Sound the mount, trumpeter," he shouted, gleefully, as, booted and spurred, he sprang into saddle. "Bring the command straight to head-quarters, Treacy," he called to his wondering second. "I've got to show my orders to the general."

And so it happened that valuable hours of that vital day were spent by a fuming old dragoon with some long-suffering troopers at his back raiding the lovely Virginia valley for an old stone house owned by a Mr. Hunt some two miles from the river, embowered in roses and trees and other rural attractions, a house that all this time was in the hands of Colonel Belden's Keystone troopers in the valley of similar name on the Maryland side, which fact Major Foulweather learned only after he had well-nigh exhausted his vocabulary of expletives, and as a last resort could only bethink him of Heatherwood.

No wonder he was in the worst of humors when he got there. No wonder there was trouble in store for all who held it dear.

CHAPTER XX.

In the scattered cavalry commands of the Army of the Potomac everybody seemed to have heard of the hot altercation between Belden and Foulweather and of the latter's discomfiture. As has been said, there was anxiety in the minds of many a good soldier, especially in that of noble old John Buford, still serving in his capacity as chief of cavalry, lest they should meet again, for Foulweather's threats had been heard far and wide.

Eager to overtake the fugitive Virginian, the impetuous old trooper had never thought to inquire about any Hunt place in the valley of the Maryland Catoctin, and had searched the Loudoun County "Kittoctan" only to meet discomfiture,—to learn that the Hunt place was on the Maryland side and, before heading for Heatherwood, that Belden's men were in actual possession of the haunt he supposed Belden knew nothing about; furthermore, that they had been in possession for several days, a squadron camping in the dreary, leafless orchard. It was then that Foulweather bethought himself of Heatherwood. Whether he found Fairfax or no, he might find *something* and could make his order from the War Department an excuse, even an authorization, to search the once beautiful old mansion from cellar to garret.

The little detachment of infantry volunteers on duty as guards had, of course, no obstacle to oppose to the actions of a field-officer of regular cavalry with a whole platoon at his back, and, indeed, in some individual cases had to scurry out of the way in undignified haste to avoid being trampled under the heels of the horses. These—the volunteers—stood there now sullen and scowling at the weary but impassive faces of the troopers, who had dismounted and were silently awaiting the further orders of their officers. The latter by this time, accompanied by a corporal and two men, had been swallowed up in the broad hall-way, where a one-sided controversy was going on between the burly old major of regulars and the somewhat inexperienced lieutenant of volunteers, the officer of the guard. The junior was young but plucky. No such person as the major referred to could possibly be there without his knowledge, said he, and he objected to the search, but he was silenced by Foulweather's disdainful production of the Stanton telegram. "Come on!" said the major, shortly, to his tall, lath-like adjutant, and the heavy spurred boots began the ascent of the stairs. Already the evening shadows were falling without, and the hall was nearly dark. Foulweather stumbled at the landing and swore characteristically. Yet even in his vengeful mood he suddenly halted within a step or two of the top, for there, dim and shadowy, but in her gentle dignity commanding his respect, stood the revered mistress of Heatherwood, and though her voice was low and almost pleading as she spoke, she none the less seemed to confront the intruders, and bid them pause.

"Pardon me, gentlemen," were her first words. "I possibly did not understand the message brought me by my servant, or she misunderstood you, but my daughter has been very ill, and I know that you would not wish to disturb her. What is this about Captain Fairfax?"

"Captain Fairfax, ma'am, escaped from prison at Point of Rocks this morning and is somewhere in hiding in this neighborhood. I am ordered by the Secretary of War himself to make strict search and leave no stone unturned to find him."

"Captain Fairfax was here, as you have doubtless heard, sir, and refused to go when his comrades of the First Virginia came with a horse for him. Since the night Colonel Clark took him away under guard to Point of Rocks he has never set foot on this place."

"He may be here now without your knowledge, ma'am," said Foulweather, indomitably, "and I thought it civil to tell you what my orders were. Search we must, and at once. I will send the other men through the cellar and first floor. Only these you see with me will be allowed to come higher. Corporal Dixon, put Devlin at that landing with orders to let no one come up until I tell you." And with that the blunt soldier would have resumed the ascent, but her white hand upraised and the suffering in the pale and patient face again compelled his respect. Rapid footsteps were heard on the rear stairway, too, and, flushed and panting a trifle, Laura came hurrying along the hall, and in silent defiance took her place by the side of her beloved aunt.

"Go down, Mr. Wilson," said Foulweather, sternly, to his tall staff-officer, "find that rear stairway at once, and put a sentry there with orders to let no one either up or down. Then join me again here."

Down went Wilson, none too briskly. Police duty with Foulweather was anything but to his liking.

"One moment, sir," the gentle voice went on, as the sound of the adjutant's footsteps ceased at the portico without. "If your search must be made, I pray that you begin below. Then I may have time to prepare my child for your coming up here. It will take but a few minutes. We will offer no objection, and resistance is of course impossible."

There was good in the old war-horse, after all. Surly, exasperated, bitterly disappointed as he was, the major felt his resolution ebbing at the sound of that sorrowing plea. For a moment he hung there irresolute, then raising his battered forage-cap, he said, "I wish I hadn't to disturb you at all, ma'am, but we'll begin below anyhow." And turning, he actually tiptoed down the stairs, a thing he probably never was known to do before in his life.

Five minutes later a dozen troopers, under his

orders, were ransacking with lighted candles in the cellar, store-rooms, and kitchen, and one of them proved an expert. In a little chamber off the hallway, and near the kitchen door and back stairway, he had made a discovery. The brick chimney that passed up from the cellar through this room was fully five feet wide just above the mantel and fireplace, yet the fireplace was small, one of those tiny niches apparently made for use in connection with what was called a Franklin stove. The stove was gone, and as Trooper Feeney poked his candle up the dark and narrow chimney and peered after it, he began tapping with the butt of his revolver at the brick-work. Presently he popped out, a bit grimy, but full of importance. "There's a holler in there of some kind," said he, "and I think this boarding by the fireplace opens." Already he was eagerly tapping at that and looking for concealed flap. "I've got it," he suddenly cried. "Give me a big knife, or a sabre." Only a little prying was necessary. A whole panel slipped easily out of its place, and, sure enough, there was a recess, and the first thing visible therein was a chamois sabre case, standing upright in the corner, and a sole-leather valise. In a moment these were slung to the bedstead; a sword blade forced the lock of the latter while eager hands drew from the chamois case an almost brand new cavalry sabre of the finest make, an officer's, while, one by one, the contents of the valise proved to be a handsome new uniform coat with the shoulder-straps of a captain of cavalry, a pair of light-blue trousers with the narrow yellow welt on the outer seam, as worn then by officers of the Union horse, a rich crimson sash, a new sword belt, a forage-cap of fine quality, with the crossed sabres of the —th cavalry in front, rich gilt spurs, handsome gauntlets, a small cavalry saddle-cloth, a binocular field-glass, with some white shirts, collars, gloves, etc., and a change of underwear; these completed the outfit. The valise was marked, in painted black letters on both ends, "J. L., New York City." The letters J. L. were embroidered on the shirt, and the collars bore the letters in indelible ink.

Wonder, perplexity, and excitement were in old Foulweather's face as he carefully searched the pockets of the uniform for further clue, while Feeney prodded for more treasures in the great recess, but the search of both was fruitless. The pockets were empty; the watch pocket below the waistband of the trousers, on which tailors ordinarily write the name and address of their customers, had been carefully snipped off, apparently with scissors. The buttons of the trousers and a little silken slip inside the collar of the coat gave the name of a prominent military tailor of Gotham as the maker. The cap bore the stamp of Warnock, at that time a leading dealer in military supplies. The case of the sabre and the boxes of the sash and belt showed that these articles were bought of Tiffany, who during the war added such items to the usual stock of gems and silverware, but the owner's name could only be guessed at from the initials on the valise. There was no waistcoat and there were no suspender-buttons on the band of the trousers, and these to Foulweather made valuable evidence. "That's the way those damned West Pointers dress," growled he to himself, in growing excitement.

Full of his discovery, he again ascended the stairs and sought brief interview with the mistress of Heatherwood. From her daughter's room she came to the head of the stairs, patient and gentle as ever, while Laura, standing protectingly behind her, looked daggers at the blunt-spoken soldier in the despised Union blue. It was easy to see that Foulweather's surprise at the treasure trove was slight compared to that of Mrs. Heatherwood's. She was astonished.

"Certainly no officer of the Union army has been an inmate of my house, nor do I know how to account for the presence of these articles," was all that she would say; and when Foulweather, still full of suspicion as to Belden, would have cross-questioned her, she gently but firmly repeated what she had said before, that she had never met or known an officer of that name. As to Foulweather's declaration that he must take these treasures with him to the provost-marshal, Mrs. Heatherwood had no objection to make. She had known, she said, of the niche or recess in the brick-work ever since her honeymoon. She told him of others, but they contained nothing unusual or suspicious. "And now," said she, "if the *major* is still determined to search the upper story and garret, he can do so." And Foulweather, in a shamefaced, hurried, and perfunctory way, made a visit, yet barely glanced through the open rooms. An old suspicion had been rekindled in his breast. He was becoming with every moment more eager to return to Point of Rocks, and within an hour of his arrival he rode away at the head of his men, leaving behind a thankful and relieved household, for in Belle's own sanctuary, hidden in the depths of one of her trunks, was a flat tin case, tightly strapped, that she had been charged to hide where none could reach it, and the owner once more lay in the little field-hospital down under the westward bluffs.

It was late in the evening when Foulweather's tired troopers reached their camp, and, after grooming, watering, and feeding their dust-covered chargers, were permitted to attend to their own ablutions, get supper, and then roll into their blankets, but there was no rest for their raging major. Stopping only long enough to get a fresh horse and a drink, he rode on to Point of Rocks, followed by a brace of orderlies, one of whom bore all the way on the pommel the sole-leather valise ravished from Heatherwood, while the other carried the sabre. The provost-marshal had turned in, but turned out again at sound of Foulweather's rasping voice.

"Well, what news of Fairfax?" was the immediate

question, as he stumbled down the little flight of wooden steps in front of his quarters.

"Damn Fairfax! He has more hiding holes than a prairie dog. But I've got something to pay for our chase."

"Damn that!" as politely replied the provost-marshall. "Here's the War Department wiring me all day long every few hours to know what you had accomplished, and where you'd gone. Thank God they sent Clark to take charge of the guard here, or I'd have been on the way to Fort Lafayette. *He* isn't, though. He's got one of the sentries behind the bars already. They say the fellow was bought out,—that Leesburg and Frederick contributed over a thousand dollars to bribe this very man. We couldn't keep a thousand men under lock and key to prevent their being approached. It's plain that those bars were unscrewed, probably between three and four o'clock this morning, and then as deliberately screwed in again by somebody while somebody else spirited the prisoner away through that back alley and across the Potomac. Think of rebel sympathizers among our men!"

"Think of 'em among our officers, by God!" was Foulweather's fierce rejoinder. "Look at this outfit that we gobbled at Heatherwood, and then promise you'll take a ride with me in the morning."

The official had no objection to looking over the outfit, whatever doubts he might entertain as to the propriety of his riding forth with Foulweather.

Valise and sabre were borne into his shabby quarters, and great was his surprise and curiosity when he learned where and how the articles had been discovered. Then Foulweather insisted on the provost-marshal's promise to ride with him "not farther than Knoxville" in the morning. The marshal scented mischief, and would only agree to consider it, and before the major could resume his entreaties heavy footsteps came quickly up the little porch and into the hall, and, with gloom in his eyes, there stood Colonel Clark. He had never fancied Foulweather, and it stung him to meet him in this hour of his humiliation and distress. Clark had keen wits. He well understood that the "regular" rather delighted in the misfortune that had befallen the New Hampshire regiment, and his greeting was cold and formal. Quick as his clumsy hands could do the work, the major had thrust everything into the valise again as he heard the coming footsteps, and his back, bending over the task, was towards the colonel as he entered the dimly lighted room. Foulweather seemed actually embarrassed, an unusual thing for him.

But Clark barely glanced at the valise. As for the sabre, except that it was new and bright, there was nothing uncommon in the sight. "I heard you were here, sir," said he, very quietly. "I fear you have not met with success."

"Well, rather," was the half-taunting reply. "Your bird had too many hours the start. How many of your men were mixed up in the conspiracy, do you suppose?"

"That remains to be seen," said the colonel, calmly. He well knew how aggravating it would be to Foulweather if he showed no sign of chagrin. "We are fortunate in so early discovering the culprit,—a fellow whose captain and comrades have suspected of rascality more than once before, and as he has been to Frederick twice in ten days, and been seen in conversation with prominent sympathizers, he was pounced on as the defaulting sentry. The wonder is that he did not desert at once and try to get away. Probably he thought the chance would be better later on. Possibly he couldn't get all the money promised him. Five hundred dollars was paid him, and it was found to-day hidden under a brick in the old walk close to his post. He dared not have it about him, of course, and had hid it there for the time being. I've no doubt the thing has been planned a week at least, and that Fairfax is far over in Virginia beyond Aldie by this time. Sentries on the railway say they heard the muffled sound of oars about four o'clock, dying away towards the other bank, but it was too dark to see anything. My regret is that you could not have started earlier. You would have stood more chance of recapturing him."

But Foulweather would not be mollified by courteous words. He knew Clark did not like him. He knew that he did not like Clark. It was high time now to be getting back to camp. He had meant to leave the valise and sabre in possession of the provost-marshal until morning, but Clark might become curious as to what the valise contained. "I'll write a couple of despatches, if you please, major," said he to the official, "then go back to camp." So saying and stepping to the door, he called to his men, "Come in here, one of you, and get these things," whereat spurred boots clicked their way across the rude sidewalk in front and up the steps, and just as the soldier entered the provost-marshal placed a candle on the table. Its light fell full on the end of the valise, on the painted letters, "J. L., New York City," and as the trooper stretched forth his hand the voice of Colonel Clark was heard, sharp and commanding:

"Stop one moment. Don't take that. Why, Major Foulweather, I know that valise. How on earth came it here?"

"Oh, I suppose you could have seen it any day at Heatherwood, if that's what you mean," said Foulweather, indifferently. "That's where I found it this evening,—and its precious contents. The man that owns them things has an explanation to make to me to-morrow."

"You got that at Heatherwood, Major Foulweather? Why, sir, the last time I saw it was at Monadnock, my home in New Hampshire, and its owner was killed at first Bull Run."

CHAPTER XXI.

GRAVE changes came in the Army of the Potomac within the next few days. McClellan, relieved from command, was succeeded by Burnside. Clark and his New Hampshire men pushed on to the front, brigaded with other new and big regiments. The court for the trial of Captain Fairfax was broken up and ordered to rejoin the corps or regiments of the respective members, their deliberations being done with, thanks to the unfeeling conduct of the accused, who had succeeded, so said jubilant Southern women at Leesburg and Frederick, by long and devious route, in rejoining his comrades. Every member was made to feel in some indefinable way that the Iron Secretary considered that altogether too much time had been consumed; that they should have sat without regard to hours, in fact without regard to orders, and that proper attention to duty on their part would have resulted days before in the conviction of the rash Virginian and his summary execution as a spy. Stanton's heart was hot within him over the daring raid of Stuart, followed so speedily by this most unaccountable escape of one of his most prominent and distinguished officers, captured within our lines unquestionably in the capacity of a spy. As it was, he held, or seemed to hold, that the court had allowed Fairfax to escape as easily as Stuart got away, and that was a matter that rankled, and no wonder, in more breasts than one at the War Department. Gloom and depression reigned in Washington. Other distinguished generals had been relieved from command, and some of them ordered to be tried for no less an offence than misbehavior in the face of the enemy. Lee and the Southern hosts were falling back, to be sure, but only to the old line of the Rappahannock, where they were thoroughly at home, and could make things lively for their opponents with small loss or trouble to themselves. A new general was charged with the defence of the line of the Potomac and the Baltimore and Ohio road. Belden's fine regiment of Pennsylvania cavalry went on to report to one brigade, while Foulweather, still an unappreciated major of regular horse, received, with disgust unspeakable, the order to rejoin the little band of veteran troopers of the old army, and his days of independent action were done with. But one of his men still lingered behind, apparently wounded in mind as well as body, and that was Trooper Bell.

But meantime, several things had happened north of the Potomac of more immediate consequence to those whose fortunes or misfortunes we have been following. First, that inevitable meeting between Belden and Foulweather occurred just as every man said he knew it would, and but for Clark's foresight and prompt action worse consequences might have ensued. Early in the morning following the escape of Fairfax, the grizzled major galloped in among the camps at Point of Rocks, followed by his orderlies and a most unhappy looking adjutant, and once more he importuned the provost-marshal to go with him, and this time to no purpose. The provost-marshal pleaded official duty. All the same, he had curiosity enough to urge Foulweather to reveal the object of his journey, and as Foulweather would not tell, and rode away swearing disgustedly, his suspicions that something unpleasant was in the wind were confirmed, and he had sense enough to go and warn Clark.

"Did he have that valise and sabre still with him?" asked the colonel, who had taken as strong a fancy to Belden as he had imbibed dislike to his comrade trooper and inveterate enemy. "Yes," said the provost-marshal, whereat Clark ordered out his horse, his adjutant, and orderly, and, inviting the provost-marshal to join him, the four quickly took the up-river road to Pleasant Valley and trotted hard after hard-riding Foulweather. At the Catoctin crossing they learned from Belden's vedettes that their colonel was at the camp of the third squadron, two miles up the valley, near the Hunt place; that a major of regulars had gone up there not twenty minutes ahead of them; and Clark's quartette put spurs to their excited horses and galloped like mad.

None too soon did they reach the spot. The group in front of Colonel Belden's tent was in a ferment already, and well it might be. In brief, what had already happened was this: Belden had just finished breakfast and was engaged in writing a letter at his field-desk, when his attention was attracted by hoof-beats on the half-frozen ground and the sudden appearance in front of his tent of Major Foulweather, with "Lanky" Wilson and two orderlies. The major was off his horse in an instant, Wilson and the valise-bearer more slowly finding their feet on *terra firma*. The second orderly held the four horses, and both he and his mate, who followed Foulweather valise in one hand and cased sabre in the other, looked as dejected as though before a garrison court, while poor Wilson almost wished himself in Libby, for all three admired Belden far more than they did their own leader. Belden's orderly, a sturdy volunteer from the Susquehanna valley, looked dubiously at the arriving party, but saluted, as he had been taught to, when Foulweather stalked straight to the open flaps of the colonel's tent, while Belden's blue eyes grew steely, a flush mounted quickly to his forehead, and there came a curious corrugation of the skin between the heavy eyebrows. Without rising, he half turned in his camp-chair and confronted the party. Foulweather advanced to the planking in front before he spoke. Then the words came with a snap:

"Captain Belden," he began, discourteously refusing to recognize that officer's volunteer rank, "you are unattended, I see, and what I have to say to you you may prefer to have your own witnesses to report, in case you should have the hardihood to bring the matter before a court-martial. I'll wait till you can summon them."

There was no need to summon. Already, at sight of Foulweather, a squadron leader and the regimental adjutant were coming "on the jump," and reached the spot almost at the close of the major's opening remarks.

"I have had one visit too many from you already, sir," said Belden, coldly, "but as we are our own masters here, I know of no better place for a meeting." And there was the significance of the old army in the way Belden used the word, as, saying it, he slowly and deliberately rose and, stepping out of the tent, confronted the glowering major, who, indeed, had to fall back a pace to avoid collision. "Now what do you want?" he went on, and it must be admitted that neither in word nor tone was Belden either conciliatory or civil. Promptly the Keystone captain and Belden's soldierly young adjutant ranged themselves alongside their colonel, with fight in their kindling eyes and clinched fists. Foulweather noted, but without alarm. Fighting was his joy.

"I accused you some weeks ago, sir," said he, "of clandestine visits to the Heatherwood place." Foulweather wasn't quite certain what clandestine meant, but he had heard the adjective frequently used in qualification of that very noun, and it sounded well.

"You denied it, and I was reprimanded for circulating malicious stories. You still maintain you were never there, I suppose?"

"I decline to have any further words with you on the subject."

"No doubt," said Foulweather, triumphantly glancing at the Pennsylvania officers, and then turning and beckoning the trooper to come forward. "You have caught sight of some of my evidence, and it's staggered you, I presume; but that's not all, by a damned sight."

"Use only civil words, sir," or I'll be compelled to have you escorted out of this camp less ceremoniously than you were once before."

"Not much you won't, Captain Belden," interposed Foulweather. "You'll be wise if you hasten to write your resignation." Then suddenly turning to the Pennsylvania officers, now reinforced to the number of half a dozen, "Gentlemen," said he, "your commanding officer, whom I have known years longer than you have, declared on honor he had never visited the Heatherwood place. Your commanding officer, while he was still serving with his proper regiment, came back to camp after a few days in Washington with a cock-and-bull story about having been robbed at Willard's of a new sabre and suit of uniform."

"We know all about that," interrupted a captain, hotly, "and it's true."

"I'm here to prove that he wasn't robbed. I'm

here to say that, as the army's on the move and court-martials can't be held, that he'll save widespread scandal and disgrace by tendering his resignation here and now. Open that sabre case and that valise," he ordered, turning to his orderly. "Here's your stolen sabre, Captain Belden. Here's your new uniform, and I found the whole outfit last night secreted at Heatherwood."

Belden, towering over the bulky major, had stood there blazing at first with wrath, then turning contemptuously cool; but at sight of the glistening sabre and the uniform coat, which the orderly reluctantly unfolded and displayed, a gleam of interest shone in his flashing blue eyes.

"Bring those things forward," he coolly said, and, stooping once more, the orderly advanced with his burden. Belden calmly took the sabre, examined hilt, guard, blade, and scabbard, then put it carefully aside, threw off the double-breasted frock he was wearing, took the captain's uniform coat from the orderly's hands, donned it in a trice, buttoned it from throat to waist, and the fit was almost perfect. He carefully looked at the trousers, noted the disappearance of the watch-pocket, tossed them aside, and then, as the orderly held the valise open before him, he tried on the cap,—another perfect fit,—examined belt, sash, and gauntlets as deliberately as he did the cap, and all this time not a word was spoken. Foulweather, breathing hard, seemed at first swelling with assured triumph, but as Belden waxed calmer every moment and more indifferent to his accuser as he grew interested in the garments and equipments, it seemed to the major that the climax was not as dramatic as he had planned. Belden was curiously studying the marking of the few shirts and collars. These he tumbled with the sash and belt back into the valise, took off the coat, deliberately handed it to his servant, who had come a wondering spectator, "Pick up those trousers," he ordered the boy, "lay the coat, cap, trousers, and sabre on my bed.—They are my property," said he, turning to the officers. "I know nothing about the rest. Ordinarily one rewards the man who returns stolen property, but you, sir, came here as an enemy. Now take your plunder—and yourself—off."

The silence that followed was brief enough, but men who were present long remembered it, and how furiously Foulweather broke it.

"Damn your infernal impudence!" he began, when a white, muscular hand seized him by the throat; two hands, in fact, were at his collar in an instant, and before them all, despite his furious struggles, Foulweather was seized, throttled, shaken as a terrier shakes a rat, Belden uttering never a word the while, and no man interfered save when Foulweather strove to drag his revolver from its holster. Then the Pennsylvania adjutant made a quick spring and, knocking the hairy paw aside, possessed himself of the weapon, and the throttling and shaking went on. Wilson, looking almost ready to cry, began to plead. One of the troopers, who had followed old Foulweather all over the plains, actually wept with excitement and distress of mind, and just when it began to look as though the major stood in danger of being choked to death, for his eyes were popping and his face was black, there came a dash of horsemen into their midst, and Colonel Clark took in the situation at a glance.

"Stop this, instantly, Colonel Belden," he cried, his voice ringing loud and commanding. "Release that officer. Gentlemen, I order you both under arrest," and, as Belden obeyed, his almost exhausted victim tottered and would have fallen but for the support of the nearest men, on whose arms he leaned, gasping and gurgling. Then Clark dismounted and came straight into the group. "Give him a chair and some water," he said, indicating Foulweather, and the scared servant jumped out with a camp-stool. "Colonel Belden, you at least are able to speak; give me your word this matter shall go no further."

"I give you my word, sir, that unless that man keeps away it shall go very much further," was the calm reply. "Major Foulweather knows where he can find me any time he desires; for the present I must observe your arrest." And with cool dignity, yet panting a bit from the lively exertion, the stalwart young colonel retired within his tent.

It was some minutes before Foulweather could be moved. For a time it looked as though an apoplectic seizure might result, but Clark presently shook him up and ordered him instantly to mount and return with the provost-marshal to Point of Rocks. The moment he could speak at all, Foulweather demanded that the uniform and sabre be restored to him, but Clark promptly refused. "You declared your belief that they belonged to Colonel Belden," said he. "Colonel Belden substantiates your statement, and you have restored them to the owner; you have no right to them whatever."

"For evidence—when he's tried—I'll never rest—till he's court-martialed," sputtered the raging old soldier. But Wilson, at a sign from Clark, took his bridle-rein and led him away, the provost-marshal on the other side, the orderlies following sorrowfully. Even among the Pennsylvanians there was sympathy for the broken-down old fire-eater of a dragoon.

And later that day Clark found him sleeping in his little tent down by the Barnesville road, and bent over the grizzled face of the man who moaned wretchedly in his heavy, almost stertorous slumber. He had been drinking hard,—his only solace, poor, lonely old fellow,—and his throat was bound with a handkerchief steeped in diluted arnica. Treacy came to see the colonel and inquire for particulars. He didn't mind being in command, but, "What the divil had the ould man been doin'?" And Clark briefly explained, then asked to see that mysterious valise, carefully studied the inscription, the lettering on the shirts and collars, had one each of the latter sent to his camp, and rode forthwith to Heatherwood.

That evening Madam Heatherwood repeated to him that she had no idea that any such valise had ever been under her roof, but when told that it was marked "J. L., New York City," and asked if she could account for its being there at all, the gentle and beloved lady became greatly agitated.

"I suspect; but even if I knew, colonel, I could not tell, bound by a promise as I am."

Clark tried to see Miss Heatherwood, but was told that she was still far too weak and ill to receive a visitor, much less to be questioned. Then he sought a word with Laura, who had not been seen since his arrival; but Clark had heard laughing talk among the men, and so made at once for the orchard, and there a crippled corporal stood attention on his crutches, and was not unkindly told to go back to hospital, which both Miss Waddell and Mr. Pettingill much resented, and the latter confided the cause of his annoyance to that queer fellow Bell, who was again convalescent and sitting up. And when, after a half-hour's cross-questioning of the saucy Virginia girl, Colonel Clark came riding down to the field-surgeon's bailiwick, and again spoke kindly and cordially to Pettingill, the latter melted at once. But when that colonel went through the big tents, speaking pleasantly to the wounded, several cots were empty, Bell's among them, and no Bell could they find when the colonel expressed a desire to see the man who fought so gallantly to save Pennington's gun.

But that night Colonel Clark wrote a rather long letter, which, addressed to Mr. George Lowndes, New York City, went off *via* Baltimore next day, and found no such person at the big gloomy old mansion. Father and daughter, the Lowndeses, had left the scene of their sorrows and gone abroad. That was why for months no answer came to Clark's missive. In two weeks more he and his regiment were on the Rappahannock, and Belden and Foulweather—long since released from arrest, as it was understood that the latter would attempt no further meeting with the colonel, but had reduced his grievances and charges to writing and the consideration of the War Department—they, too, were well away by different routes on the march to join their brigades, and still newer troops moved into the valley of the Monocacy and up the Potomac towards Harper's Ferry. The night before Clark marched he called to say good-by to the gentlewomen of Heatherwood, and there he heard a piece of news that Madam Heatherwood told him with tears running down her cheeks. While her boys, Ralph and Tighlman, were still imprisoned in Washington, Floyd Fairfax had succeeded in rejoining Stuart and his old regiment, only to find himself ostracized, "cut," a Pariah among soldiers and gentlemen, accused by Montfort and Garnett of shirking danger and duty with his men and accepting dishonorable captivity under the roof which sheltered the lady of his love.

CHAPTER XXII.

Evil days had come to Heatherwood, as well as to those who loved it and so long had made it their home. The gloomy winter of '62-3 opened early. The blue Catoctins had been shrouded in a snow-cloud before November was fairly a week old, and the old household physician, riding over from Frederick two or three times a week, an object of suspicion to every new sentry or guard despite the numerous passes and vouchers he never dared to leave at home, finally shook his head over the slow recovery of his patient, and asked her devoted mother if it were not possible to remove her to Baltimore or Washington. Laura sang no longer in the orchard, where a meeting and parting of the romantic sort had taken place when Pettingill received sudden orders to accompany a party of convalescents to the distant front, and he and silent, stern-faced Trooper Bell were marched away by slow stages to reinforce the army. Burnside was massing in front of Fredericksburg for the senseless slaughter yet to come. Ralph and Tighlman still sighed in their soldier prison and were refused exchange, despite the fact that scores of their comrades were being sent back to Virginia. Foulweather's charges against Belden, though they fell flat where the gallant accused was concerned, seemed to have redoubled the ire of the Secretary of War and confirmed him in his belief that the Heatherwoods had rewarded kindness with treachery. As ill luck would have it, the officers who best knew the gentle mistress of the old manse were mostly of the class that clung to McClellan, Porter, Stone, and others whose names were, for the time being at least, clouded in Stanton's eyes. Nothing they could say in her behalf appealed to him. Nothing others could urge proved potent enough to outweigh two things,—first, Mrs. Heatherwood's calm and determined assertion that she could not say who it was that had spirited away Fairfax's farmer disguise and had hidden in that chimney niche the uniform and equipment of a cavalry officer; indeed, she said that she did not know; and, secondly, Miss Heatherwood's equally calm and determined reply, weak though she was when visited by the staff-officer sent to investigate, that she *would* not tell, though she admitted that she did know. The question of their removal from Heatherwood was settled for them without further reference to the doctor, and the three ladies, carefully yet courteously guarded, were escorted to Baltimore, where old friends received them with open arms, only to become, in turn, objects of suspicion themselves, and to find their home, their movements, their very lives, dogged by detectives and secret service people. It could not be otherwise. It was one of the inevitable consequences of the war. Away into December the head of the War Department would boil over with wrath and indignation when Stuart's raid was mentioned, or some one spoke of Fairfax. Well was it for Colonel Clark, with all the splendid record won during the first year of the war, that he had been summoned to Harper's Ferry and was away at the moment of the Virginian's escape. Even as it was, Stanton seemed to hold that the colonel should have foreseen and prevented any possibility of his soldiers being tempted by the wealthy friends of the accused. The New Hampshire "boys" went into the hopeless assault on the heights of Fredericksburg under the spur of Stanton's intimation that they had a disgrace to wash out, and if the blood of half their number were atonement sufficient, as Clark sadly wrote that bitter night, then were they indeed absolved.

Left in charge of poor old Chloe and her aging spouse, with a caretaker from Poolesville and frequent domiciliary visits from curious soldiery passing that way, Heatherwood Towers, as the Marylanders poetically called it, drowsed through the dreary winter, yet found itself not altogether friendless. The major-general commanding at Baltimore, a man somewhat of Stanton's type, would order no guard for its protection, but there were invalids in the field-hospital under the height who day after day had eagerly awaited the visit of its gentle owner, whose sweet smile and soothing or encouraging words had sustained them in the fevered days of the autumn. Mindful of the many little delicacies that she had brought them, and of her affectionate care, they now, in their slowly regaining strength, organized among themselves, after hearing of depredations and robberies, what they called the Heatherwood Guards, and with the full knowledge and approval of the surgeon in charge, who also had learned to bless her coming as much as they, stoutly posted their crippled sentries night and day and taught the evil-disposed a lesson that prolonged the life of the once lovely old place through the bitter winter, until there came a day when once more the orchard was in full bloom and the orioles and blue birds were flashing in the sunlight from tree to tree, when their numbers were so far reduced that they were powerless against the new and relentless foe, and all their loyal tribute of affection and gratitude was in vain.

No need here to tell of the increasing gloom at Washington over the disasters, one after another, that befell the gallant, patient, ever-ready, yet long-mishandled Army of the Potomac, or of the corresponding joy and increasing hope and defiance in the social life of Baltimore. All through the long, anxious winter the Heatherwoods lived there in monotonous seclusion, diversified, perhaps, by the arrest of Miss Waddell for irrepressible impudence to the provost-guard after the news of Fredericksburg. Her release was speedily ordered by a laughing, gray-haired colonel, who drove her to the verge of fury by demanding of his juniors what possible harm the little spitfire could have done; and she was really pining to be court-martialled and jailed as a rebel and a martyr one minute, even while secretly praying for news of Pettingill the next. He was first sergeant of his company when Hooker made that admirable move to Chancellorsville the last of April, and, still as first sergeant, commanded it when it slowly fell back with the fiercely fighting line on the third day of that headless battling. "Young and green" as he was at the start, the fighting blood of Concord Bridge and Bunker Hill was coursing in his veins, and Clark, though himself wounded and well-nigh broken-hearted over the disastrous moves that had robbed him of one-third of his officers and men, wrote to the governor that First Sergeant Pettingill deserved promotion more than any man he could think of in the ranks.

And Baltimore was mad with ill-concealed joy and delight when, close upon the heels of the news of Chancellorsville, there came the thrilling whisper, "Lee is coming! Lee is coming! The victorious army of the South will be across the Potomac—at our very gates—within a fortnight!" And Belle Heatherwood's pale cheek flushed with strange emotion—hope? love? anticipation?—who could say? Twice had letters been brought to her from Fairfax, a vindicated man. The letters of friends at Leesburg, Poolesville, and Frederick, backed by those of Madam Heatherwood herself, all spirited through the lines by the mysterious agencies existing both in

Baltimore and Washington, had established his innocence of the allegations laid at his door, but, in his wrath at Montfort and Garnett, he had refused further service with them and had fought superbly on the staff of A. P. Hill until the officers and men of a sorely depleted regiment of Virginians urged his acceptance of a vacant lieutenant-colonelcy, and he led them like a lion when they struck the corps of Howard, crushing it like an egg-shell, the fatal first day of Hooker's one battle in chief command.

But over and again there was a question on the mother's lips that was checked by Belle Heatherwood's uplifted hand, by the piteous plea in her sad, sweet face. Much her mother suspected that one man had risked life and honor to save Floyd Fairfax for no other reason than that he believed the Virginian's death as a spy would break Belle Heatherwood's heart. The nimble escape with the condemning disguise, the later relapses, and the well-assumed mental break-down essayed to prevent his being called as a witness before the court,—these, together with the daring and devotion he had earlier shown in their service, plainly told their story,— that Trooper Bell was a lover Quixotic, even, in self-abnegation, and so unworthy in his own eyes as to ask no word of hope, and only in one way able to find means to relieve his over-weighted heart: he could not woo or win her love, but her gratitude, her respect, he could and would command. Firmly believing, ever since the night he witnessed her agony over the capture of Fairfax, that it was because she devotedly loved him, he had first secured, then dashed away with, the fatal disguise, had later managed to head off every effort to produce himself as a witness, and had finally and silently gone his way to rejoin his regiment without one word of blessing from her lips, without one glance from her beautiful, grateful eyes. From him no further line or message had come. Foulweather had sent the valise with its contents to the War Department, where it was speedily relegated to a rubbish heap, bigger game than that demanding the efforts of every man on duty; and now the Heatherwoods knew not whom to ask; indeed, they knew not but that inquiry for a Union trooper on their part might blast his name and prospects even as their own seemed ruined. Unable to relieve their own anxiety on his account, they were ill equipped to lessen that of others, yet there came a day, just when for the second time Lee's hard-marching infantry once more swung their battered hats and cheered at sight of the blue Catoctins of Maryland, when Belle Heatherwood, reading aloud to her wearied mother as the latter lay by the open window, fanned by the soft Southern breeze, was startled by the slow opening of a door leading into the hall, and there, hesitant, timid, yet with a world of sorrow and pleading in her face, dressed still in morning, stood Florence Lowndes.

One moment she hung there irresolute, as Belle slowly rose from her chair, her face whiter now than that of her unlooked for visitor, her slender hands pressed to her temples, her eyes filled with bewilderment. Then with one impulsive gesture she threw out her arms, and in an instant the girls were locked in each other's embrace, every bitter word of the past forgotten.

Later that long June afternoon, their sorrow-weighted hearts relieved through nature's blessed floodgates by the torrent of their tears, they were seated at a window commanding a view of the wide and crowded thoroughfare. All Baltimore seemed thronging into the open air, thrilled with exultation, they whose loved ones marched with Lee, or silent with apprehension, they whose hearts and hopes were bound up in the Union. Wild rumors were afloat on every side. Newsboys yelled shrill mendacity, as they darted, "extra" laden, through the crowd. Gayly dressed women exchanged congratulations, even daringly flaunted the rebel colors on their dress, laughing gleefully as their bright eyes flashed defiance at the blue-uniformed officers hastening to and from the general's head-quarters up the street. A band was playing spirited music at the base of the monument in the adjoining square, and a roar of delight went up from a thousand throats when it suddenly burst forth with the strains of "The Bonnie Blue Flag." The rush of the provost-guard was all that stopped still further demonstration, and a regiment, with bayonets ominously fixed, marched in grim silence through the square, formed line in front of head-quarters, and stood at rest, leaning on the muzzles of the long muskets and peering sternly out from under the black visors of the worn blue forage-caps at the occasionally jeering swarm along the opposite sidewalk. For reasons of her own Mrs. Heatherwood refrained from coming to the windows this day, and remained at the rear of the house. Another perplexity had come. Well she knew that in this unheralded return from abroad Florence Lowndes and her father had at last received Clark's important missive, and were there to question. Surely there was something strange in the fact that Jack's valise, with some of his clothing, together with the uniform of another officer, should have been found at Heatherwood. Florence was confident that Jack had only one such valise, and that he took it with him when he went to the front at the first call. Well she remembered her tearful parting with him and her dread of her father's anger should he discover that his daughter had dared seek his banished son. It had hurt her that the news came as it did. She could hardly explain why, except that "Mr." Clark, as she persisted in calling the now famous brigade commander, beloved and honored in the hard-hit, hard-fighting army, had never understood Jack, and had even prejudiced her father against him. Reasoning it all out, she well knew that after her bitter words to Belle and her refusal to answer the latter's sad, womanly letter she had no right to expect the Heatherwoods would write again.

She had never notified them of the project of going abroad, where, finding no comfort in the beaten track, father and daughter had sought the by-ways, and had gone to what were then remote places. Clark's letter awaited them in Rome on their return from a long, lingering journey up the Nile; and so, while, sobbing, she told Miss Heatherwood of the tidings sent by Clark, it never seemed to occur to her that for over a year Belle had known all about the valise and other and far more vital matters and had made no sign. She accepted as all sufficient Belle's half-choking explanation that it was found at Manassas where mother had gone to nurse the wounded. She seemed to attach no significance to the fact that Mrs. Heatherwood had avoided her all the afternoon. It was but natural that the fond and gentle woman should think best to leave the girls together for hours, that the reconciliation might be complete. Her father was to call at eight and talk with Mrs. Heatherwood himself. He wished to seek her aid in the discovery of important papers Jack probably had in that valise at the time of the capture of the baggage-wagons by the exultant Southerners. No one would more readily assist him in his search than this noble woman who was so honored by soldiers both North and South. And so as the afternoon wore on Belle's nervousness began to disappear. Florence asked no questions that grievously embarrassed her. Together they read the ominous extras. Together they clung, standing at the window watching the increasing crowd and excitement in the street. Timidly Florence began to ask for tidings of Ralph and Tighlman, and finally of Fairfax, and quickly she noted the faint color that stole to the soft cheek of the Maryland girl at mention of the Virginian's name. Together they were seated at the open casement when, with flashing eyes and flaming cheeks, Laura Waddell came bounding in all athrill, her light silken jacket thrown back, revealing on the bosom of the gossamer gown beneath the scarlet, blue, and white of the "Stars and Bars." The sight of the stranger only slightly checked her impulse.

"Belle! Belle!" she cried; "look out yahnduh! Here comes that very fella you wouldn't tell me about at home; and he's got to be a general!"

The clatter of horses' hoofs added to the clamor in the streets. At quick, spirited walk, almost verging on the jog-trot, a little party of Union horsemen came riding towards head-quarters. Right and left the throng stood still and stared, though the sight of generals wearing the single star was no novelty. It was the superb form, face, and bearing of the young brigadier foremost in the array that riveted all eyes upon him and left but casual glance for the few staff-officers and orderlies who followed. Erect and graceful, manly strength and confidence in his pose, sitting his spirited horse like a centaur, his keen blue eyes gleaming from under the visor of his jaunty forage-cap, his uniform, evidently new, fitting him without a flaw, his yellow sash and gold-barred belt, his handsome sword, boots, and horse equipments, all the perfection of soldierly style, yet impressing no one with the idea of the soldier dandy, his handsome, clear-cut face bronzed by the hot Virginia suns, his mouth concealed by the sweeping blond moustache—no wonder even rampant, rebel Baltimore stared and admired. With blanched, incredulous face, Belle Heatherwood gazed, lost to all surroundings, forgetful utterly of the girl at her side, until suddenly recalled to herself and her friend by the piercing cry in which wild joy, amaze, unbelief, aye, even dread, were mingled. "Jack! Jack! *Brother!*" And then with outstretched arms poor Florence fell as though suddenly struck a mortal blow and hung lifeless over the sill of the open window.

It was long before they could restore her. When at last consciousness returned, her father, too, was bending over her, and his stern, sad, rugged old face was piteous in its anxiety and distress. Almost her first words were, "Did you see—Jack?"

"Hush, my darling!" he answered, brokenly, and the tears started to his eyes. "We have heard all about him. I wish to God it were my Jack. That was the Pennsylvania cavalry officer who won such fame, and his general's stars, on Stoneman's raid. His name is Grosvenor Belden.

CHAPTER XXIII.

"Up from the South" in the long June days came the long gray columns of Lee. Less than a year had sped since, shattered, yet undismayed, they had recoiled from the shadows of the blue Catoctins and retired to the old intrenchments of the Rappahannock, whence, triumphant and with self-confidence tenfold increased, after the bloody lessons given the Union arms at Fredericksburg and Chancellorsville, once more they essayed the conquest of Maryland and the dash at the Northern cities. Once more the daring advance guard bridged the Potomac, and the famous old lieutenants led their grimy corps through the streets of Hagerstown and on towards the lovely Cumberland Valley of Pennsylvania,—all save one; Jackson, most daring of all, had crossed a still more shadowy river, and was resting forever under the shade of the trees. Not yet had the knightly leader of the Southern host begun to realize the extent of his loss. There had been no general engagement since the grapple in the thickets south and west of the old Virginia hamlet. Not yet had he fully realized another thing,—that the eyes of the latest commander of the Army of the Potomac had been opened to the need for better use of the eyes of the army; that master hands had been reorganizing the Union cavalry; that the sloths and fossils were being replaced by keen-witted troopers who knew their trade and were ready to ride, scout, and fight night or day, and were praying for no greater boon than a chance to match the "Cavaliers" of Stuart against the "Ironsides" of the North. John Buford, impatient of staff duty, rode at the head of one division, Kilpatrick and Gregg of the others, while gallant young soldiers had been chosen to step up to the stars of the brigadier, and Merritt and Custer, boy captains but a day ago, donned the yellow sash, and regular and volunteer, their brigades hailed the new commanders with cheers of pride and confidence.

At Beverly Ford and Brandy Station the troopers of the North and South fought their first battle royal, and Stuart saw how great a change had been wrought within the few months. Brainy men were now directing the blows of the Union horse, and brawny arms were delivering them, and for the first time in his war history the Virginian met his match and knew it. Yet, even at the moment when it dawned upon the Southern commander that at last the Union had a cavalry force worth his consideration, and the Army of the Potomac was possessed of a right arm it lacked the year before, even when it was most likely they would need their own, did Lee and Stuart plan a separation. Even as the head of the Southern army of invasion came in view of Maryland Heights, while the Army of the Potomac, marching night and day, strove hard to interpose between the rebel battle-flags and the alarmed and threatened halls of government at Washington, the screen of Stuart's cavalry slipped away from between the parallel columns, and, passing entirely around the rear of Hooker's hindmost brigade, went gayly away on a raid of its own that bore it close under the guns of Washington, and so on up through Maryland and Pennsylvania, lost to Lee for many a day when most he stood in need of it, only to return in time for the last hour's bitter work at Gettysburg and to be ground to earth and battered and slashed and sent whirling from the field, completely overmastered by Gregg and the Second Division, backed by Custer with the Michigan men.

Yet changes had come in the Union horse that were not all for the better. A wail went up in many a camp when gallant "Grimes" Davis met his soldier fate, heading the dash at Beverly Ford. A growl of remonstrance rose from many a bearded throat when Belden accepted the yellow sash and silver stars and went to Washington, transferred to a new command. ("Lost," said his trooper friends, "in the infantry.") Yet this was before young cavalry captains were getting their brigades, and Belden was wise. Furious things old Foulweather was saying, as he led his regiment, the —th Regulars, on the march to Maryland, but when he read the order that made his junior (a captain of the Second) instead of himself (a major of the —th) full brigadier-general, and assigned him to the command of the regular brigade, the old fellow's wrath and misery were well-nigh complete. "They might as well kill me outright," said he to Treacy and Hamlin, who had heard the news with secret joy, "as to let me die by slow torture and mortification as they are doing." And a far more serious matter was it beginning to prove than at first his brother officers supposed. Envy, jealousy, disappointed ambition, hate, and heaven knows how many other things, were telling on the rugged old trooper, and as the brigade crossed the Potomac and reached the Maryland shore the surgeon came to the commander.

"Old Foulweather," said he, using the pet name so well known throughout the army, "is in the grasp of a high fever that may prove very serious. He should be sent at once to the nearest hospital."

And so that very evening a yellow ambulance clattered up the towpath and turned in under Heatherwood Height, and the escorting troopers, three in number, asked for the doctor in charge of the field-hospital still maintained there for the benefit of the sick or possible wounded among the troops detailed to guard the canal and the many fords and ferries, and from the depths of the dust-covered vehicle they lifted as tenderly as possible a raging, raving, struggling old soldier who swore hideously at surgeon, steward, sergeant, and all, but was overpowered and borne to a shady, airy tent, and there almost forcibly put to bed.

Three hours later, when, refreshed and rested, their horses fed, watered, and groomed, the escorting troopers would have taken the road to Frederick to rejoin their regiment, one of their number was missing, and the sergeant inquired, after the manner of war-time troopers far and near, "Where 'n 'ell's Bell?"

To which answered the other words to the effect that "you never knew where Bell was 'cept in a fight,—then he was *there!*"

Inquiry among the convalescents seated in the slanting sunshine watching the signal-flags waving on the westward heights evoked the information that a "feller" answering their description had gone up the path to Heatherwood half an hour before, whereat the sergeant emulated his now prostrate commander and blasphemed vigorously.

"That damned Beau," said he, "is more trouble than the rest of the troop put together just so soon as we get north of the Potomac. South of it he's all right. I might have known he'd be losing himself."

"What'd you bring him for?" asked his subordinate, unfeelingly.

"I didn't; the lieutenant sent him, and told me he knew the best road and all about the country, and now he's gone and we are ordered to be at Frederick to-night.—Who lives up yonder?" he abruptly asked an invalided sergeant hobbling by, and the volunteer stopped for a chat with the regular.

"Family named Heatherwood, from Baltimore.

House has been vacant for a long time until this week. Now there's several people there, they say. The old hands here used to look after it and kept guard there, but there's only one or two of them left. They post sentries from that regiment over yonder up there every night now since the folks come back, and no one's allowed in or out."

"Well, I'm going up," said the sergeant, stoutly. "I've lost a man, and they say he went up there. You watch the horses and traps, Jim," he called over his shoulder to the private trooper. "I'll be back in twenty minutes."

Following the pathway through the leafy woods, Sergeant Black began the somewhat steep ascent among the trees until he emerged from them at the edge of a little sloping bench of cleared and once cultivated ground, beyond which stood the barns and enclosures, and beyond them certain weather-beaten sheds and a corn-crib. Not a soul was in sight, and after a moment's quiet reconnoissance and a long breath or two, the war-worn soldier pushed ahead. He found the barn and barn-yard empty and the last vestige of forage gone. The storehouse, corn-crib, etc., had long since outlived their usefulness, every crumb or kernel having been devoured or swept away. Out in the orchard the sun was throwing his last rays through the blossoming trees and gilding the old sun-dial and tipping the hedge and that relic of a fence with gold. The kitchen door was open, so was one that led to the cellar, and somewhere thereabouts there was an occupant, for he heard the crooning sound of a darky song. War is the foe of conventionality, and, never stopping to knock, the soldier strode across the threshold. Here there were signs of life and action, for a brisk fire blazed in the stove, and pots and kettles gave forth the appetizing odor of a bounteous supper. Then from the depths of the cellar the darky song came crooning nigher, a woolly head, enveloped in glaring bandana, hove in sight up the mouldering stairs, and two staring, goggle eyes met his in evident disapprobation.

"I am looking for one of my men who came up here a few minutes——"

"I doan' know nuthin' 'bout your men," was the instant interruption of Aunt Chloe. "Lord knows we'se had trouble 'nuf between the lot of 'em," yet, with odd inconsistency, added, "Wha's he like, anyway?"

"Tall, fine-looking young fellow—handsome, I suppose you'd call him. Don't look like—most of us."

"I ain't seen nuffin' handsome since Marse Fairfax and Marse Ralph, an' such gen'lemen, was wid us," was Aunt Chloe's almost disdainful answer. "Go long! You're only lookin' for somefin' to eat."

But the sound of the colloquy had attracted others to the spot,—two others,—for the hall door suddenly opened and, to the amaze of the trooper sergeant, two young women, winsome, sweet, attractive young women, prettily gowned, as even he could see, ladies, as he knew at a glance, stood there at the threshold, looking not unkindly down at him. In an instant off came his cap.

"I beg your pardon," he faltered, "but I had to come up to inquire if anything had been seen of one of my men who wandered up here a while ago. It is time for us to be moving."

"You are cavalry, are you not?" asked the nearest. "No cavalry soldiers have been near here since we came a few days ago. We have infantry guards at night and some crippled soldiers whom my mother nursed long months ago. They are all out in front."

"Thank you, miss. I'll hunt them up," began Sergeant Black, backing towards the door. "I didn't mean to intrude."

But it was Miss Heatherwood's turn to inquire. Half-timidly she asked, "What command—what regiment is yours?" and her soft eyes were full of interest, even of anxiety, as she spoke.

"—th Regulars, miss. Major Foulweather was commanding. We've brought him here, sick, to the hospital below."

And now a sudden flush leaped to the questioner's face. Then, though an eager light shone in her eyes, the color died away and left her pale. "What was he like—this—soldier?—what was his name?" she faltered. And in surprise, if, indeed, no other emotion moved her, the fair girl by her side looked suddenly, searchingly, into Miss Heatherwood's face.

"A tall, fine-looking fellow, miss, with blue eyes and handsome face,—Bell he calls himself."

"Oh, no, no!—No, indeed!" was the hurried answer. "I'm—I'm sure no such person has been here; and I would know him. He has been here, you know. It was he who saved the gun the day Stuart's men so nearly got it."

"The very man, miss. There's no better when it comes to fighting. But this isn't the first time we've lost him, and there'll be trouble if he leaves us now, when every man is needed."

And still silently, searchingly, Miss Heatherwood's companion, a fair-haired, blue-eyed girl, whose garb told of recent mourning, gazed fixedly into Miss Heatherwood's face, and noted the signs of agitation there and in the rapid rise and fall of her bosom.

Then with sudden effort, and as though conscious of scrutiny, Miss Heatherwood, despite her fluttering heart, rushed into eager question again. "Can you give us any news, sergeant? Can you tell us where Stuart has gone? or when we can get back to Baltimore? Secretary Stanton gave us permission to spend only three days here, and, when we tried to return, Stuart had cut the railway to Baltimore. The horses we hired at Frederick are gone, we don't know where. My mother has sent word of our plight to the commanding officer at the nearest camp, but no help has come, and my friend here, Miss Lowndes, should have joined her father in Washington yesterday. We have sent our old negro servant to Frederick to hire anything on wheels that will carry us, with one trunk, for mother's word was pledged to the general commanding at Baltimore——"

"Will the ladies ride in an ambulance, behind army mules?" was the sergeant's eager inquiry, as he stood buttoning his trooper jacket, hitherto thrown open at the throat and chest. "We have the ambulance that brought Major Foulweather. We can take you to Frederick, and then you can go by first train to Baltimore."

"Oh, most gladly! most gratefully! Could you wait just a moment until I can tell my mother?" asked Miss Heatherwood. "We'll be ready almost any time you say, if she approve."

And Sergeant Black said he would wait, indeed must wait, until he had found out about Bell, and with a scraping bow that, in its very awkwardness and spurry entangling of his dusty boots, was the acme of soldier devotion, he hastened past Aunt Chloe and around to the front of the house, where, dozing and chatting under the now dingy portico, were three or four of the old hands, men too reduced by camp ailments or long-unhealed wounds to be ordered back to the front, and of them he sought, all unsuccessfully, tidings of the missing trooper.

Meantime, Miss Heatherwood had scurried up the back staircase, her companion more slowly following, and tapped lightly at the door of her mother's room. Grief, anxiety, and care had so told upon the aging, loving gentlewoman, that night or day, whenever possible, sleep had been enjoined upon her as nature's best restorer, and never would they suddenly arouse her. No answer came. Noiselessly the daughter opened the door and peered within. The bed was unoccupied, the lounge as well. The room was without a tenant. Hastily Miss Heatherwood searched the upper floor, calling "Mother!" as she did so, but without success. A shawl was missing, and it was evident that while the girls were busy with their own affairs earlier in the long afternoon, the gentle mother had slipped quietly out of the house. A sudden light dawned on the daughter and shone in her brightening eyes.

"Stay here, Florence, dear. I know where she's gone," she cried, her excitement manifest in the glowing cheeks, and, darting through the kitchen, she sped swiftly along a winding path through the shrubbery, down the slope to the north of the homestead. Half-way down was a little arbor and rustic seat, once a favorite resort, but now dismantled, if not well-nigh ruined, and there, smiling through a veil of tears, her mother slowly rose to greet her, while a broad-shouldered form in dusty blue burst through the shrubbery beyond and fairly leaped out of sight in the shelter of the grove.

That lovely June evening, an hour after sunset, the dust-covered ambulance drove away down the winding road escorted by Sergeant Black and a single trooper, the former mystified beyond expression and unable to say a word. Miss Heatherwood had so eagerly accepted his offer to convoy the little party to Frederick that he expected similar alacrity on part of the mother, and was surprised at the length of time that elapsed before her appearance. Then her gentle, appealing voice and manner charmed him at once, as it did everybody, and the rough soldier stood respectfully attentive to her words. By this time he realized that this was the woman of whom so many a comrade, regular or volunteer, had spoken with blessing on his bearded lips. Gladly she availed herself of the offer, yet there was embarrassment, hesitancy, something amiss, and at last, as the girls seemed to cling about her, she stepped with him through Chloe's oft-invaded sanctum, and he saw and they saw she had that to say to him which others should not hear.

"I have a favor to ask you, sergeant. We can be ready to start in half an hour, if need be, but all the roads from Edward's Ferry towards Frederick would be crowded with marching columns. Delay will be inevitable. Trooper Bell is with you. Will you tell him at once we are to go with you in your ambulance, and bid him ride ahead and notify my relatives, the Tighlmans, that we are coming? He knows their home."

And then Black recalled the vague rumors he had heard in the troop about Beau Bell's long sojourn at this very spot, and knew that he must be another of Madam Heatherwood's grateful patients.

"He shall go if I can find him," was the prompt answer.

"You will find him," was the confident reply. "He was here to see me, but there are reasons why my children, and she smiled fondly as she included Florence in the endearing word, "should not know of it to-night."

Hastening back to the field-hospital, the sergeant found that Trooper Bell was there on hand as Mrs. Heatherwood had predicted. There was no time for rebuke. Bell received his instructions with evident surprise, but without a word. He quickly saddled, mounted, and rode away while the ambulance was being hitched. A tempting supper was set for Black and his comrade in the dining-room when they arrived, and, despite their soldier rations not so long before, they could not turn from Aunt Chloe's chicken and coffee. At eight they drove briskly away with their precious freight, not ten minutes before a lieutenant and a dozen men from the aqueduct guard came clambering up the westward slope. "Gone?" said the officer, in dismay, responding to the brief announcement of a crutch-propped invalid. "Why, my God! I've just come with orders to see that they don't go! They're to be taken to Washington under guard to-morrow."

An hour later, plodding slowly along up the Monocacy Valley, hemmed in, front and rear, by solid columns of dusty troopers, many of them sleeping in saddle, the occupants of the ambulance heard the oft repeated caution "Halt!" and for the twentieth time they stopped a moment before trundling on again. The open door-way of the uncouth vehicle was towards the southeast, and the horse of the squadron commander following dropped his weary head and rubbed his nose against the sill. Then a voice was heard to break the silence: "Lieutenant, ain't that a fire back yonder?"

"More'n likely," was the weary answer. "Fires are frequent enough, God knows."

Miss Heatherwood was supporting her mother's head upon her shoulder at the moment, but the latter was up in an instant, and together they edged to the door-way and gazed out into the night.

Away to the south a dull-red glare was spreading over the horizon, and the southwest slope of Sugar Loaf gleamed through the blackness of the night, its jagged side aglow with the reflected blaze. Each moment the reflection grew stronger. Then, as though fresh flame had burst through wooden roof or wall, the rolling smoke cloud drifting eastward glowed with sudden force, and even the distant heights at Point of Rocks threw back the ruddy sheen. Then high aloft over the valley a pillar of fire soared into the southern sky, and from within the hooded wagon in his front the squadron leader heard a woman's sob and the half-stifled words, "Mother, it's Heatherwood! Oh, I know it's Heatherwood!"

And then, growlingly repeated down the column, came the same relentless order,—"Forward!"

CHAPTER XXIV.

FIERCELY over the smoke-crowned ridge the midday sun is beating down. Far as the eye can penetrate the eddying, sulphurous mist to north or south, black-muzzled guns are rudely aligned, some along the relics of stone wall, now splintered in a hundred places, rent by solid shot and shell, some at the edge of the westward slope. There is a throb and concussion in every second borne on the heated air from across the low, flat valley, seamed diagonally by a broad, straight road, dotted towards the southward with two or three farm-houses of stone, all more or less shattered, and one of them—the nearest—ablaze. A cloud-bank of pale blue, perhaps a mile away, spans the valley at the west and extends from far down to the left away up to, around, and beyond a cluster of roofs and walls, of wood and stone, nestling in the heart of the northward valley. Here, there, and everywhere that opposite line of low-hanging smoke cloud is rent and torn from beyond by dazzling flashes of fire. The heavens give echo to incessant roar and thunder from the trembling earth. The quivering air is pierced by scores of shrieking demons that, unseen in their flight, come plunging like death-dealing meteors among the silent batteries, or bursting in mid-air, with flame and crash, into hissing fragments that tear their way earthward or fly far over the fertile plateau that stretches away in graceful undulations until hemmed by the line of distant forest at the east. Only the week before this very spot was the scene of rural, peaceful beauty; this placid old Pennsylvania village drowsed in the summer sunshine throughout the long June day; the blue hills, stretching from Maryland away northeastward to the Susquehanna, framed the lovely picture towards the setting sun; the cattle browsed in the sloping fields in the long shadows of the leafy groves; the birds sang to heaven their pæans of rejoicing from morn till night; the cloud shadows sailed over waving fields of wheat and bearded rye, and deepened the dark-green foliage of the orchards; the farm boys whistled at their tasks, and around the tavern porch at eve the honest burghers told their tales of how last October they and the home guards sent the rebel raiders—Jeb Stuart's cavalry—"flyin' out of the valley and back to Virginia where they belonged." Yes, all Gettysburg believed it was the sight of the undaunted front of the local militia that bade the triumphant Southron pause in his mad career of destruction, and history records the fact that not until his advance rode into sight of the steeple of the old Dutch church did Stuart turn and hark back full speed for the Potomac. But a different tale is being told to-day. Stuart, once more riding and raiding through southern Pennsylvania, has passed far beyond, gone away northward to the bridges of the Susquehanna by way of York on one side, while one-legged Ewell, with Jackson's old "foot cavalry," has trudged every inch of the way to Carlisle on the other; and June goes out with famous John Buford and his devoted troopers jogging through the now alarmed and bustling town, bent on seizing the roads to the west and on "fighting like the devil" to head off these advancing hosts, until Reynolds with the left wing of the army can come up to his aid. Two days of mortal grappling, of desperate hand to hand fighting, have turned the old town and all the fields and slopes, groves and orchards, into morgues or hospitals, and now at last has come the time for Lee's supreme effort. One after another, in assault after assault, Ewell, Hill, Hood, and Longstreet have been hurled back from the rocky flanks of that stern blue line; and now it recalls the old guard at Waterloo, for the great Virginian, the idol of the Southern host, calls on Virginia to do what other States have failed to do. He sends Stuart, returned at this eleventh hour, to burst through the thin veil of cavalry out on the Union right and sweep down upon the trains, reserve batteries, and the rear of the battling line, while Pickett, with that glorious division of Virginians, held in leash until the very last, led in brigades by such knightly soldiers as Armistead, Garnett, and Kemper, and supported on the right and left by brigades and divisions less famous, perhaps, yet made up of fighting men under tried and skilful leaders,—Pickett is ordered to pierce that blue line at the centre, then sweep it from the crest.

For two mortal hours, as preliminary, the fiercest cannonade ever heard on the Western Continent has shaken the earth and rent the heavens. For two mortal hours a rain of bursting shells has poured upon the long, low ridge fringed by the Union guns. Providence thus far has sided with the South, for the soft wind from the northeast has banked the smoke down in the valley in front of the guns of Lee, blazing along a line two miles in length, while on the higher crest, where stand the Union batteries, it floats away, leaving them exposed to view. From the slopes behind their guns the Confederate generals can see the effect of their fire, and direct such changes in elevation as may be needed, while the Union guns have had only the smoke-bank at which to aim, yet their response has been deadly. Wise leaders have solved the meaning of this tremendous long-range battling, however. It is but the overture to a terrible drama soon to begin, and Hunt, chief of artillery of the Potomac army, has ridden along his flashing line ordering "Cease firing!" Ammunition must be saved, guns must cool, or there will be failure in the hour of greater need.

And now, towards three o'clock of the hot July day, a silence ominous and forbidding has followed the furious clamor, a silence broken only by the low-toned words of command, or the moan of almost countless sufferers borne from among the guns to where the surgeons, red armed, ply knife and saw in the charnel pits at the rear. Havoc and destruction have reigned among the batteries. Here and there a shattered wheel or axle has dropped a cannon on the foremost line, but it is among the limbers and caissons at their back that the effects of the furious shelling is most apparent. Horses lie with stiffening, outstretched legs in bloody heaps, some few still madly plunging in their agony. Here and there a wreck of splinters tells where some ammunition-chest has exploded and wrought death and mutilation on every side. Mopping the black sweat from their swollen faces, brawny men in shirt sleeves have thrown themselves upon the ground among the guns, others are clustered sadly about some dying comrade, others kneel in soldier grief at the side of the dead. All along the line of the ridge behind the batteries, crowding into the rare intervals, battalions of infantry sorely reduced in numbers are lying prone to escape as much as possible the hissing fragments of the shells. Out in a little grove south of the still smoking guns of Cushing and Woodruff a new brigade has been stationed, and these Green Mountain boys take their baptism of fire with awe and wonderment; yet, confident of their leader's judgment, hold their ground like veterans. Away to the left on the rocky sides of the Round Tops there is a flutter of color over jagged ranks of dark blue, that promises the wearied line along the ridge that no enfilade can come from that quarter, and the gray-clad bodies stiffening among the rocks in the gorges at their base, or among the trees of the curving heights at the north, tell how fierce was the Southern effort to force a way on both flanks,—and how ineffectual. In rear of the line are occasional groups of horsemen, though most officers are dismounted,—common sense dictating where Confederate shells do not; yet there are generals and staff-officers already again in saddle, sure of vigorous work ahead. Some have not dismounted at all, even in the storm of missiles; others are quietly mounting now, for the fury of the cannonade is over, the fire is dying out. The great drama of the day is coming; it is time to reset the stage.

Hancock, superb as ever, rides among his faithful men and reins in his horse to say a word of cordial greeting to the heavily bearded brigade commander who, seated on an ammunition chest, is stoically submitting to the reslinging and dressing of an arm severely lacerated in the fierce battling of the day before. A soldier every inch of him, despite his years of plodding at the law, Colonel Clark insists on his right and his ability to lead his men this vital day, though it may be months before he can again draw sword. Spurring up from the Round Tops another brigade commander, whose sash and stars have not yet known the tarnish of the battle smoke, eagerly accosts the famous leader of the Second Corps, and out goes Hancock's hand in welcome:

"Belden, this is glorious! How did you reach us? Is your brigade here?"

"Not yet organized, general. I was doing duty in Baltimore, but got permission by telegraph to join, and rode out from Westminster this morning." Curious eyes following the new-comer mark how like to Hancock is the young general. "Just as though they were brothers with not ten years difference in their ages," says Clark to himself, as, together, the two stalwart soldiers ride away in search of General Meade, for Belden comes to tender his sword and services in any capacity, and there is need, sore need, of every man the Union can throw into the fighting line, and the time is drawing nigh.

Three o'clock, and now at last the Southern guns are still, and slowly, very slowly, the smoke veil drifts aside, goes sailing out of the valley into the opposite woods, and so the curtain rises on the last great act, of the last great day,—the climax of Gettysburg has come.

Away down to the left, out beyond the orchard from which Sickles yesterday was driven with such heavy loss, a new division has moved silently forward, and as the smoke cloud lifts, and anxious, haggard, yet fiercely gleaming eyes peer forth to the distant fields beyond the pike, in two long extended lines, five thousand soldiery in dingy gray can be discerned, crouching or lying upon the shot-ploughed turf. Almost two-thirds of a mile in length in line of battle, five to six thinned regiments to each, are two brigades easily distinguishable by the bits of color where at regular intervals the St. Andrew's cross flutters on the dull red of the Southern battle-flags, and by the groups of horses that, in rear of each command, tell where regimental and brigade leaders are waiting with their few staff-officers the signal for action. Back of them, three hundred yards or so, a third brigade, also in long extended line, stretches from north to south. It is Pickett's magnificent division, all Virginians, Kemper and Garnett commanding the foremost line, Armistead the second,— gallant fellows, one and all. Only this morning have they reached the field, fresh and confident,— men who never yet have been denied when it came to headlong attack, and Lee has called on these, his "statesmen," his neighbors and friends, his kith and kin, to perform the last supreme act of devotion, to charge and pierce that wearied Union line at its very centre, to burst through the barrier that blocks their march to the cities of the North, or to die in the desperate yet glorious effort.

And that Pickett may have ample support in an assault that all men know must be hazardous in the extreme, and may be disastrous, Wilcox with his strong brigade is ordered to cover him on the right, the southern flank, and Wilcox at this moment it is who leads forward his lines from the skirt of the woods, from under the shelter of the guns set almost hub to hub along the opposite slope, and once clear of the batteries halts his command even farther back than Armistead, to await the movement of the Virginians. On Pickett's left, or northern, flank, too, he must have strong support, and here no less than six brigades, led by fellows who have already been fighting hard, are slowly pushed forward into one long line of battle whose front is covered by a heavy force of skirmishers that come well up to the pike and almost under the silent breastworks towards the northern flank of the Union position. These men are mainly North Carolinians, Pettigrew commanding, and it is their formation that reveals to keen-eyed Hancock and his alert subordinates that the main attack will come at the centre of the line, right out here at Ziegler's grove, directly in front, probably, of that protruding clump of trees where Stannard and his Green Mountain boys are kneeling, and here where Andy Webb's Pennsylvanians, back of the stone wall, are aligned in front of Cushing's guns. Only slender ranks are here to meet them, yet the whole western front of the Union line is threatened by the dispositions of Lee, and not until the attack is centred on some section of the crest is it safe to order one single regiment to move or leave its post in order to strengthen some other.

Aye! There it comes, some unheard signal from across the vale. No one can see Pickett's solemn farewell to Longstreet or read the grief and reluctance in that veteran's face. He cannot, will not, give assent to an assault he deems a hopeless sacrifice. It is Lee's order, and that is all sufficient. Down towards the pike are the smouldering ruins of an old farm-house and its outlying haystacks, the spot where

Humphreys's line was so fiercely battling but the day before. There in heaps lie the swelling carcasses of Seely's horses, just where they dropped in rear of his heated guns, and beyond that scene of fire and carnage, and beyond the death-strewn pike, as one man Pickett's division springs to its feet and the next instant is seen to be in motion. Shimmering through the burning heat of the July sun, with the gleam of sloping muskets, the flutter of proudly carried banners, the rhythmic swing of marching veterans, yonder comes a battle-picture that will live forever in the eyes of those who gazed this vital day, that will go down in history as the grandest pageant of an immortal struggle. Saluted by the guns on Little Round Top, almost instantly followed by many another along the Union lines, superbly indifferent to all, Pickett's Virginians, as though on division drill, begin their stately "passage of the lines," and in utter silence, in cadenced step despite the shells that burst above their devoted heads and shower them with whirring fragments, they pursue their chosen course. Steadily, aye, with almost disdainful deliberation, they move north towards Pettigrew's waiting ranks, and not until opposite the centre of the Union line do they form column of attack. Here Kemper, throwing out a strong veil of skirmishers, is seen to have halted. A broad gap begins to yawn between him and his comrade brigade, and into this gap, up from the rear, calm and unhurried, marches Armistead; and now, in the proud old order of attack they love so well and have essayed so often, the three brigades, their foremost regiments aligned, once more are given the word, and Pickett and his splendid legion are facing their soldier fate. Hearts beat hard and lips are compressed. No sound comes from the serried lines, but the remorseless tramp, tramp of near ten thousand, and the half-stifled groan with which some poor fellow pitches heavily forward, or the awful, indescribable, crunching, crushing whish and whirr with which huge fragments of iron tear through the stern, solid ranks, rending flesh and bone, sweeping away files and sections, yet never checking the calm, steadfast, indomitable majesty of that matchless advance. "Good God, isn't it superb!" is the cry that goes up everywhere among the watchers at the Round Tops and the sheltered right; but along the stone walls and among the black-mouthed guns that line the threatened crest, grimy fellows in long ranks of blue grip tight their fresh-capped rifles and whisper, "Remember Fredericksburg."

And now Kemper is across the pike and his right swings out to pass the flaming ruins at Cadori's, and as Armistead's men breast the low ridge of the roadway that crosses their front, and Garnett, too, comes sturdily tramping over, all the Union guns in front of them depress the muzzles, and canister is rammed home in place of shell. Another minute and that superb sacrifice will be within the range of the lighter missiles; but all of a sudden, to the wonderment of a whole army, the division halts in its tracks; Pickett finds it is heading a little south of the point he is ordered to probe, and right there on that open slope, deluged with shot and shell from guns that rake his ranks from right to left or hurl them in the very faces of his men, the Virginia leader dares to order, as though on drill, an oblique change of front, a sort of left half-wheel that brings Kemper's southern flank almost agraze of the little grove wherein, still silent, Stannard holds his breathless Vermonters. Then once more, "Forward!" is sounded, and now may God be with the right! for despite the storm of shot and shell that has strewn their bloody path with dead and wounded, determined, undaunted, magnificent in their disciplined daring and devotion, the brigades resume their grand advance, still so strong in numbers, so glorious in their faith in one another and in their leaders, that victory and triumph seem perched upon their waving banners, and the thin blue line that spans the crest must burst asunder or be brushed away before the human flood.

Once across the pike, the nimble skirmishers have been recalled and at the run go darting through the narrow intervals between the ranks. Over the dull gray undulating columns a dull gray cloud is hovering, half sulphur smoke from the bursting shells, half powdery dust from the sun-baked slope. Only four hundred yards away now. Already half the mounted officers are unhorsed, and Armistead, struggling from underneath his stricken charger, leaps out in front as though to show his devoted men no shot can harm him, and with hat high lifted on his sword-point, exulting, waves them on. "Forward! Forward! Touch to the centre!" are the only orders. Not once does the iron discipline relax; not once does a subdivision halt to fire, even when Kemper's leading battalions come abreast of Stannard's bristling grove, and to the furious barking of the double-shotted guns along the crest is added the sudden crash of musketry on the right. Even now, with company commanders, right guides, and dozens of gallant fellows tumbling to earth under the scorching ambuscade, even now the proud morale of the sons of that historic commonwealth is proof against the soldier impulse to wheel and volley into that death-jetting clump of timber. Edge away from it they must, for, remorseless still, the guns of Cushing tear huge gaps in the nearing front, and with every stride the advancing columns narrow. Gallant little Cushing! Mortally wounded though he knows himself to be, mortally wounded as is his devoted classmate, Woodruff, only two years out of West Point, they fight their guns to the very last and die like heroes at their post of duty. Three hundred yards, and still no quickening of the pace; still that steady, measured, inflexible advance. But now comes the test that tells. Webb, mindful of the tactics of Bunker Hill, has sternly held the fire of his Pennsylvanians, and at last he gives the word.

Added to the sputtering crash of Stannard, a fierce volley bursts from the stone wall, and the gray ranks reel and stagger, the battle-flags are bowed one instant, and only one, for now at last the spell is broken, now at last the word is given, now at last the thrilling shout of "Charge!" is taken up and echoed throughout the column, and, yelling like demons, the Virginians break their stern array, and with levelled bayonets come dashing up the slope. Huge human wave, rolling, surging, sweeping, resistless it bursts and breaks upon the slim barrier at the edge, where despite blood-tipped bayonets, clubbed muskets, hurtling rocks,—every device of hand to hand combat,—the blue line is swallowed up and washed backward with the gray as over the wall it comes, and in among the smoking guns it rolls, while afar back across that death-strewn valley mad cheers of joy and triumph rend the heavens and the mighty heart of Lee wells up in thanksgiving, for the colors of his beloved State are waving frantically over the captured guns,—the grand assault of Pickett has pierced the Union line!

O short-lived triumph! O bitter close to all that valiant effort! O cruel, fruitless sacrifice of priceless blood and treasure! With half her number prostrate along the path or stricken here among the foe, Virginia stands alone upon the summit won at such immeasurable cost. Wilcox has wandered with his brigade too far to the south and is out of supporting distance; Pettigrew's North Carolinians have recoiled before the defenders of the northward ridge, and the ringing chorus of victory that hails the sight of Pickett's battle-flags, waving on yonder flaming crest, proves but the knell of their defeat. Unsupported right and left, they are hemmed in now on three sides by cheering and exultant lines in blue. Hancock and Gibbon, sore wounded, have gone down before their rush; Webb's temple is seamed by their hissing lead; hundreds of gallant officers and devoted men are dying among the Union guns, but all to no purpose for the cause for which Virginia battles. Every instant adds to the thronging numbers of her foes. One after another the worshipped battle-flags are dropping. One after another the beloved leaders are missed. Armistead falls dying on Cushing's body. Garnett is shot to death at the wall. Kemper, severely wounded, is being borne by crouching comrades back down the smoking slope. Colonels, majors, and captains by scores are gone, and only a little remnant of the proud division hears the sternly shouted orders to surrender. They have done their best. Never in all the history of warfare did men dare or do more, but they are all exhausted now. Huddled together, leaderless, blind, panting in the hot, stifling smoke, surrounded on every side by hostile ranks, by bearded, blackened faces that even in the flame and fury of battle glow with admiration of such undaunted heroism and soften with pity for such hapless fate. It is all over. The cross of Saint Andrew, that waved so madly but a moment ago, droops defenceless now. One by one the rifle-stocks are lifted in mournful token of surrender, and, drifting backward from the slope, Pickett, broken-hearted, finds himself, with one lieutenant-colonel and a band of stragglers, all that is left of Virginia's grand division, —all that is left but a name that can never die.

In the solemn joy that hovers over the worn and wearied lines on Cemetery Ridge this night there is no sound of cheer or triumph. Such victory costs too dear. At sunset a young Union general, bending over the dark, pallid, clear-cut face of a Virginia colonel, motions the attendant soldier to fall back.

"In God's name, Fairfax," he murmurs, "why did you let yourself be taken? Do you not realize what is hanging over you?"

For answer the prostrate officer draws from his holster his stained revolver, every chamber black and empty. "I had not a shot left—for myself. Your bullets would not hit me. It was the butt of a musket that knocked me senseless. I had hoped to die with my brave—my murdered boys."

CHAPTER XXV.

BALTIMORE again, and every hospital is thronged. Mid-July has come, and Lee has gone, once more permitted to retire unharassed across the Potomac. Once more the Union lines are stretched along the canal, and a picket post is stationed on the height where towered stately Heatherwood, now a pile of blackened, melancholy ruins. Once more Bob Hamlin's troopers ride through the dusty lanes that, less than a year before, they traversed at top speed in chase of their Virginia foe, but no longer rages old Foulweather at the head of column. To the amaze of all he had turned up in time for the fierce battling of the second and third day, but shot and sabre-stroke have laid him low and left him, swearing still, a bandaged and bewildered invalid at Hanover. Treacy it is who commands, and Treacy who signs the report that tells of the splendid charge they made to hold the rebel right when Hood launched his columns at the Round Tops.

"Again it is the duty of the regimental commander to refer to the gallant conduct of Trooper Bell" (Bob Hamlin writes it all), "for, when the sergeant standard bearer was shot from his horse in the midst of the rebel line, it was Bell who rescued both, bearing the wounded sergeant to a place of safety, and then, standard in hand, rejoining in time for the second dash, in which he was unhorsed and seriously wounded, yet managed to toss the precious emblem to a comrade and eventually to crawl back to our lines."

Again is Beau an impatient patient in the surgeon's hands, transported, as are many of the wounded, to Baltimore. He recovers rapidly, for hard knocks seem to have no lasting effect on his vigorous constitution. He is up and hobbling about the tented enclosure in which so many comrades lie suffering through the long, hot days. Surgeons are few enough, and nurses sorely needed. Farther north, by hundreds, noble-hearted women crowd to the hospitals and press their services, but the bitterness of this bitterest of wars is heaviest here in the proud old Southern city, and many a stricken soldier longs in vain for the soothing touch of a woman's hand. Far to the front the able-bodied and the convalescent must soon be hurried, but for the time the twin triumphs of Gettysburg and Vicksburg, told in thunder on the glorious Fourth to a rejoicing nation, seem to hold the hand of the Union leaders, as though reluctant further to smite so brave, so suffering a foe. All through the hot July days, east and west, the columns of Meade and Grant are held in leash, as though the merciful, the tender-hearted Lincoln were stretching forth his hand imploring the erring children of the South to come to him that he might indeed bind up the nation's wounds and care for him who had borne the battle; for him, or the loved ones left to weep for the soldier who would never fight again. A paralysis of pity has swept over the armies of the Union, and made them powerless to follow up their victories. For weeks the cities swarm with slightly wounded or furloughed men, and provost-marshals cease to demand papers and passes through sheer fatigue. Back to the old familiar lines slowly march the war-worn veterans of Lee, a mournful remnant of the proud and triumphant array that swung so jubilantly north the month before, and there comes a fortnight in which even stern military justice seems forgotten, in which there is no longer thought on vengeance, a fortnight in which Floyd Fairfax lies within his guarded tent, visited by sympathetic friends, nursed by gentle hands, encouraged by more than one old comrade of the blue, before the Iron Secretary seems to realize that once again the spy of Heatherwood, the escaped prisoner of Point of Rocks, the daring Virginian who had cheated the gallows almost under the shadow of his wing, is here again, a wounded leader of Pickett's legion,—here within his grasp.

By this time, too, the Virginia colonel is quite able to reappear at the head of his men. A crashing blow of a gun butt on his uncovered head, a knee sorely wrenched by the frantic struggles of his dying horse disembowelled by a shell at the pike, make up the sum total of his casualties, and from these he is well-nigh recovered, but there can be no hope of exchange. Heatherwood and Tighlman have finally succeeded in effecting their transfer, for the South had far the best of it in prisoners after Fredericksburg and Chancellorsville, but no such luck can be hoped for in the case of Fairfax. Even in the Union army there are men who tremble when they think of the fate that will surely be his the moment Stanton becomes aware of his recapture, and one of these is Belden. The draft riots in New York and other cities have called for the presence of many of the regiments of the Potomac army, and the new-made general, whose bravery and whose example were so conspicuous at the forefront among Gibbon's men, still finds himself without a command. Fort McHenry and the post at Federal Hill are heavily garrisoned. A major-general of volunteers makes his headquarters at Baltimore, while his command is mainly strung along the Potomac from Edward's Ferry to Cumberland, and to him has the young West Pointer been ordered to report for assignment to duty; but West Pointers are things that double-starred statesman holds in aversion ever since the day he was forced to listen to the comments of one of their number upon an amateur attempt to attack a battery with a regiment in column of platform cars. He greets the new brigadier with cold civility, tells him to make himself at home at Barnum's until something turns up, and dictates a newspaper editorial upon the prevalence of padded, pigeon-breasted graduates of the National Academy in the corridors of the hotels, while the heroic volunteers of all ranks are found only at the post of danger,—at the front. Meanwhile, the recruitment of the new regiments of Pennsylvanians that were to have formed Belden's brigade seems to have languished, and good honest burghers throughout the Keystone State believe the war is over and clamor for the return of the troops already in the field. Belden writes vehement letters to Washington and Harrisburg,—to fossils at the War Department and to friends at court,—but with little effect at first, for the former are set against the detachment of young regulars to the command of volunteers, where they speedily win distinction far above that accorded veteran bureau officers, whom they may soon outrank in the permanent establishment; and the latter seem to share the belief of all Bucks County that the South has never recovered from the drubbing it received on Pennsylvania soil at the hands of Pennsylvania men, and further enrollment is unnecessary. They have good cause for pride in the valor of the sons of the Keystone State, God knows, for Meade was defending his own fireside; for the grandest soldier of them all, though he would not take the command of an army divided against itself, died on the foremost fighting line, repelling the fierce onset of the first day on the soil of his native State; for officers and men in scores from the lovely valleys of the Juniata, the Delaware, the Susquehanna, and the west slope of the Alleghanies laid down their lives in willing sacrifice for the sake of the Union and the glory of the old commonwealth; for it was Webb's Pennsylvanians who opposed their sturdy front to Pickett's overwhelming rush, fighting like devils even when hurled back by weight of numbers. There were days when General Belden could have torn the stars from his shoulders and gone back to take command of his old squadron. There came a day when he would have done it, such was his wrath and indignation, but stars, straps, coat, and all were gone for a time, and the very devil was to pay in Baltimore!

Impatiently awaiting at Barnum's the coming of telegrams or letters in reply to his importunate demands; forbidden by the general orders of the War Department to visit Washington without permission previously obtained from the adjutant-general, who seemed to see stars too many as it was and refused to encounter more; forbidden by military regulations to leave his post of duty without written permission from the general in command, to whom he will not apply under any circumstances, the stalwart young soldier fumes and rages about the Monumental City, finding his only comfort or usefulness in visiting the wounded, among whom there are many officers whom he knows. His horses and equipments he keeps at the stable adjoining the great hotel. His aide-de-camp, an enthusiastic stripling of his own name and race, is quartered with him. His orderlies—one a veteran of the old regiment, the other a strapping volunteer—are billeted with the provost-guard, and it becomes his daily custom to ride out to the camps and hospitals and to familiarize himself with such defences as there are. Men and women both look more than once at a form so graceful and commanding, and at a face so clear-cut, so handsome, so eloquent of soldier spirit and determination. Within the week of his return after Gettysburg, General Belden is far better known by sight to every officer and man of the neighboring forts and camps, and to the populace of the city, than is his senior in rank, the commanding general, who is rarely seen outside his office or his temporary home.

One soft evening in July, Belden has dismounted within a broad enclosure bounded by a high, unpainted picket-fence, and covered with the spreading canvas of a score of hospital tents. The walls are all looped up to permit free circulation of the air among the patients in their simple cots. The spreading tent-flies are propped high above each ridge-pole to shield the roof from the sun that blazes so hot at midday. The surgeon's quarters near the entrance, the guard tent on the opposite side, the entrance gate itself, and the store tents and dispensary are watched by pacing sentries, who halt and present arms as the little party enters. A young medical officer steps quickly forward to greet the distinguished arrival. A group of convalescents, reading newspapers or chatting together under a spreading awning, arise and stand attention,—a piece of soldier courtesy the young general acknowledges by lifting his forage-cap. Then stepping forward and extending a cordial hand to one or two of their number in whom he recognizes old soldiers of the regular cavalry, Belden seems to comprehend the entire gathering in the kindly look with which he accompanies his inquiries as to their improvement, their needs or wishes. It is while he is thus engaged, surrounded by the battle-scarred fellows, that a tall soldier, in natty, trim-fitting fatigue uniform, who, sitting somewhat apart from the others, has been eagerly studying the pages of a New York journal, but who, like the rest, had sprung to his feet, is now seen to slip quietly away and to walk rather rapidly, for a convalescent, around the corner of a neighboring tent, and there is lost to view.

"Who was that?" asks the general. "I've seen him before, haven't I? He has the ear-marks of the dragoon about him."

"Faith, sir," was the prompt, half-laughing reply of an Irish corporal, with the fond familiarity of that favored race, "the general has seen the likes of him every time he has looked in the glass since he joined us at old Lar'mie, and small blame to him if he looked as aften as I'd dhrink his health! That's Beau Bell, sir, that the boys would be callin' Belden, for he's the best fighter in the ould regiment—that wasn't born Irish."

"Bell, indeed!" is the smiling answer, as the general slips a generous greenback in the soldier's hand.

"We all know him, and I much want to see him. Tell him, will you, Terry? I'll ask the surgeon to let you have a little outing this evening, lads, and the corporal has—the countersign," he adds, with a twinkle in his bright blue eyes. "But remember, draw it mild, and no row with the police or patrols." So saying, he leaves them jubilant, the kindling eyes that follow his erect and graceful figure telling eloquently the regard in which the soldiers hold him. Directing his steps to a portion of the enclosure devoted to the officers, the general passes within an airy tent, then stops short almost at the threshold. It stands apart from the others. A sentry is posted at the front, another paces the little pathway not twenty feet away. The occupant is evidently a prisoner in more senses than one, yet at sight of Belden both sentries halt and present arms, and a tall, dark-bearded, dark-eyed patient, with gentleman stamped in every feature, rises slowly from his reclining-chair. "Ah! Belden, this is kind of you," he says; then, turning at once to two visitors seated near him, "Mrs. Heatherwood, may I present General Belden?—Miss Heatherwood," he adds; and then, with a backward glance at an officer in the uniform and equipments of a lieutenant of infantry, "and Lieutenant Farnham, who has no wish to supervise this interview, but, like the soldier he is, must obey his orders," whereat the young volunteer flushes, gratefully. Belden bows low and courteously, but Mrs. Heatherwood has risen before he can protest, and, coming forward with the same sweet manner and gentle voice that seem inseparable from her, holds forth her hand, exclaiming, "I am glad, indeed, to meet General Belden. There was a time when it seemed to be maintained that we had met before, and were old friends."

"And is this——? Why, what need to ask?" he says, with beaming eyes. "Of course, there can be but one Madam Heatherwood." And both his hands are clasping the slender fingers as he gazes into her pale, peaceful, tender face. "I do not know how many fellows have talked of you and blessed you, dear lady, and I envied them the knowing you. Who said we were old friends? I wish we were. I pray we may be," he goes on, impulsively, as he slowly releases her hand.

"We ought to be," is the mournful answer, "yet it was far better for you that we had never met in the past. What a tale we have to tell you, General Belden! It was your name, if not your voice, that saved our home to us a few months at least. It is all in ruins now."

"My name! my voice!" he cries, amazed, as he draws forward her camp-chair and aids her to her seat. "Why, this accords with some strange yarn I got from Washington, and then that uniform of mine that was found within your doors! What does it mean? How did it happen?"

"That—I—cannot explain—now," she answers, hesitating, embarrassed. "Yet some day you shall know, if we all live until 'this cruel war is over,' as the song goes. Colonel Fairfax can best tell you how your name suppressed them—the cannoneers—the day that Stuart passed us by,—or my daughter,—for they heard it all. I was prostrate."

"But not now," interposes Fairfax, in response to an appealing, upward glance from Miss Heatherwood's soft eyes, "not now!" And without turning he indicates by a significant movement of the hand the officer of the guard, seated unhappily by.

"Yes, the colonel is right," promptly chimes in Mrs. Heatherwood, "for we are limited to a call of fifteen minutes. Come to me,—indeed, I know you will if duties permit,—and you shall hear it all."

"Then for the moment I will leave you," says Belden, promptly, his eyes glancing quickly from Fairfax to the slender, silent girl. "You must have matters to talk of——"

"We have, general, and may we not have your counsel?" replies Mrs. Heatherwood, as promptly. Then, throwing aside all reserve, she frankly speaks: "You have known Floyd Fairfax for years. You must know he can never have been a spy. You do know the accusation against him. I ask you, is it possible that a spy would risk the loss of his comrades' respect by refusing to be safely borne away by them to rejoin his regiment in Virginia, simply because he had given his word to an officer—just as he might to this gentleman here—that he would not attempt to escape from Heatherwood?"

"I know the whole story, dear lady," answers Belden, sadly. "But it is not what I believe, or what his old comrades believe, that weighs in this case. The evidence before that old court, he himself will tell you, is sufficient to convict, and, loyal as I am to my government and my flag, I wish to God he had never risked falling again into our hands."

"Then you believe——"

"I believe Secretary Stanton to be implacable. Ah! no," he adds, mournfully, as she glances quickly, fearfully, first at Fairfax, then at him, as though she would say, in mercy do not let our kinsman hear such dreadful news, "it will do us no good to blind our eyes. Fairfax and I have talked it all over. It is nothing new to him. You still have warm and influential friends at Washington. Let me urge you to lose no time. See them or write them to be in readiness to act in mass on Stanton the instant he learns that Fairfax is here. In all his pressure of care and duty the list of prisoners has not yet been read to him, but sooner or later some one, hopeful of reward, will tell him, and then——"

"Then what, general?"

"Then his life will not be worth a penny."

The impressive silence that follows, broken only by the convulsive sobbing of Miss Heatherwood, lasts but a moment. At the door of the tent appears a corporal of the guard. "The officer of the day's compliments. The fifteen minutes are up, sir;" then, "and the sentry says there's a man here to report to General Belden."

"Tell him to wait," is the brief answer. "Mrs. Heatherwood, you will let me see you to your carriage?" adds Belden, gently. "We must respect the order, or even such brief privileges may be withdrawn."

Sobbing violently, Belle Heatherwood has risen, her fair head bowed upon her bosom, her handkerchief, wet with her tears, close pressed to her face. The young officer of the guard, with twitching lips and blinking eyes, stands awkwardly by. On the narrow walk at the side of the tent, some unseen foot stirs roughly the gravel, and a voice is heard: "Don't go; the general says wait." Then, more sharply, "Halt! I say," and the sound of quick footfalls ceases. Paying no heed to what is transpiring without, Colonel Fairfax bends impulsively and throws his arm about the quivering form of the fair girl and presses one long kiss upon her brow. There is a moment of clasping hands and choking adieu, and' then another voice. At the tent door stands a strange officer in the uniform of a captain; the gold cord on his trousers and the dark ground of his shoulder-straps announce him to be of the staff.

"General Belden," he says, respectfully, extending an official envelope.

Belden whirls quickly upon him. "Ah! Captain Wallace, orders—for me?"

"From the major-general commanding, sir. He goes to inspect the lines along the Potomac, to be gone a week, and is ordered by telegraph to leave you in command in his absence. There are instructions affecting—this gentleman," he adds, uneasily, with a glance at Fairfax.

Tearing open the despatches, Belden reads with paling face. Then both hands drop in helpless sorrow.

"Well, old man?" says Fairfax, a sad smile on his wan face, as he holds forth a long, slim, sinewy hand.

"It has come, dear old friend," is the answer, with something very like a sob. "They order you to Federal Hill. They order me to be your jailer."

CHAPTER XXVI.

SAD and anxious faces were seen on every side that hot July in Baltimore. The thrill of wild anticipation, of coming triumph, with which was hailed the news that Lee once more had invaded the North gave place to a lethargy of despair. Many households in Maryland were in mourning. Black was seen on every side in Baltimore. With fearful loss the daring army of the South had been driven from Pennsylvania, leaving behind it many a chivalrous leader and thousands of its best and bravest men. It was one thing for gentlemen to die in the battle front fighting for the cause they had espoused,— even in their agony of grief Southern wives and mothers found deep consolation in the thought,— but it was far different to see a loved and honored soldier of their faith threatened with a felon's death upon the scaffold. Baltimore went wild with grief and helpless rage over the stories spread on every side concerning Fairfax. Though still bedridden and enfeebled, he had been dragged, said rumor, from comparative comfort and a clean and airy tent, and despite unhealed wounds was thrust into a foul dungeon, the prey of rats and vermin, chained, like Bonnivard at Chillon, to a pillar below the level of the waters, denied food, raiment, the actual necessities of life, deprived of all means of communicating with friends, weighed down with cannonballs and other non-portables, subjected to daily and nightly torture, awakened every minute by brutal sentries if he slept. Just heaven! what didn't the women say and believe? Without warrant of law, without complete trial, as it was pointed out to them, even the Iron Secretary could not order his execution, and thereby were they convinced that since Stanton dared not hang his prisoner at once he meant to drive him mad or kill him by slow torture. Even Southern sympathizers knew that if a military commission could complete the trial of the hapless Virginian, there was evidence enough on which to hang him. The question was, How soon could the court get to work and finish the case? How soon might not the impatient Secretary decide to settle the matter out of court? All Baltimore realized that Fairfax was in peril of his life, in danger of a shameful death; and even the contemplation of the fact that gentlemen like André, patriots like Nathan Hale, and impulsive boys like Mumford had died for their principles at the rope's end, brought no consolation to the countless friends of the imprisoned soldier.

Yet to the privileged observer Floyd Fairfax was a happier man than the Union general charged by War Department orders with the defence of Baltimore and the safe-keeping of the spy. So far from the former's being chained in a dungeon beneath the lapping waters, he had the run of a high and airy room, cool as anything could be under the blazing sun of late July in a Maryland town. He had ice in abundance, flowers in profusion, bath-tub, books, stationery, clean linen, an excellent physician, and at least one devoted friend, his old comrade, his new custodian, Grosvenor Belden. True, only these two were permitted to visit him, only such letters could reach him from without as were inspected by the commanding general, only such letters could he send as the general could certify did not convey more than the stern orders of the Secretary would countenance. Four days had elapsed since his transfer from the hospital camp, and in no wise physically had he suffered, while Belden raged at heart over the order which condemned him to such duty, even while Fairfax thanked heaven that it was Belden and no other who was charged with his safe-keeping. What sorrow and humiliation and possible indignity had not been spared him through this knightly foe and faithful friend who came by day and night to counsel and to cheer! To Fairfax Belden strove to hold out hope of kindly consideration of his plight. To himself, who alone knew the full tenor of the Secretary's instructions, he admitted no hope whatever.

Another thing that gave him grave concern was the fact that his superior, the absent commander of the department, was ordered to hasten his return to his post, and this meant that his, Belden's, charge could be but temporary, and all opportunity for ameliorating the lot of his old comrade would be denied him with the other's coming; for, like more than one creation of the war, both North and South, the major-general, when at safe distance from the front, was tremendous in the blows he dealt the foe. Everything Belden could do through friends at Washington he had done, even to the rousing of Stanton's wrath against himself and a renewal of Stanton's warning that he'd have no more of this giving aid and comfort to the enemy. It wasn't enough that gentlemen should fight like Paladins in the field; there were statesmen, heaven save the mark! who would have had their soldiers trample on a prostrate foe, and smite, like jealous, raging women, the face uplifted to implore a victor's mercy. We had them North and South,—the men who bullied helpless wives and daughters in New Orleans, or starved and shot their captives in the stockades of Macon and Andersonville.

It was a lovely Sunday evening. The soft breeze from the Chesapeake was drifting over the heated roofs of the city and cooling the faces of the thronging soldiery at the forts. Out on the ramparts swarmed the defenders, now that the sun had sunk below the western horizon, and the flags that all day long unfurled over Federal Hill and frowning Fort McHenry had fluttered downward like gayly plumaged birds to sleep until the coming of the morrow's sun. Through the heavily barred windows of his prison Floyd Fairfax looked out over a bustling yard, bounded by rude wooden barracks and dotted here and there with snowy canvas. North and south the view was just the same,—barracks, bayonets, blue-clad soldiery sauntering ever by, many looking at his gridironed casement with not unkindly interest in their unlifted eyes; some even venturing, half awkwardly, a shy salute. Of the city, the harbor, the far green fields, the dancing waters of the bay, the distant forests, he could see nothing. Life was hemmed in, circumscribed, by the pitiless accompaniments of war, and doubled sentries, with muskets capped and bayonets fixed, paced beneath his curtainless windows, peered in, by order, every few minutes day and night, while others, supervised by an officer from his tent door not ten paces off, kept vigil at the entrance that was proof against all machinations or temptation. They were keepers of each other's honor as well as of the prisoner. There could be no buying an entire guard. There could be no possibility of escape. Even if Floyd Fairfax should evade their vigilance, every loop-hole of the fort was guarded, every approach picketed. Sentry after sentry would bar his way. One after another every scheme proposed in rebel Baltimore was given up as hopeless. Floyd Fairfax was doomed.

Just as twilight settled down an open carriage, at sight of which guards and sentries stood rigidly at attention, came driving rapidly up the dusty road, whirled unhindered past the guard-house, and drew up in front of the prison door-way. Promptly the officer of the guard opened the carriage door and offered a white gloved hand to assist the tall young general officer to alight. Even then they noticed, officers and men, that Belden's face was graver, sadder than before. Followed by the doctor who was driving with him and by an orderly who sprang, basket-laden, from the box, and escorted by the officer of the guard, the little party entered and walked on through a corridor that resounded to their footsteps. Presently out came the lieutenant, met at the threshold by his red-sashed superior, the officer of the day.

"Thank God for small favors!" was the instant salutation of the junior. "We're to be relieved from jail watching anyhow. Orders have come to send him to Fort Lafayette."

"You don't say so! When does he go?"

"To-morrow some time. A guard is to come for him at reveille."

Then sergeant looked to soldier, and soldier to his mate, and the faces showed that even then in the sympathy excited by the tidings there was greater sense of comfort and relief. The news went from group to group, from soldiers under arms and in equipments to fellows dawdling about the barracks in their shirt sleeves, to others strolling townward on pass till tattoo, and there was quite a gathering at respectful distance when once again the young commander came striding forth, his forage-cap, as was his wont, pulled well down over his eyes.

"Is it true, general?" asked the soldierly captain, whose red sash, crossed from shoulder to hip, bespoke the officer of the day.

"Sadly true," said Belden, gravely. "Dr. Morrow remains with him awhile, but I have to drive to McHenry. This weather is too hot for horseback exercise. The usual orders, captain. I'll be back later to-night."

"The usual orders, lieutenant," said the senior to the officer of the guard. "It's our last night at this kind of work, thank God! All the more reason that it be thorough. See that your men understand their night orders. I shall begin questioning before taps."

"The usual orders, sergeant," said the officer to the sergeant of the guard. "Instruct your reliefs thoroughly. I'll see to those on post." So saying, he turned to the nearest sentry, facing close before the prison door. "Your special orders, sir?"

Facing his young superior, the soldier tossed his glittering musket across his body to the position of "arms port," and, going straight to the meat of his instructions, ignoring the array of general orders that every wartime sentry knew, he jumped, as directed, to those that met this especial case:

"My special orders are to use the utmost vigilance in preventing the escape of the prisoner known as Fairfax, here confined; to permit no person to enter except the commanding general, the post commander, the officer of the day and guard, the medical officer, and the attendants they direct to accompany them."

"From whom do you take orders?"

"In general, only the commanding general, the post commander, the officers and non-commissioned officers of the guard, but no orders which may permit the prisoner to pass this door-way will be recognized except when given by the commanding general in person or by his superiors in presence of the post commander."

"No cross-questioning was needed. Only keen-witted, clear-headed men, the pick of a clean-cut American regiment, were chosen for this duty. The lieutenant found his flank sentries equally well instructed, with the addition that bullet or bayonet or both were to be used should the prisoner seek egress by the windows overlooking the sentry post. They were chatting in low tones, the officers and non-commissioned officers of the guard, as to what was the purport of this move to Lafayette, "the Bastile of the North," the isolated fortress that stood at the narrows of New York harbor, when the doctor and the orderly came forth, and the former's eyes were wet.

"Yes," he said, in answer to questioning glances. "There is a possibility that he may be removed before dawn. The general has begged that the ignominy of fetters may not be enforced, and that he may send him around by sea instead of by the scorching railway. The 'Narragansett' sails at daylight, and the answer may be here any moment."

"The basket was—all right, I suppose?" said the captain, dubiously. He could take no chances with Stanton at the head of things.

"Clean linen and the like," said the doctor, briefly. "You'll hardly doubt your general, I suppose?"

"There are generals I might doubt," was the answer, "but not him," he added, as Belden's carriage once more entered the gate-way just as the drums and fifes struck up the long, wailing prelude of tattoo.

Preoccupied and sad, Belden passed his saluting comrades without a word, and spent ten minutes in the dimly lighted room. The sentry at the northward window said that Fairfax had been writing, and gave the general two letters, after which they clasped hands and talked in low tones.

And even when the general came forth the New-Englander, the officer of the day, with the caution of his Connecticut training, sought further information at the fountain-head:

"If the order should come, general, will you bring it, or haow?"

"I shall come myself, sir," was the answer. "I have asked this favor, backed by the doctor's certificate that a hot day's journey by rail might be fatal to a man just recovering from the blow of a clubbed musket on the brain, and the department will hold me responsible, doubtless, for his safe delivery aboard the 'Narragansett.' Now, doctor, if you are ready."

The orderly sprang upon the box. The doctor stepped in by the general's side. The carriage drove rapidly away. At Barnum's their inquiry was for telegrams. Two had come, brought from head-quarters but a moment before. The first announced that the major-general commanding would return by noon the following day. The second Belden read, then crushed in his hand, while a flush of indignation leaped to his face and fire glowed in his honest, brave blue eyes. A moment later, like a caged tiger, he was pacing up and down his room, Dr. Morrow silently watching him.

"Read that!" exclaimed the young soldier, at last, as he tossed the crumpled paper to his friend. "It's as much as saying that I myself am attainted. By God, Dr. Morrow!" he continued, as he turned, with blazing eyes, upon the calm practitioner, "I'll fight for my flag as long and as hard as any man, but I'll be damned if I can be hired to kick a gallant soldier when he's down."

"Quiet, quiet, general," was the surgeon's soothing reply, as he picked up the paper and slowly spread it out upon the table. "Walls have ears, key-holes eyes; chimneys, sofas, closets, corridors are packed with spies. That assertion of yours is enough to send you to Lafayette as well as Fairfax. Let's see what the Grand Panjandrum sayeth:

"'WAR DEPARTMENT, WASHINGTON, July —, '63.
"'GENERAL G. BELDEN, U.S.V.,
"'Temporarily Commanding, Baltimore, Maryland:

"'Your request not favorably considered. The Secretary of War directs immediate and unhesitating compliance with his orders concerning the prisoner Fairfax.' Hum, So and So, Adjutant-General. Now, my dear friend, to be frank with you, I am glad of this. You've been fretting yourself into a fever over Fairfax. You don't know it, but you're a sick man this minute. I've been watching you all day. Your pulse is rattling away as it never did under fire, and your temperature is at fever heat, nothing less. Now, I can do what I couldn't do if Fairfax were to be sent by the 'Narragansett,'— order you to bed, give you cooling and soothing medicine, and fetch you out in time for the duties of the morning. Come, lad," he added, soothingly, placing his hand on his commander patient's shoulder, "I'm in earnest. No; you can't go to the Heatherwoods' to-night. You're going to bed at once. I'll send the messenger to Eutaw Street, and will follow him as soon as I've got you to sleep."

An hour later, like a tired child, the wearied, troubled soldier surrendered to the drowsy influences of the doctor's cooling, soothing draught, and Morrow tiptoed from the room. When Morrissey, the veteran orderly, stole in to get the general's boots and uniform to brush them for the coming day, the general was sleeping the sound sleep of exhaustion, and the faithful Irishman bent a long, wistful look upon the loved commander he had followed from the far frontier, and his hand trembled as, to the bundle of boots and clothing, he added the general's handsome sash and belt, his sword, forage-cap, and gauntlets.

CHAPTER XXVII.

The patrol of the provost-guard, a little earlier that evening, had halted a tall soldier in the uniform of the cavalry, who was coming briskly down the hill from the direction of the convalescent camp. So far from showing annoyance or disquietude, as was often the case at such interruption, the soldier stood with confident mien and promptly presented his papers, standing rigidly at attention while the officer closely inspected them. There was no flaw. They were all in precise and regular form,—Private Lawrence Bell, Troop "C," —th U. S. Cavalry, a convalescent patient U. S. General Hospital, etc., etc., on recommendation of the chief surgeon was granted five days' furlough, with permission to visit relatives in Philadelphia; was to return to said hospital by 9.30 P.M. on the 27th day of July, 1863, or be considered a deserter. Said soldier was six feet two inches in height, blue eyes, fair hair, light complexion, and was by occupation a clerk,—that occupation being the one almost invariably given by every enlisting soldier who had presumably known better days—but no trade. The furlough was signed by various officials, and was countersigned by the provost-marshal, so that for at least two or three days Trooper Bell was free to come and go, his own master so long as he behaved himself.

"Where are you going now?" asked the officer.

"To meet some old comrades, sir, down by Camden Station. They have a theatre pass till midnight; then I'll take the train to Philadelphia." The answer was prompt and respectful.

"You have a long walk for a man recently wounded," said the lieutenant, still glancing over the furlough.

"I'll take a cab, sir, at the square, if the lieutenant has no objection."

"Oh, of course not. It's all right if you have money to throw away."

"We never could save money in our regiment, sir," said the trooper, with a quiet smile that showed the strong white teeth underneath the drooping moustache, and lightened for a moment the tired, almost pathetic, look about the deep-blue eyes. He received respectfully, yet with an unconscious dignity of manner, the papers returned to him, saluted with punctilious deference, and then, though his fine face clouded with instant thought and anxiety as soon as he was free, went quietly on his way, followed by the regard of more than one pair of eyes in the patrol.

"That man looks soldier enough to be a colonel any day," was the muttered comment of the lieutenant, "and I've seen him somewhere—in better clothes." Then the silent squad marched on.

But the driver of the waiting cab diverged from the route to Camden Station before he'd gone three-quarters of a mile, and as the city clocks were striking eleven, reined up in a side street near an open square. The soldier sprang forth, shot into a dark alley-way, and the cab whipped up again. In ten minutes it was back, its lamps gleaming opposite the end of the alley. A gate opened a few paces away, and a woman's voice, low, intense, prayerful, murmured, "I shall spend the hours on my knees. Oh, God speed, God bless you, my boy!" There was a lingering handclasp, but no response.

"To the stable," was the muttered order, as Bell resumed his place, with a bulky parcel on his arm, and again the light vehicle darted away, this time turning sharp about and threading a course through the side streets, past shops and dwellings, dark or dimly lighted, until at last it hauled up at a corner in rear of some massive buildings, and Bell, bundle laden, stepped out, handed the driver a greenback, briefly said "Good-night," and, wasting no further words, strode calmly and confidently into the doorway of a roomy stable, passed on to a harness-room at the rear, and there, polishing a pair of high boots and hissing away, trooper fashion, at his task, sat Morrissey.

"Which?" muttered Bell, as he passed him by.

"The second, the door av it's open on this side," was the Irishman's answer, and in a moment Bell's bundle was exchanged for one that lay in the depths of a closed carriage, standing with others under an open shed. A paved court-yard lay beyond, and farther still were the walls and windows of a big hotel. Presently back came the tall trooper again.

"Now, Morrissey, there's no time to lose. The doctor's gone probably. Run up to the room for ten minutes, and then, mind now, only three drinks, just enough, old boy, so that they can see it when you order the carriage. No more till after you pick me up at the side entrance. Carrick will drive as usual, and you saddle while Carrick is hitching in."

Together, bundle laden, the two soldiers passed by a rear stairway used by the servants only, up to the corridors of the old hotel. Morrissey softly entered the general's room; Bell passed on to one a few steps beyond and locked the door behind him.

Midnight and the bells of the city had ceased their solemn chiming. The roysterers among the various resorts along the wharves were scattering to their undesired roosts before the bayonets of the hated patrol. The dark shadows of the ugly brown barracks on the height were unrelieved by the light of a solitary lamp. Out on the northward slope a pacing sentry looked down upon the placid harbor, hemmed by gloomy forests of masts and cordage, by black and frowning warehouses. The silent streets were outlined by dim, yellow dots of gas-lamps, and farther down the broadening estuary the surface of the waters sparkled with the faces of the myriad stars and the riding lights of the ships that lay at anchor, some within the point, others still farther beyond and under the bristling ramparts of Fort McHenry. There they floated, store-ships, transports, merchantmen, and, hovering close at hand, watching them like marine sheep-dogs, the few men-of-war, where,—

> "Here and there a twinkling port reflected on the deep
> In many a wavy shadow showed their sullen guns asleep."

No breath of air was stirring. A belated watch striking eight bells aboard a distant bark, full two minutes after the dull booming of the city towers had ceased, sent his tinkling knell to the departed day, sweet, clear, and vibrant, quivering like silver string upon the night, and the dreaming sentry at the gateway, his thoughts wandering far homeward to the hills of the Connecticut Valley, whirled about at the sudden crunch and sputter of horses' hoofs coming rapidly up the sharp incline, and his bayonet clashed with unusual menace as it came down to the charge, while stern and sharp the challenge rang out, "Who comes there?"

"Frind wid the counthersign," responded a loud, jovial, yet thick Milesian voice, as the coming horseman slackened speed.

"Halt! Dismount! Corporal of the guard, frind wid the counthersign," responded the sentry, keen to the customs of war in like cases, yet, because of the interruption to his visions of home and loved ones, venting his spleen in mischievous and not unrecognizable imitation of the Celtic accent. "It's the general's orderly, Morrissey," he muttered, as the corporal came darting out of the guard tent, rifle in hand, to inspect the midnight intruder.

"Boonesborough, and be damned to ye!" was Morrissey's intemperate response to the demand for the soldier credentials required by the regulations; "and I can lick the wooden clock-maker that masquerades there as a soldier on yon post. D'ye hear that, you?" and it was patent to the military eye and ear that the general's orderly had had a drop too much; "an' I'd do it now if ye'd sthep out av your belts and onto the grass yonder, but that the gineral's jist behind. Turr'n out your gyard, ye lousy son av a wooden nutmeg——" But the coming crash of hoofs and whirr of carriage-wheels put sudden end to his impudence. The senior officer of the guard came springing from his tent within the gate-way. Several of the guard seized their rifles, as though expectant of the order to fall in. The carriage reined up almost in their midst before the lieutenant had time to further question its exhilarated advance guard. The light of the guard lantern fell full on the clear-cut, soldierly face at the right window of the carriage; on the forage-cap pulled down to the brows of the keen blue eyes; on the well known drooping moustache sweeping outward at the ends and the pointed imperial; on the muscular throat, with the velvet collar of the general officer; on the broad, square shoulders dotted by the glistening silver stars.

"Fall in the guard!" shouted the sergeant at the sight, but there was instant protest in low, firm tone from the carriage window.

"Never mind the guard, sir. I do not wish to inspect. Let my orderly ride in ahead, if you please, and keep the gate open a few minutes for me. He has given the countersign, I presume."

The lantern was withdrawn, the officers and the men stood at the salute as the carriage again moved on. There was another and briefer parley at the tent of the officer of the prison guard, and the sentries at the door-way of the rude wooden building in which Fairfax was confined faced outward and stood at the carry, while the well-known form of the handsome young general emerged from the closed carriage, halted one moment as though to assure the lieutenant, who hastened to join him, and then passed on into the dark interior, followed by the officer and his sergeant with the keys.

In a moment these latter came forth and found Morrissey once more in saddle, and, consequently, even more independently truculent than if only in liquor, saying opprobrious things to the silent sentries about volunteers in general and Connecticut Yankees in particular. A general officer's orderly is a man of consequence, even though garbed as a private soldier, and while the lieutenant hastened away to notify the captain and officer of the day of the important arrival, the sergeant strove to smooth things over. "Any other Mick," he said next day,

"I'd have flattened out with the butt of my gun, but General Belden's man was sacred." To the scandal of the service, after sarcastic reference to the warriors at the outer gate, Trooper Morrissey had the hardihood to produce a flask from his saddle-bag and to take a long, gurgling pull at the contents by way of drinking health and better manners to his hearers, who, hailing from the land of steady habits and thrifty occupations, were a living reproach to so representative a son of the sod and of "the old arrmy."

"You'll be so drunk in ten minutes you'll tumble off your horse, man," said the sergeant, in dismay. "The general can't help seeing you're half-seas over now. Hush! He's calling.—Yes, sir, I'll send him right in." But the tall, commanding form appeared at the door.

"Morrissey, ride down to the wharf and see if the boat is in from the 'Narragansett,' and let me know at once."

"Yis, gineral." And the Irishman, with impressive salute, clattered away to the gate. The officers of the day and guard were hastening together to the prison at the moment and heard the orderly as he started.

"The general sent him to see if a boat was at the wharf from the 'Narragansett,'" was the sergeant's explanation.

"Thank God!" said the junior officer again. "They've got some mercy for the poor fellow after all." On tiptoe the captain stepped within the hallway, but the door to Fairfax's room was again closed. A faint light gleamed through a crack at the sill, but he could hear or see nothing without standing there and lifting the hinged shutter to the grated aperture, and something told him that this was not appropriate in presence of the general commanding. Chatting in low tones, once more the officers stood together under the starlight. The sergeant spoke of the evident intoxication of the Irish orderly, and wondered that the general hadn't seen it. The driver explained,—the same who drove on the open carriage at dusk,—"Morrissey," said he, "is a character. He was the general's orderly in his old regiment out on the plains, and he hasn't touched a drop for weeks, but he thinks almost as much of this Mr. Fairfax as he does of the general. They were both his officers in the same regiment until Virginia seceded. Morrissey took a drink or two when the permission came to send Mr. Fairfax round by sea. Don't mind anything he says. He'll be sorry for it in the morning, and I'll look after him all right."

"When'd the telegram come?" asked the captain.

"I don't know, sir. Morrissey routed me out about an hour ago; said the general wanted the closed carriage at once. It'd just got there then, I reckon. What keeps 'em, d'you s'pose?"

The officer of the day stepped round to the flank where the sentry was silently pacing. A faint light, but no sound, came from the barred window. Only by standing on a bench could he look in, and this he shrank from doing. "I stepped up there, sir," said the sentry, "when I saw the light, but the general, he came to the window and told me never mind, he'd come with news for the prisoner."

News, indeed! Starting from a troubled sleep at the touch of a hand upon his arm and the murmur of a voice, Floyd Fairfax gazed up eagerly at the dimly outlined form bending over his bed, and stammered, "Who-o-who says this? I do not understand. Who are you?"

"Ask no questions, Fairfax," was the whispered answer. "Your life depends on it. Make no noise. I'm here to lead you to safety. Your friends are waiting for you barely ten miles away. My carriage is here at the door under a general's orders and escort. None dare stop it. Listen, I say," for the Virginian would have interrupted. "I must strike a light in a moment and you must hurry into your clothes. Now, I warn you solemnly, not an exclamation, not a sound!" And with that the shadowy visitor turned to the table. A match scratched and sputtered. The blue flame feebly shone a moment; then clear and strong a yellow light spread over the curtainless room and revealed in outline the tall, stalwart figure of an officer in Union uniform. His waist was girt with the yellow sash and gold-barred belt of a general. From the bed came a gasp of incredulity and amaze, but the stranger never turned. He lighted the candle. Then leaving it on the table all." On tiptoe the captain stepped within the hallway, but the door to Fairfax's room was again closed. A faint light gleamed through a crack at the sill, but he could hear or see nothing without standing there and lifting the hinged shutter to the grated aperture, and something told him that this was not appropriate in presence of the general commanding. Chatting in low tones, once more the officers stood together under the starlight. The sergeant spoke of the evident intoxication of the Irish orderly, and wondered that the general hadn't seen it. The driver explained,—the same who drove on the open carriage at dusk,—"Morrissey," said he, "is a character. He was the general's orderly in his old regiment out on the plains, and he hasn't touched a drop for weeks, but he thinks almost as much of this Mr. Fairfax as he does of the general. They were both his officers in the same regiment until Virginia seceded. Morrissey took a drink or two when the permission came to send Mr. Fairfax round by sea. Don't mind anything he says. He'll be sorry for it in the morning, and I'll look after him all right."

"When'd the telegram come?" asked the captain.

"I don't know, sir. Morrissey routed me out about an hour ago; said the general wanted the closed carriage at once. It'd just got there then, I reckon. What keeps 'em, d'you s'pose?"

The officer of the day stepped round to the flank where the sentry was silently pacing. A faint light, but no sound, came from the barred window. Only by standing on a bench could he look in, and this he shrank from doing. "I stepped up there, sir," said the sentry, "when I saw the light, but the general, he came to the window and told me never mind, he'd come with news for the prisoner."

News, indeed! Starting from a troubled sleep at the touch of a hand upon his arm and the murmur of a voice, Floyd Fairfax gazed up eagerly at the dimly outlined form bending over his bed, and stammered, "Who-o-who says this? I do not understand. Who are you?"

"Ask no questions, Fairfax," was the whispered answer. "Your life depends on it. Make no noise. I'm here to lead you to safety. Your friends are waiting for you barely ten miles away. My carriage is here at the door under a general's orders and escort. None dare stop it. Listen, I say," for the Virginian would have interrupted. "I must strike a light in a moment and you must hurry into your clothes. Now, I warn you solemnly, not an exclamation, not a sound!" And with that the shadowy visitor turned to the table. A match scratched and sputtered. The blue flame feebly shone a moment; then clear and strong a yellow light spread over the curtainless room and revealed in outline the tall, stalwart figure of an officer in Union uniform. His waist was girt with the yellow sash and gold-barred belt of a general. From the bed came a gasp of incredulity and amaze, but the stranger never turned. He lighted the candle. Then leaving it on the table so that when he faced the astonished Virginian its beams would fall upon his back, he calmly twirled upon his heel and stood before the prisoner, erect, silent, almost stern.

"Belden! Belden! In God's name, are you mad?" was the stifled cry, as Fairfax, with staring eyes, fell back upon his pillow, and now there was command in the stern low tone and uplifted hand.

"Silence, man! and dress instantly! What you see your guards see, and believe," was the whisper. "Now I have orders to give, but you get up at once."

Yet when the general returned, having despatched Morrissey on his errand, Fairfax still sat like one in a daze, a look of awe, if not almost of terror, on his face, for now the light, dim though it was, fell full on the features of the visitor as he re-entered. Shrinking back, the Virginian stared, speechless one moment, then came the words,—

"Face and form you are Belden. Voice and carriage you are not. Only one man I ever knew had your voice, and he—— In God's name, who are you, if not Jack Lowndes risen from the dead?"

"Jack Lowndes, whom you killed at Bull Run, but forgot to bury," was the placid response. "Now, will you dress, or go to Lafayette at reveille and be hanged as a spy the next day? Damnation, man, if you're not dressed in five minutes, I'll call my guards and pitch you into the carriage, neck and crop!"

Just as the solemn bells of Baltimore were striking one, and in silvery, mellow tinkling the swarm of ships chimed their double strokes, there issued from the dark portal of the prison two tall and manly figures, the one on the right buttoned to the throat in the double-breasted frock of a general officer of the Union army, his belt, sash, and shoulder-straps gleaming in the light of the sergeant's lantern, the one on the left, leaning slightly on his conductor's arm, attired in worn Confederate gray.

"I relieve you of your charge, gentlemen," said the former, in the same low, grave tones. "Captain, will you kindly assist Colonel Fairfax? That leg won't bear much weight as yet."

"May I not thank you, gentlemen," said the Virginian, with high-bred courtesy, as he took his seat, "for the consideration and kindness that you have shown me?" He extended his slim white hand. Captain and lieutenant both grasped and shook it, and wished him happier fortune. "Morrissey will return for the colonel's luggage in the morning," said the general. "He should be here now. Good-night, gentlemen."

"Good-night, sir." And with these parting words the carriage whirled quickly towards the gate, and past the post of the main guard. Here there was a momentary halt and parley.

"I beg pardon, general," said a voice; "I'm officer of the guard, sir; I'm afraid your orderly's been drinking. He's just tumbled off his horse, and I don't think he can mount again."

"The scoundrel!" exclaimed the brigadier, impatiently. "Where is he?" And Morrissey, limp and protesting, was lugged to the carriage door.

"Sure, the gineral knows I can ride anything on four legs, drunk or sober," was his maudlin cry, and then his own long legs gave way under him.

"Here, pitch him right in, sergeant! I've had to pull the old rascal through many a scrape before. Give me the rein of his horse and give the horse a whack when we start, and he'll follow all right. Go on, driver. Lie still, there, Morrissey. Good-night." And so down the incline they sped to the silent street below, and away towards the deserted wharves. But the minute they were out of sight and hearing of the sentry-posts, Morrissey sprang up and began to squirm out of his trooper jacket, and the general spoke,—

"Off with that uniform, Fairfax! Once more you don the Union blue, sir. Once more you've got to ride for your life in an old Second Cavalry saddle. Think of the night the Comanches chased you into camp on the Wichita, and ride like the wind for old Carrick's place—you remember it—out towards the Point. You'll be on the Eastern Shore, safe and sound, at daybreak."

But still the Virginian hesitated. "One moment, Lowndes. You've learned your part and my past to perfection,—at Heatherwood, I suppose. What rank you hold, what name you bear on the Federal rolls, I cannot guess, but this night you're in masquerade as Belden. Give me your word that he will be in no wise involved, or by God! I go back to prison."

"You can't. You're my prisoner. General Belden is sleeping in his bed, the doctor by his bedside. It will be proved he never left the room."

"Then you and this gallant old friend and comrade, Morrissey. Your honor as an officer—his liberty."

"All that was officer in me was killed at Bull Run. As for Morrissey, nothing can be proved but that he was obeying the orders of the man everybody believed to be the general commanding. A plain drunk is the extent of his offending,—a soldier sin he'd venture any day for a thousandth part of what this will net him."

And still Fairfax hung back and strove to repel the efforts of Morrissey to aid him out of his coat. "There's one thing more I've got to know, Lowndes," and the dull glare of a gas-lamp shining for a swift moment on his face showed the tension of his thought. "Before Bull Run I believed you stood—between me and my most cherished hope. What does it mean that you, a Union man, are daring, God only knows what penalties, to save me?"

"It means simply," answered his companion, slowly, as the carriage sped by the switch-lights of the railway, and jolted over rough, unpaved streets at the outskirts, "that no Union man who knows the truth would have you hanged as a spy. We fight in fair field, sir. You assumed that disguise for—a woman's sake, not for Virginia or the South."

For another moment Fairfax could not speak, his voice failing him through the force of his emotion. Words of further gratitude sprang to his lips, yet died there. At last, "Lowndes," he murmured, "may God grant me life to show my appreciation. I have misjudged you utterly. But if I should be killed——"

"You *will* be if you are not out of that dress and into this in five minutes. Your pass as orderly is in the right hand saddle-bag, the countersign is Boonesborough, in case you meet patrols, as you probably will. Quick now, you have to mount and we must leave you in a minute. Carrick's boat is waiting for you at the old bank; the Heatherwoods planned it all."

And though the speaker's lips set tight as he finished the words, he went on unflinchingly. Three minutes later the carriage stopped.

"I can go no farther, sir, without danger of being heard by the guard at the cross-roads," murmured the driver.

The occupants stepped out upon the dusty side street. Away to the northward, behind them, a dull glow in the sky and the dim lights underneath marked the site of the city. Around them were open fields and scattered houses. Quickly Morrissey, as he would have done of old, brushed the dust from the saddle of the wondering horse, then held the mud-flecked hood of the stirrup. Slowly, painfully the tall Virginian swung into saddle, and sat there, attired from top to waist in the uniform of the Union trooper, and his dull gray trousers, thrust into long boots, would hardly be distinguishable at night from dusty blue. Around his waist Morrissey clasped the sabre-belt. "Lord love ye, sorr, I was niver a finer-looking arrderly meself, even when I sthrutted in the thracks of Colonel Lee."

A hand-clasp and hearty shake to the sympathetic Irishman, and then, drawing off the gauntlet, Fairfax bent down to the other side.

"Lowndes," he murmured, as his slim hand was somewhat loosely clasped, "there is something yet I must ask, something I cannot fathom,—What has Miss Heatherwood to do with this—infinite service you are doing for me?"

And the answer came with but a moment's delay: "Pretty much everything. Remember now, you are riding for her sake."

CHAPTER XXVIII.

THE devil to pay in Baltimore, indeed! The sunrise guns had hardly boomed from Federal Hill and Fort McHenry, when General Belden, accompanied by his aide-de-camp, who looked somehow as though he'd been up all night,—which it subsequently transpired he had, playing poker with a jovial coterie of junior officers not a block away from Barnum's,—and followed by an orderly and a closed carriage, in which sat Dr. Morrow, rode past the saluting guard and in among the barracks, and looked surprised to see no sentries at the prison.

"Where are your men?" he briefly asked the captain who hurried to his side.

"Why, we took 'em off, sir. I didn't suppose they were to be kept on after the prisoner was removed."

"Prisoner removed! What do you mean?"

The captain turned various colors. Was it possible that Morrissey's whiskey had befuddled the general too.

"Colonel Fairfax was the only prisoner in there, sir, and you took him away at one o'clock."

Belden was off his horse in an instant. "*I* take him off! Man alive, you're dreaming! I haven't been here since ten o'clock last night." And he sprang up the steps and into the dark hall-way. For a moment the officer of the day seemed stricken dumb; then he shouted for his lieutenant and the sergeant of the guard, who came on the run, just as Belden reappeared, pale as a sheet, his cap off, the perspiration starting from his brow. "Quick!" he ordered. "Tell me what you mean? When? How——?"

"Why, General Belden, I'm not dreaming," cried the officer. "These gentlemen were with me. They know. They'll corroborate what I say. It was you, sir, came with a carriage just like this, and Morrissey —only Morrissey had been drinking. Surely you remember, sir. You were dressed exactly as you are now. You had the same carriage, but a different driver. You know, lieutenant. You saw it, sergeant." And with consternation in their faces, the subordinates murmured assent. Morrow had sprung from the carriage and was standing, actually trembling, by the general's side; the latter stood apparently stunned.

"Do you mean he's gone?" gasped the doctor.

"My God! sir, I mean the general himself came and got him,—the only man who *could* take him came and got him," moaned the Connecticut officer, gazing from one to another, as though ready to believe himself the victim of some foul conspiracy against the government.

"And he had this carriage—and Morrissey?" cross-questioned the doctor.

"Yes, sir, this very one."

Morrow looked to the driver, who sat wondering and embarrassed, flicking with his whip-lash at the flies alighting on his horse's twitching flanks.

"It was out, sir, till nearly three o'clock, Carrick driving. 'Twas all covered with mud when I was called this morning. It took four niggers twenty minutes to clean it. Morrissey wasn't to be found anywhere."

Five minutes more and the general was spurring to head-quarters. In half an hour telegrams were flashing to Washington. By six the provost-guard was searching high and low, and secret service men were boarding every boat and train. Morrissey, limp and bedraggled, was hauled from the stable loft, half dazed with whiskey, yet loudly damning everybody for disturbing his rest after he'd "been out wid the gineral half the night." "Where's me haarse? Shure the gineral let him go, afther he'd ordered me to dismount and get inside, breaking the heart av me that had taught him all the cavalry tricks he ever knew. Who was wid us? Nobody but jist Loot'nant Fairfax takin' a ride wid his ould frinds till I went to slape and niver knew nothing till we got back to Barnum's, and the gineral went to his room an' I followed to get his boots and clothes. No man can say I was dhrunk when I could tind to all me jewties like that."

Worse and more bewildering grew the situation as the morning wore on. Morrow declared that, returning from a visit to friends at midnight, he peeped in at his patient and found him soundly sleeping; that again he visited the room at one and at two, and there the general lay like a tired child. Yet hotel employés declared that only a few minutes before twelve, in complete uniform, with sash, belt, and sword, the general had descended to the ladies' parlor, and had then taken Carrick's carriage at the side entrance. The night watchman declared that shortly before three the general returned by the same route and went up to the third floor, Morrissey lurching after him, but without the cap and jacket, belt and sword with which he started. He wore instead a flannel blouse and a battered hat, and was plainly drunk. The general seemed angered at him, yet permitted him to follow to his room. Towards four o'clock the watchman saw another soldier, who had been with Morrissey earlier, go down the back stairs with him from the servants' quarters, where the orderly had a little sleeping-room. This other seemed trying to help the Irishman to the stable, and that was all.

At noon there came officials from Washington to conduct investigations. At 12.30 the major-general returned from the West and was closeted with the new-comers, while Belden, still half dazed and all distress and apprehension, paced in restless misery the adjoining room. At one o'clock all Baltimore was athrill with the news that during the night Colonel Fairfax had been released from prison by General Belden himself, and at two that Belden was in turn a prisoner. Other Union generals accused of disloyalty had languished without trial, one, at least, at Lafayette,—why not Belden? Twice before had he incurred the suspicions of the War Secretary, and no amount of heroic service in the field seemed to counterbalance the attaint of lukewarm patriotism at the rear. Small wonder, either, with treason stalking unrebuked throughout the streets of Northern cities, preached by more than one paper in many a State, practised by mobs of foreign-born citizens and spread far and wide through the venom of the copperhead. Harassed as he was, front, flank, and rear; prejudiced as he had grown to be through reports of Belden's previous record,—his altercation with that sturdy patriot Foulweather; his old comradeship with Stuart, Fitz Lee, Hood, and Fairfax; his early teachings in the old regiment under Sidney Johnston and Robert E. Lee; his alleged intimacy with the Heatherwoods; his avowed sympathy with Fairfax and persistent efforts in his behalf,—these were enough to poison the mind of milder men than Stanton. And when soon after one the despatch reached him over the wires that the returned major-general considered the evidence against Belden such as demanded immediate arrest, the order flashed back instanter. At three that afternoon, overwhelmed with consternation and dismay, General Grosvenor Belden was shut in a close room at head-quarters, with bristling bayonets at the doors, no arrest on honor being deemed sufficient in his case. The Connecticut officers, deprived of their swords, were confined to their tents as possible accomplices. Dr. Morrow, shadowed by secret service men, was fuming about the hotel and head-quarters, protesting against the whole affair, and swearing that Belden had never left his bed from 10.30 until dawn; and Morrissey, also swearing, but after the manner of a pirate, and fighting like a mad man, was lugged to the guard-house, "a thing of shreds and patches."

"All this on or about the 25th day of July, 1863, in or about the city of Baltimore, Maryland," as the laboriously drawn specifications later said. Then, away down along the south shore of the Patapsco was found that very morning a riderless horse with the government brand and cavalry equipments, an orderly's pass for one, Trooper Morrissey, in the off saddle-bag, which receptacle was half-full of soldier traps, including a flask of portentous size, itself half-full of whiskey. "Timothy" was grazing contentedly by the roadside when gathered in by a Maryland farmer, whose face was guileless as he answered the sharp questions of the swift-coming scouts. A famous place for oyster-boats were the flats of the Chesapeake, despite the fact that July was not the famous month for oysters, and the "Narragansett" ploughed her way through quite a fleet of sails after she weighed anchor in the early morning. The soft bosom of the bay was dotted by peaceable craft in dozens, for crabbing was good and so were clams, and old man Carrick's fishing-place seemed to have been alive at a very early hour that morning, too, for when the scouts came galloping thither between six and seven and asking eagerly whether he had fitted out any parties that morning, Carrick was fain to admit that there were "no less than three come down before sun up." His boys had them somewhere along shore now; but Carrick didn't say for whom was engaged his best boat and oars and oarsmen two days ahead, or who came trotting thither in the dark hours before the dawn and was out of a Yankee uniform and into a Secesh coat before you could say Jack Robinson. That uniform, weighted with stones, was dropped overboard when the little craft was half-way over towards Sparrows' Point. Another, a worn Confederate gray coat, was loaded with railway spikes and pitched over the bridge rail by Morrissey on the homeward way, after which the carriage had rolled swiftly back to Barnum's. Sparrows' was a point on the northeast side of the bay, and while two lusty oarsmen pulled silently out over the dark waters, keeping well away from the riding lights of many a shadowy hull, yet peering eagerly through the faint mists that rose from the placid surface, the old man blessed the stars that had given him such plucky sons, and led the wondering cavalry horse well out upon the roadway, headed him for the dull glow above the westward city, and, with a resounding thwack or two across his outraged haunches, sent him clattering homeward. Long before the "Narragansett" left a streak of foam between the old fishing-pier and the glowing eastern sky, the boys were back and ready to take folks a-fishing should they come,—as speedily they did,—and he who had been their passenger was safely under hatches on a little coasting schooner, far over towards that dreamy, sleepy, old-fashioned region, low lying across the Chesapeake, and known as the "Eastern Shore." Easier was it to find a needle in a haystack than an escaped Confederate when once he reached the drowsy confines of Kent, Queen Anne, or Talbot.

That Colonel Fairfax had been aided by the concerted action of many friends in Baltimore was of course the prompt conviction of all the Union officers. That Belden could have lent himself to the plot was readily believed by quite a number who had no previous knowledge of the man, of the old army, or of the customs of war. The major-general commanding had no doubts whatever, and sneered at those who ventured to entertain them. The men who knew Belden and believed in him were either at the distant front, where they belonged, or languishing from wounds in far-away homes or hospitals. For forty-eight hours the papers were full of exciting detail, and their editorials of denunciation and dismay consequent upon this new exhibition of treason in the camp. For forty-eight hours the name of Belden was held up to execration all over the North, and that of Fairfax as a triple-turned spy and traitor. For forty-eight hours the secret service officials swarmed about the homes of many a prominent family in Baltimore, and once more the Heatherwoods were forbidden to leave their doors. For forty-eight hours loving hearts were praying fervently for further tidings that should have come, signalled or sent through that mysterious agency that proved so subtle and so strong throughout the long four years, yet seemed to falter now. For forty-eight hours at a dozen hearthstones in the old Southern city there dwelt an agony of suspense, for the news so prayed for came not. They whose joy had overflowed at the whispered tidings of the escape now clung to one another shuddering at the vigor of the pursuit, the energy and wrath of the Union leaders, and the probability that prompt action had defeated their well-laid plans and cut off the fugitive's retreat. For forty-eight hours no one entered the Heatherwood house except on government business or by military authority, not even "the butcher, the baker, and the candle-stick maker," and three unhappy women kept their rooms in the second story or gathered for comfort and support by the couch of the gentle mother who seemed at last to have lost hope and courage and to have broken down. By her side knelt her daughter, pallid, silent, tearless. At the window, watching, cat-like, the passers-by and the little groups that, despite the orders of police and patrols, would gather and stare, Laura Waddell, with blazing eyes and burning cheeks, knelt for hours at a time. A light in an opposite dormer-window by night, a shade withdrawn by day, would mean that Fairfax had reached in safety the farmhouse of some trusted friends, by whom he would be safely hidden until opportunity came of slipping over into Virginia again beyond the Union lines. But the longed-for signal was not shown. Once a sad, white face appeared at a lower window just at the gloaming of the second day, and Laura started nervously, eagerly, yet with her hand warned Belle away. Only a mournful shake of the head answered the appealing gaze from the windows of Mrs. Heatherwood's room. There was no news of Fairfax, and, had all been well, they should have heard full thirty-six hours before. It was then that Miss Heatherwood, too, seemed to break down under the strain, and, throwing herself on her knees at her mother's side, burst into a passion of tears.

"Mother! Mother!" she cried; "I must know what it means! I cannot bear such mystery. Who aided him to escape? Who released him from his prison? You know, and you are hiding it from me. I must know. Is Jack alive? Was it Jack? Mother, mother, in mercy tell me," she sobbed aloud. "Where is he? Why do I never hear of him now?"

And drawing the weeping girl to her heart, her own eyes welling over, her pale lips quivering with grief, Mrs. Heatherwood could only answer, "Belle, my child, I wish I did know, I wish I could tell. Just now, even more than news of Floyd, whom I believe to be safe, I would welcome news from Jack."

And that night at 9.30 the officer of the guard sat in his tent, overhauled the few passes, and inspected the few men who had been permitted to leave the enclosure for an evening stroll, and the sergeant checked off the names on the list and sent the returning convalescents to their tents. The half-hour passed and the gates were swinging to when the lieutenant lifted up his head and voice. "Hold on a moment there!" he said; "there's a man short. Oh! Bell's the name. He was due here at 9.30. Five days' furlough. Hasn't he come in?"

"No sign of him yet, sir," was the prompt reply.

"Very well, close the gates. He may turn up within the hour. I'll give him a little leeway, anyhow,—trains may be late."

But the night wore on without him. Another morning flamed on the eastward sky. Again the distant boom from Federal Hill saluted the rising sun, and far and near the first notes of the reveille called the soldiers to the duties of another day. Forty-eight hours, lacking but a few minutes, had passed since the discovery that Colonel Fairfax had been stolen from his guard, and now opposite the name of Trooper Bell on the report submitted for the signature of the surgeon in charge was the single word, "Deserted."

CHAPTER XXIX.

A TROOPER'S LETTER.

"PHILADELPHIA, July 27, 1863.

"MR. GEORGE LOWNDES,

"Willard's Hotel, Washington, D. C.:

"DEAR SIR AND SIRE,—This letter will not startle you as it might have done two years ago, because at that time you believed my troubles—and yours on my account—safely ended. Since then, however, thanks to Colonel Clark, you have felt constrained to renew your search for the missing papers, if not for the missing son, whom, but for the doubt as to those documents, you would have been well content to know was buried.

"So far as you were concerned, it was my intention that that son should be, for all time, dead. His name, his rank, and something, at least, of his past were buried at Bull Run, and you would never again have been troubled by his ghost (and the words with which you drove him from your roof were full warrant for his determination) had not fate reserved him, and you, for unforeseen complications. The life, the honor, the happiness of men and women whom I hold dear are now at stake, and you are the only person I know who can promptly set things right. You, as a man of wealth and social position and a power in local political matters, are now in touch with the Secretary of War. You can establish justice and promote tranquillity. To assure the Honorable Secretary of the truth of all that follows in this letter you have only to cause the following-named officers to appear in person at Washington, to wit:

"Brigadier-General Grosvenor Belden, United States Volunteers, in unmerited arrest, Baltimore, Maryland.

"Brigadier-General Joshua Clark, United States Volunteers, commanding brigade, —th Division, Second Army Corps.

"Major Foulweather, —th United States Cavalry, and be damned to him, in hospital somewhere with a broken leg when it should have been his neck.

"First Lieutenant Robert F. Hamlin, commanding squadron, —th United States Cavalry.

"Major W. H. Morrow, Surgeon United States Volunteers, under the shadows of Baltimore detectives and Barnum's Hotel.

"Then there are ladies, including my sister, whose names need not be dragged into the matter at all.

"As you did me the honor to say that only business propositions would ever be entertained by you in the future, I tender you, for your good offices in this matter, first, the restoration of letters you have vainly sought for,—those in which my mother pleaded with you for justice to me, and promised and vowed certain things in my name which you refused to entertain, and thereby transformed into dead letters. Second, the unexpended portion of the little sum my mother placed in the Park Bank for my use, all of which I drew out in April, '61, and intrusted to other hands. So long as I pursued a course that would bring credit to her son and honor to the name I saw fit to assume, I cherished the first named and drew upon the second. Having now taken upon myself, an enlisted soldier of the United States, the functions of a general court-martial, of the reviewing authority, and of the Secretary of War all in one, and having tried, acquitted, released, and thereby done my best to restore to the cause of the Confederacy, as it happens, a gentleman held as a spy, I am no longer worthy to hold such position of trust and emolument under the general government. I therefore voluntarily withdraw from it, and am no more worthy to be called her son, though quite good enough in my own opinion to be yours. In plain words, sir, I, Jack Lowndes, *alias* Lawrence Bell, a private trooper of the —th United States Cavalry, have given aid and comfort to the enemy by compassing the escape of Colonel Floyd Fairfax, —th Virginia Infantry, and then and thereafter deliberately deserting the service of the United States.

"How did I do it? In this wise: Ever since the week of my most untimely taking on with the regular army old hands have spoken to me of my strong resemblance to their former first lieutenant, Grosvenor Belden, then a captain on General Hooker's staff, later a colonel of Pennsylvania cavalry, and now a brigadier-general of United States Volunteers, always a gallant and distinguished officer and gentleman. The fancied resemblance pleased me, though it didn't flatter. I saw the gentleman in Washington and had the remarkable opportunity of releasing from pawn certain articles of his apparel placed there, candor compels the admission, not by himself, but by an employé of the hotel, who found them too big for his individual use. It pleased me to attire myself as Captain Belden, simply to see if people would recognize in the resurrected militiaman and volunteer, left for dead at Bull Run, and the disinherited knight of your household the resemblance to an officer and a gentleman. In Virginia I had fallen, first, into the hands of the enemy, who, believing me dead, would have buried me alive, thereby reversing the decree of my friends, who, believing me alive, would have buried me dead. Then fate—was it my mother who pointed the way?—led to the scene two of her old and devoted friends, Hester, Lady Heatherwood, and Florence, Lady Fairfax. It was the former who nursed me day and night until she was able to have me transferred from the battle-field to the home of her friend and kinswoman at Leesburg. You will not be grateful to them for their ministrations, but the world will say I should be, and I am. Also am I grateful for their solemn promise that Jack Lowndes should remain numbered with the dead, and for my own that Lawrence Bell would live to serve them loyally. They, under sore stress, have kept their promise to reveal to none but one woman the story of my resurrection. I to the bitter end have kept my self-recorded pledge to lose no opportunity to befriend those they love, even as my mother loved me.

"In the dress and authority of Belden I bore an urgent message from Heatherwood to the Hunt house in the Catoctin Valley. In the guise of Belden I ordered our gunners to withhold their fire on Stuart's battery the day they rode by Heatherwood, and, finally, in the uniform, the equipments, the carriage of Belden, accompanied by Belden's orderly, whom I had first befuddled with liquor and then ordered to call Belden's own driver, I assumed Belden's sole prerogative and set free a gallant soldier, the son of one benefactress, the kinsman of another. If this were not reason enough, there is still one more, to me the most potent of all, but it would probably have no weight with you.

"And now, the Honorable Secretary will not willingly or readily release General Belden, restore him to command, and publicly wipe out the stain. Disaster in his eyes, as we know, has ever demanded a victim. Nor will the newspapers now maligning that gallant and brilliant officer tender the faintest amende when the truth is known. These wrongs are hard for a soldier to bear, and for my share in their infliction I tender General Belden the expression of my deep sorrow that things had to be so. But, under similar circumstances I would do the same again, and down in the bottom of his heart General Belden will thank me for having saved his old friend and cherished comrade from the felon's death that would have been his lot.

"No lighter sentence would have suited our Iron Secretary. The circumstances of his disguise, the place of his capture, the character of the papers found in the pockets of the farmer garb I strove to drown in the Monocacy, but that Foulweather's fellows fished out before they were fairly soaked, all rendered imperative a finding of guilty of being a spy within the Union lines, yet General Belden knows, and I know, spying was the last thing Floyd Fairfax had in view. Belden, being an officer and a gentleman, could not, without dishonor, act on his convictions. Trooper Bell, being only a despised enlisted man, without name, home, or fortune, could and did do what his superiors dare not. The Secretary will say it was a crime in me to release him. I say it would have been a crime to hang him, and that his crime would have been far greater than mine I will submit to the decision of that Immortal Judge in whose sight Edwin M. Stanton and Jack Lowndes, *alias* Bell,—head and foot, respectively, of the army of the United States,—stand on the equal plane of miserable sinners.

"The Secretary and you will say that if I thought

I was right I should have stood my ground and faced my accusers, taken my punishment, and not added the crime of desertion to my already clouded name. In the first place, I have no name. In the second, I have no confidence in military justice as practised under civil supervision such as Stanton's; and in the third place, I do not propose to spend ten years at Dry Tortugas or some other prison because I did what I knew to be right. As to the stigma of desertion that must attach to me, I shall look at it from the point of view of the philosopher in the ranks. The men who knew and served with Jack Lowndes at Bull Run, who charged with Lawrence Bell at Gaines's Mill and Hanover Court-House, who fought by his side the day we saved the gun at Heatherwood, and who were with him in the dash on Hood's right flank at Gettysburg, will say that, even though he has seen fit to wind up his record with the Army of the Potomac by tricking the guards at Federal Hill and retiring from the service of which he was so bright and not over-particular a star, the credit side of his account outweighs the debit. This sounds immensely egotistical, but I mean every word of it.

"In fine, sir, I feel that, so far from bringing discredit on either of my names, I have done honor to both, and as I am now about to assume still another, I hope to cover that, too, with distinction. In another army and another field and with another name, I mean to do battle for our flag 'till the last armed foe expires,' or words to that effect, and should the third name under which I have served my country become eventually known to you as that of a fellow who fought hard and well for the Union's, if not for his name's, sake, I picture the self-complacency with which you will congratulate yourself on having furnished no less than three able-bodied soldiers for the common cause,—all from the one son you kicked out of your house.

"And now, sir, to conclude. I had hoped that my beloved sister would never have to know of my reappearance on this earth unless I could come to her with a record so proud that even you would have been silenced, but I have seen fit to surrender my prospects, the main hope and inspiration thereof being deader than I was at Bull Run. By this time her grief would have been assuaged, and she might have ceased to mourn. To her I shall write by another hand, as I do to the loved household among whom, when banished from your doors, I found shelter, welcome, and infinite patience and mercy. This done, I have but one other obligation to discharge. So soon as General Belden is exonerated you will receive the order for the items of which I spoke.

"This letter you will doubtless consider bitter, insolent, most undutiful, and, as of old, will attribute its tone to over-indulgence in liquor. In this you will err, as you often did before. Wine mellowed what you termed my intractable spirit, filled me with faith, hope, charity,—made all men, even you, my friends. These lines are penned under the austere influences of an abstinence that has been total ever since I got drunk ten months ago, as a man does to neutralize snake-bite, in order to delay my having to testify against Fairfax, at Point of Rocks, until his friends at Frederick could buy off one or more of his jailers.

"Posting this and other letters at midnight, I shall leave Philadelphia at once, and become, as you used to suggest, 'another man.' Your friend, the Secretary, and his friends, the secret service fellows, will lose time in looking for me. With due respect,

"Your son,

"JOHN LOWNDES."

This was the letter placed in the hands of the Secretary of War at noon on the 28th of July. Pallid, trembling with emotion, his eyes full of trouble and dismay, the New Yorker seated himself while the Secretary read. What passed between them later was not told. At one o'clock a despatch was received by an astonished major-general in Baltimore, directing that Brigadier-General Belden be released from arrest and ordered to report in person, accompanied by Surgeon Morrow, to the Secretary of War the following day. So suspicious of trickery was the department commander that he demurred. Not until four P.M. was the order communicated to General Belden, on the arrival of certain officers from Washington. With them came a portly civilian, prominent as a member of the Union League, and held in high consideration by the government. Mr. George Lowndes sent his card to the young brigadier, begged the favor of an interview, was closeted with him and Dr. Morrow half an hour, and then the trio drove to Barnum's, Belden declining to stop and accept the congratulations of the commanding general. Later, an orderly was despatched with a letter to Eutaw Street, where it was received by a young damsel with black eyes and rosy cheeks, who seemed mad with delight and mischief, and who perplexed the shy volunteer by demanding, "You Yankees goin' to hang Floyd Fairfax now, or wait till you get him?" for the shade to the opposite dormer-window was raised, and people with beaming faces had been throwing surreptitious kisses and joyous glances at Madam Heatherwood's window for over an hour. And later still, while the two fair girls were clasped, sobbing, in each other's arms, and Belle and Florence poured out their heart-load of sorrowing confidences, their hopes, their fears, their almost idolatrous praises of Jack's heroism, Jack's self-abnegation, Jack's marvellous exploit as described by Florence,—never realizing, woman-like, the gravity of his offences from the legal and military point of view, never dreaming of the peril in which he had placed himself,—a sorrow-stricken father held long conference with Mrs. Heatherwood in the parlor below. To him at last she recounted the strange events of the two years past, of her discovery of Jack among the desperately wounded, of the promise extorted from her as soon as he could make himself understood,—that she would keep his recovery a secret from all but Mrs. Fairfax and Belle, until later on he could absolve her; of the desperate nature of his case at first,—shot, as he was, straight through the right lung; of how reckless he had later been in her service, even to the extent, all unknown to her, of having the officer's uniform and equipments kept there at Heatherwood; of his donning it for Belle's sake in order that he might ride to the Catoctin Valley, where his pass as orderly would not carry him, and so warn the Hunts to tell Fairfax of how Heatherwood was surrounded and to forbid his coming; of how Jack later managed to destroy Belle's missive to her Virginia kinsman when Foulweather found the trooper at the mansion; of how he saved them from a cannonade and had striven to destroy the evidence against Fairfax. Her tears welled up as she spoke of that night, and of his later conduct, or misconduct, while in the hospital. From the night of Fairfax's first arrest Jack had never seen Belle, nor had he written to her, and when he came as one of the escort with the fever-smitten major, it was only herself, Madam Heatherwood, that he had sent to ask to meet him at the old arbor on the hill-side. It was only herself to whom, later, he unfolded his plans for the release of Fairfax from prison at Federal Hill. She had instantly conferred with the colonel's friends in Baltimore, and, once the prisoner was safely away to Carrick's, the rest was easy. A thousand times over the devoted fellow rewarded her for the little she had done for him, said Mrs. Heatherwood. Yet, as was the case with her daughter, woman-like, she could not see that he had utterly sacrificed himself. Surely the nation, the people, even the government at Washington, would forgive him when they knew all. But how were they ever to know—all?

And in the midst of their conference a card was handed in. General Belden begged to be allowed to pay his respects to Mrs. Heatherwood on the eve of his departure for Washington, and even as the gentle woman turned to greet and welcome him, Aunt Chloe went wheezing up-stairs with a note for Miss Belle.

Not five minutes later, before the first greetings were fairly over, before Mrs. Heatherwood had ceased again to marvel at the resemblance which the silent father sat so mournfully studying, there came the sound of a sudden and heavy fall in the room above. Mrs. Heatherwood looked up in alarm, and then hastened to the hall, for the voice of Florence was heard calling for help. Not knowing what might have happened, Belden himself led the rush up-stairs, but turned back at the door,—it was only a fainting girl who lay there prostrate, and the letter later explained it all, even to that which the loving mother half suspected, yet so long could not understand.

That night, as Mr. Lowndes and the young general paced slowly back to the hotel, the latter heard the full particulars, as related by Mrs. Heatherwood, of the story of the "double" whose existence he had suspected for many a long month. He took the sad old gentleman by the hand. "So far as I am concerned, sir," said he, "your brave son has full forgiveness. I wish I could say it for the authorities. But if ever he need a friend, he can count on me. I shall do my best to find him just so soon as the hue and cry are over."

But neither Belden nor the father had seen the letter over which, late into the night, a loving, sorrowing woman, kneeling by a beloved daughter's side, wept and prayed for hours.

" PHILADELPHIA, July 27.

"There was a time in your past when you told me that a great renunciation was needed before I could hope to win the love of any woman worth the having.

"The day I rode for you to the Catoctins I read such new, sweet promise in your eyes and words that my heart bounded with a hope I never knew before. That day I dared to take your hands in mine and dared to press one kiss upon your forehead,—the first, the last, all in one. The message I bore forbade his coming; your eyes and lips invited me, even though I wore the humblest dress in the hostile blue. That was one day.

"Then came another when, unseen by you, I

watched your agony at your lover's capture, and what I saw and what I heard were more than enough. You and your ever blessed mother had kept my secret, and I had vowed that, come what might, if fate should throw in my way the chance of saving those you loved, I would stop at nothing to keep the faith. I saw again the proofs that your heart was bound up in Floyd Fairfax the day when stern orders compelled me to stand by that open tent and listen to your sobbing, and to hear later—thank God I could not see it!—how his arms enfolded you, how his kisses swept away your tears.

"It was possible for just one man to save him to you, and—it is done. My promise is kept, and though the love I craved is given to a happier man, I have made my great renunciation. It is now, farewell.

"JOHN LOWNDES."

CHAPTER XXX.

A GENERAL court-martial assembled at Fort McHenry, Baltimore, late in August, for the trial of Trooper Luke Morrissey, —th United States Cavalry, "and such other prisoners as may properly be brought before it," and the odd part of the affair was that there were officers who sought the distinction of being brought before it, and who were denied the luxury. An officer might demand a court of inquiry, said the sages of the War Department, and the President might or might not accord it as he felt disposed, but no officer could demand a court-martial. Consequently, released from arrest and restored to duty, the Connecticut officers were denied the privilege of being vindicated by a jury of their peers,—no one of whom, it was asserted, could possibly have distinguished between Lowndes and Belden were these two now famous personages attired exactly alike. High and low and unavailing was the search for the deserter, who had vanished, leaving not a trace behind. True to his word, an order for "the items above referred to" came with a sad, fond letter to his sister Florence, who wept over it for days, but dutifully obtained and restored to her father the stout, leather-encased packet, so long reverently guarded by Miss Heatherwood. No word of reproach did the daughter utter as she handed to the broken-spirited old man the precious case, and with it the check for the balance remaining in a Philadelphia bank to the credit of "Lawrence Bell." The father's hands trembled as they opened the former, and great tears trickled down his furrowed cheeks as he reread one of the fond, pleading pages, and then bowed his head on his arms and brooded in silence. By his side knelt Florence, striving to soothe and comfort, but he would none of it. "Her last plea," he moaned, "was for Jack, and yet I steeled my heart. I thought I knew him best. I thought his will should yield to mine. I never thought to reason with him."

In the personal columns of leading journals, east and west, were inserted for weeks appeals to Lawrence Bell to communicate with his friends and that all should be made right ; but if the appeal met the ex-trooper's eye he probably had his doubts as to the ability of even so prominent a member of the Union League to make right a clear case of desertion, or possibly he scented a trap on part of the detectives. Not one clue would he give as to his whereabouts, yet there speedily came proof that he was keenly watching the course of events, and that was during old Morrissey's trial.

Here, indeed, was a problem. Twenty years had that veteran followed the flag without other reproach to name or fame than the semi-occasional spree so characteristic of the Hibernian trooper of the old army. Wounded in the war with Mexico when he rode with the dragoons; extolled in general orders for heroism in Texas when, at the risk of his own gallant life, he stood by a wounded sergeant and fought a swarm of yelling Comanches, being himself twice wounded in the successful attempt to save his comrade; lionized in the new regiment as the nattiest orderly ever chosen by cavalry adjutant for detail with such honored officers as Sidney Johnston, Robert E. Lee, or dear old Major Slowtrot Thomas; distinguished, as were hundreds of our rank and file for refusing commissions in the army of the Confederate States, even when importuned by officers they loved as Morrissey loved Fairfax; and, finally, renowned in the regular brigade for his daring and devotion in many a charge or scrimmage in the bitter war then waging, Morrissey's record of twenty years of heroism was now being weighed in the balance against one tremendous accusation,—that of having compassed the release of a rebel officer who stood accused of being a spy within the Union lines. Without his co-operation, drunk or sober, it would have been next to impossible for Bell to play the part of Belden. Evidence was adduced showing that Bell and the accused had had two or three long conferences the evenings preceding the 25th of July; that when Carrick would have declined his job as driver of the general's carriage, Morrissey offered to "go bail" he'd make it worth Carrick's while in more ways than one. Evidence of his furious denunciation of a man who spoke of Fairfax as a spy was produced, and of his declaration in a public place (Moriarty's Shades) that the man that would hang Floyd Fairfax as a spy should be "put in diapers for an immachurist;" which when related by the witness simply convulsed the court. But there was none but himself to tell how Floyd Fairfax had watched and even nursed the old fellow when down with fever in the Red River bottom. There was no one to step forward and tell that court under oath how indignantly the grizzled soldier had refused to touch one penny of the money the friends of Fairfax had raised.

All the same, there came a letter to the judge advocate from the missing trooper Bell, and a swarm of witnesses to testify to Morrissey's past record and character. Of the latter were both Belden and Foulweather. The letter of Trooper Bell could not be admitted as evidence, but was read with absorbing interest by every member of the court. All the blame, it said, should be charged to him, Bell, precisely as, in the case of other deserters, it was then the custom to charge every missing article on the ordnance or quartermaster's returns, from a howitzer to a halter-strap. Morrissey was simply the tool with which he wrought. It is easy to persuade an Irishman to risk his own life for the sake of the man or the cause he holds dear, and, having risked his life a hundred times for the government, he was induced to risk trial and punishment to save the neck of his old commander, for no amount of hard swearing could ever convince him, Morrissey, that Fairfax deserved the fate of a spy.

Belden's testimony in behalf of Morrissey was eulogium, so was that of Treacy and Bob Hamlin, but Foulweather, as might have been expected, gave but reluctant praise. To the quick wrath of the accused soldier, the good words of the swarthy major could only be dragged from him by dint of earnest effort on part of the judge advocate, who finally waxed indignant at the obstinacy of his witness; and then followed an unlooked-for and startling incident.

Angered at the attempts of the judge advocate to extort from him reluctant admission that the accused had been a most valuable and trusted soldier for twenty years, old Foulweather blurted out, "I don't care what a man's past services may have been, the moment he gives aid or comfort in any shape to any creature connected with this damnable rebellion I'd hang him high as Haman! I'd stamp out his name as I would a snake! I'd——"

"Silence, sir!" thundered the president of the court, with a whack of his sword on the table. "Confine your remarks to answers to the questions put by the judge advocate. We need no firing the heart of the North in this presence."

"Bedad!" was the astonished interjection of old Morrissey, as he rose from his chair, quivering with mingled wrath and emotion. "There was no need in firing Heatherwood, but ask *him* who done it!" And in the midst of an awkward and solemn silence the prisoner pointed square at his erstwhile commander, who turned, scowling and furious, on the excited Irishman.

"Sit down, Morrissey!" ordered the judge advocate, almost springing at him. "Not another word, sir!—Sit down, major!" he continued, as old Foulweather arose as though determined to address the court. "This is no place——"

"Place or no place," shouted Foulweather, "I am challenged and I shall answer here!" Over the instant hubbub in the court, over the stern orders of the president for silence, his harsh, sonorous voice rang out invincibly. "That place was the hot-bed of treason,—the home of spies and traitors. They conspired with their kind in our army to deprive me of command. They put me in charge of a surgeon, but couldn't blind me or stop my ears. They were ordered arrested by the War Department. Traitors in our uniform set them free,—helped them away, by God! in the very ambulance that brought me there! D'ye s'pose I'd lie bedridden when I heard that! I was out of it and up that hill, and those New England soldiers knew a loyal officer when they saw one, and they did my bidding. War is war, and if I'd had my way that rebel hole would have gone up in smoke a long year before."

That night, hours after the temporary adjournment of the court, in the corridors of the hotels, in the crowded streets of camp, men stood and talked of Foulweather's boast, and of Foulweather's fever-crazed deed. Fever might have accounted for his possible craze that night in June, but not now. Long weeks had elapsed since his hammering at Gettysburg. He had so far recovered as to be allowed to visit Washington and invade the War Department and inveigh against the miscreants promoted over him, and to vaunt his own deeds until ordered as a witness to Baltimore. This night, piling Pelion upon Ossa, he was found to be drinking heavily, and this complicated matters still further. Ordered to report at McHenry for further examination on the morrow, the major at three o'clock in the morning was forcibly borne to a room and put to bed, Treacy and Hamlin mounting guard with solemn faces. Was this to be the realization of a fear each, unknown to the other, had felt for months past,—that the stanch old fighter had fairly worn himself out, and that envy and jealousy, blasted hope and blighted ambition, all had conspired with over-much whiskey and more than enough of hard knocks to unbalance the veteran's reason. Certain it was that when the doctor came with the morning he found his patient unconscious, breathing stertorously, his veins black and swollen, his face suffused. There was no Foulweather to answer the call for the witness when court convened that morning. There was no recognition in his blood-shot eyes when Treacy and Hamlin, ordered to rejoin their squadrons at the front, called to see how their old major was and to say good-by. Whatever might have been the extent of his malady when sent to hospital at Heatherwood, there was left no room for doubt of its severity now. Foulweather was too ill to rejoice even when poor old Morrissey's sentence was later read. The court had no volition at all. Compelled by law to sentence in accordance with the degree of the offence, it had accorded him a long term of imprisonment, with ball and chain, in the dismal casemates of Fort Lafayette, but coupled with this award an earnest plea for mercy.

And even then the veteran seemed little discomposed. "Whist!" said he. "There is wan to spake yet that niver turned his back on a poor privut. Wait till the Prisident hears what they've given old Morrissey." And hear it he did before the setting of another sun. Poor old Foulweather! The news that came a few days later that the veteran trooper had actually been pardoned and restored to duty would have crazed him had he not gone daft already. That winter saw the old regiment in new hands, for the raging major never joined again.

Meanwhile, the summer's sun had driven many Baltimoreans out of town, and, as might have been expected, both Mrs. and Miss Heatherwood were sufferers. Sorrow and anxiety are poor companions with which to encounter the humid heat of the Patapsco shores, yet day after day, as soon as relieved from the restrictions that confined her within doors, Mrs. Heatherwood was again making her tireless round among the sick and wounded. It could not last long, and Mr. George Lowndes, absent on a sad quest in Cincinnati, received a telegram from her physician recalling him at once. Since the hour Jack's farewell letter came, Belle had left the house only when taken out for an occasional drive in the early evening. Florence, despite the heat, refused to leave her friend, and by mid-August the three women looked, as sympathizing neighbors expressed it to one another, "like perfect frights." This time Lowndes would not take no for answer. He bundled the three into an evening train and settled them at Cape May. It was sorely against Mrs. Heatherwood's will, but she was prostrate and could make no active resistance. There were cool, soft breezes and entire rest; all three could look for benefit. Meantime, the aging father returned to the West and resumed his sorrowful inquiries.

Profiting by the inaction of the Union leaders in the East, Lee dared to detach one of his three corps and sent Longstreet to Tennessee to the aid of Bragg, with the result that, midway between the scenes of the great Union triumphs of Gettysburg and Vicksburg the South came up smiling after its supposed annihilation and dealt the direful blow of Chickamauga. The war, then, was anything but ended, and once again Baltimore thrilled with joy.

Mid-October came, and, older, grayer, sadder still, Lowndes came back from weeks of fruitless searching among the hospitals of Kentucky, and, gathering up his household, took them to the old home on Fifth Avenue. Another clew had reached him, and he was eager to go to Chattanooga, but Chattanooga was shut off from the outside world by the bold besiegers. Yet no sooner did Grant burst through, with Sherman at his heels, than the inert mass starving or sleeping in the shadows of Lookout Mountain seemed to spring to life again, and just as the early snows were sifting down about the roofs and spires of Gotham, hope and enthusiasm reawakened in the North over the news that Bragg's besieging army was swept like chaff from Mission Ridge, and only the old flag now was floating down the Tennessee. That grand victory of Grant's came just in the nick of time, for far and near all over the loyal States the pall of despond was spreading. The South had fought too hard and long and well.

Bivouacked on the very crest of the ridge, close to the dull red earthworks on which they had planted their colors during the day, a strong regiment of far Western men was singing and rejoicing about the blazing cook-fires. Every now and then the groups nearest the dusty roadway would rise and cheer some general or staff-officer as he rode rapidly by, and all along the line the exultant shout would be taken up. They were cheering everybody, anybody, the evening of that glorious day, but they sprang to their feet again and swarmed like bees and swung their caps and shouted madly at sight of a stocky, broad-shouldered, sharp-featured little fellow in a major-general's coat, who laughed and shook his head at their characteristic yells for a speech, but he said thrilling words to those who grasped his hands and hugged his booted legs and crowded about his horse, and they cheered again like mad, for this was Sheridan's division, as undivided a command as ever stood the shock of battle. Presently it transpired that he wanted to see the man who bore their colors up the height after the sergeant was shot down, and there was a yell for Corporal Hoe, and the corporal couldn't be found. The regiment had wavered a minute, it seems, midway up the slope, for Bragg's men gave them a crashing volley or two from a zigzag line of parapet a hundred yards beyond them. The color-bearer reeled and fell, but passed his silken treasure to the hands of a tall, brown-bearded corporal in the rear rank of his guard, and this man, tossing away his rifle, sprang out to the front full a dozen yards, swinging and waving the brilliant banner high over his head and shouting, "Come on, men! Come on!" In an instant, too, an officer had rushed to the front, the young colonel commanding, waving his sword and shouting, "Forward!" The line burst ahead with a yell, yet could not overtake that tall, athletic leader. Every inch of the way to within a few feet of the summit he kept in advance, leaping the shallow rifle-pits, scrambling over log breastworks; and just how he escaped death was a miracle, for the flag was riddled, the staff splintered with bullets.

Yet this night, when Sheridan wanted to shake

hands with him, Corporal Hoe had disappeared. "Tell him to come to me in the morning," said the little general, as he rode away, and then the men began to talk of Hoe.

Who he was, where he was from, nobody knew, and Hoe wouldn't say. All the information given by the meagre muster-roll was to the effect that he had enlisted in such a county on such a day in August, 1863, but the "batch" of recruits made up of drafted men sent down to join just before Chickamauga were able to add that Hoe had enlisted as substitute for a well-to-do father of a numerous family, and they told a story to the effect that the officials said that the substitute was worth ten of the original. Tall, splendidly built, a soldier evidently, the officers were quick to see in the silent, blue-eyed fellow a man with a history. But good men were too valuable to be made restive under importunate questioning. Hoe's reserve was respected. His cool courage at Chickamauga made him a corporal. His stature and steadiness took him at once into the color-guard, and only in one way had he betrayed anything by which his antecedents could be conjectured. There had been hardly any time for drill before the recruits went into action with their regiment, and in loading Private Hoe made a half face to the left, threw the butt of his long rifle back in rear of the left foot, with the barrel sloping to the front instead of, in the language of the drill-sergeants, "bringing the piece vertically in front of the centre of the body, barrel to the front, butt between the feet." "See that?" said Captain Rogers. "That man learned the manual of arms before the war." Of course, they asked him where, and Hoe, smiling quietly, replied, "In a militia company," which was perfectly true, yet helped them not at all.

That night the colonel called to the adjutant, "Sheridan has sent for Corporal Hoe to come to his head-quarters. Better make him color-bearer at once and stave off his being detailed as orderly."

Yet the colonel need not have worried. Hoe had already declined to leave his regiment for any other duty. The spring of '64 came on. Grant and Sheridan had been summoned to the East, and, with Sherman to head the army of the West, these three sons of Ohio set forth on that momentous campaign that was to prove the beginning of the end, and from Atlanta went a paper, backed by the endorsement of famous brigade, division, and corps commanders, in which the colonel urged that Sergeant-Major Hoe be commissioned because of conspicuous bravery and marked ability, and so it happened that at Franklin he rode at the colonel's side as adjutant of the regiment, and that at Nashville, where Thomas turned the tables on his old regimental comrade, Hood, it was Hoe who led the dash of the attenuated battalion when colonel and half the captains were gone. Yet all this time, reserved, silent, and, as all could see, sad, he had remained a stranger, for to no man did he tell the story of his past. They honored him, believed in him, and would eagerly have sought his confidence and friendship, but, while scrupulously courteous and considerate, he maintained what they all felt was an incognito.

The morning of the second day of the grapple had come, and Hood's astonished army, that on the previous dawn was defiantly facing north and threatening the proud capital of Tennessee, had been sledge-hammered out of its encircling earthworks to the west, and now, hanging with grim desperation to the bristling redoubts at the eastward end of their line and the strong post of Overton's Hill, confronted the dim blue ranks of Thomas. Who would have said five years before that these fellow-soldiers in the same regiment in which rode Sidney Johnston and Lee, Hardee and Thomas, Hood and Garrard, Fitz Lee and Johnson, Belden and Fairfax, that here within hail of the hospitable Southern city two great armies would be fighting to the death,— Thomas, the sturdy battalion commander, at the head of one; Hood, his erstwhile dashing lieutenant, at the head of the other; while two of the divisions engaged on the Union side should be led by Garrard and Johnson, old friends and comrades,—adjutant and subaltern respectively. Fierce and bloody had been the battling at Franklin a fortnight before. Sharp and stern the struggle of yesterday, and now one more united effort was needed and Hood's last prop would be swept away.

And yet this is almost an improvised army that

Thomas has at hand. Many a new and untried regiment is here. Three or four brigades and brigadiers were strangers not three weeks ago, and the veterans of the Fourth Corps look askance at the new blankets, overcoats and knapsacks of a brigade that marches by an hour after dawn. "Johnny Raws," say the grinning files of the rearmost line of a Western regiment, whereat the brigade commander, a massive, bearded, soldierly fellow, whom their practised eyes are quick to recognize as a veteran, turns half laughing in his saddle and shakes a gauntleted fist. "We're to go side by side, you rascally Badgers," he cries. "Let's see if my 'raws' will be done any quicker than you." Whereat there goes up a shout of good-natured chaff and applause. A bumptious man, an ill-tempered rebuke, would have roused the ire of the soldiery. The laughing challenge wins their sympathy instanter. "Bully for the general!" goes up the cry, and several officers turn to see what the shouting means.

"I never saw that general before," says the senior captain, who has had command since Franklin. "Who is he?"

"One of those Army of the Potomac fellows," answers their own brigade leader, himself only a colonel. "They take our best generals to plan their doings for them, and then send their new ones out here to learn how to fight. That's General Clark, though they do say he's a good one."

And at sound of the name the tall adjutant, who

has been seated making some memoranda in his notebook, springs to his feet and, with paling face, stands gazing after the marching column.

"What is it, Hoe?" asks the brigade leader. "Have you ever met him?"

For a moment there is no answer. There is, indeed, significant silence. Then at last comes the reply, "I have seen him—somewhere before."

Three hours later the sulphur clouds hang low over the scarred slopes to the south of the lately beleaguered city, and the roar of battle is giving place all along the line to exultant cheering. Gun after gun, battery after battery, has been enveloped by the charging battalions in the light-blue overcoats, and everywhere on a front of over three miles the waving banners of the Union are pressing onward. Everywhere the dull gray ranks are breaking and drifting away, save at one point. At the edge of a clump of trees, in a strong earthwork, half a dozen light guns are still playing on the halted brigade that has essayed their capture, for several plucky but sorely thinned battalions stand firmly in support and sweep with their fire the westward and northward slopes. Raging at the unlooked-for check, a division commander rides furiously along the sullen, unresponsive ranks crouching for shelter at the foot of the slope.

"It's no use, general," says a veteran colonel, dejectedly. "These fellows have charged twice, and look there!" he adds, pointing with his sword to the corpses strown along their front away up almost to the black embrasures. "They are fought out. Another charge would use up what's left of them."

"Then, by God! let 'em lie there and see better men do their work!" is the savage rejoinder, and spurring at the gallop to his right, the general dashes up to the bearded brigade commander. "General Clark," he shouts, "change front to the half left and drive those fellows out of that grove! You can do it—Crandall's men are pumped."

Not five minutes later and with grand enthusiasm the leading line of the new brigade, two strong regiments in front, is sweeping steadily up the slope, and the Southern guns and musketry turn savagely upon them. Half-way, and they waver, for men are falling fast, and out rides their brigade commander, colors in hand, his voice ringing magnificently through the roar of artillery. Fired by the sight, the remnant to their left seems all on a sudden to spring to its feet as though to show the division commander the colonel has maligned it, but all eyes are on the splendid form of the adjutant of that Badger regiment. Leaping on the horse of a wounded major, seizing the old battle-worn colors he had borne at Mission Ridge, out he dashes full twenty yards in front of the reviving brigade, and with a deafening yell it rises and follows him, and so it happens that in the surging rush that goes over the battery, battalions and all, Clark's "Johnny Raws" and Crandall's crippled veterans tumble in side by side, their inner flanks huddled together indistinguishably, their voices mingled in exultant cheers. Almost at the same instant, it seems, these two grand leaders, the general and the adjutant,—the general from the Army of the Potomac, the adjutant from none knows where,—their horses shot from beneath them, their flags still waving high, come leaping through the fire-flashing bank of smoke, their paths converging, their cheering men close following at their heels. Over the thin and crouching ranks in gray the victors sweep, shouting hoarse orders to those attempting to escape to stop in their tracks or be shot down, and almost before they realize it three thousand rejoicing men in Union blue are captors of the battery, its supporting brigade, and of the battalions lining the earthworks to the south, who, taken in flank, can neither fight nor run. For a moment Pandemonium reigns. Hats, caps, and colors are tossed in air. Popular officers are raised on the shoulders of their cheering men, and borne to the parapet. A major-general and his staff come galloping to the scene to join in the jubilee. Right and left the aides and officers are darting, receiving the swords of the captive Confederates and marshalling their sorrowing leaders before the division commander. And then, still panting, General Clark bursts his way through groups of enthusiastic men.

"Where is the fellow that led on our left?" he demands. "I want to shake hands with him."

And a soldier, pointing to where half a dozen officers are kneeling about a prostrate form, says, "This way, general," and Clark joins them, kneels, and, looking into their anxious faces, queries, "Is he badly wounded?" Whereat a surgeon gravely nods and goes on with his work. Belt and sash have been unloosed, the coat thrown open from throat to waist, and now as the doctor unbuttons a shirt already soaked with blood, and bares the broad, muscular chest, a reddish-blue mark catches the professional eye. A locket, pendent from a fine gold chain, is revealed to all. "This gentleman has been shot before, and if he could recover from that, he can, please God, from this," says the surgeon, solemnly, as he finds a welling fountain farther down on the other side. "It is loss of blood that has used him up," he adds, as with skilful hands he begins to stanch the wound, while an assistant raises the drooping head and applies a flask to the pale lips. Feebly a hand is uplifted and the flask is thrust away.

"Drink, sir," says the surgeon, "just a sip or two. It's brandy. No, I insist," he continues, as again the half-unconscious officer seems striving against it.

"Hoe never drinks," murmurs Captain Rogers. "That's what's the matter." But the surgeon's order prevails.

"What do you call him? What is this gallant gentleman's name?" asks Clark, bending forward, his eyes ablaze with new and eager interest. "I—think I've met him before."

"Hoe—John Hoe, our adjutant, by gad!" says

the battalion commander, proudly; "and we'll match him against anything in the army, east or west."

But Clark moves still nearer, and is peering intently into the bearded face just beginning to receive faint color, and then, dreamily, the eyes unveil, and faintly, half-consciously come the words, while the ghost of a smile seems to flit about the corners of his mouth,—

"Hoe—yes—John Hoe—Ivan Hoe, don't you see, Clark—Desdichado—the Disinherited Knight."

And then, with a cry that startles the groups on every side, the bearded general throws his arms about the swooning man. "Jack! Jack! Thank God we've found you at last!"

* * * * * * *

The lilacs were in bloom again in many a little court-yard in Gotham. The grand army had come drifting home for muster out after the final parade in Washington. The streets and avenues were filled with men in faded blue, the clubs with uniforms. A bearded soldier, double-starred by brevet for gallant and meritorious services in the battle of Nashville, had stopped on his homeward way to call on his old client at the Lowndes homestead, and to shake hands over and over again with a tall, soldierly, yet pallid man whose brave blue eyes and clear-cut face, whose imperial and moustache, were oddly like those of the bronzed and bestarred young general who seemed almost as great an object of interest in the household as his now acknowledged double, the son and heir. Big and roomy as it was, the old brownstone mansion was filled with guests this lovely day in '65, and yet there were more to come. It seemed as though the father could not summon friends enough to do homage to Jack. It had seemed, weeks before, as though that helpless invalid could not be brought to realize the truth that, stern and implacable as he had seemed, that father loved him and had long forgiven the faults and follies of his youth. When at last Jack could see how gravely he had misjudged his father, his humility and penitence were indescribable. Only Florence saw their reconciliation; only to one friend did she describe it,— one whose lips but rarely spoke his name, and then only with betraying quiver. For weeks after the great battle they nursed their invalid at Nashville, and not until April had they ventured North, and then only as far as Washington and Baltimore, where an "Iron Secretary" found time to see and shake hands with the young major by brevet of volunteers, whose commission recited heroic deeds and was made out in the name of John Hoe. "Congress will have to straighten out his various names and titles," said the Secretary, now a care-worn and grizzled man, "but I can 'tend to the removal of that charge of desertion against Trooper Bell and—certain other deviltries," to which even now, it seems, he could not allude without a grimace. There was a disposition in Baltimore to do homage to the returned volunteer, now recognized as the man who had saved the life of Fairfax, but this the convalescent refused. There was a week in which Florence trod on air lest she should disturb certain interviews, that occasionally became murmurous, between her hero Jack and her Maryland friend. There were more such weeks when, along in May, the Heatherwoods, mother and daughter, and Colonel Ralph were made to come to Gotham as the guests of George Lowndes, Esq., and the reunion of the blue and the gray began forthwith. There was more of it when Belden dropped in just as Clark returned from the West, and, though there were fortunes to be repaired and shattered homes to be rebuilt, and many and many a grave over which to mourn, there were sunshine and blessed peace, and the heart of one noble woman overflowed with thanksgiving as she looked around with swimming eyes upon the loved ones reunited.

They sat clasping her hands one night, Florence on one side, Belle on the other, when the men for the moment, after the fashion of the day, were lingering over their cigars in the dining-room, and to them came the butler. There was a soldier would like to speak with General Belden, and there at the door stood old Morrissey. The exclamations of delight with which that astonished veteran was seized and dragged into the parlor brought a rush from the table in the room beyond, and both Belden and Jack nearly shook his arms loose when they reached him. Then he was fairly hauled into that brilliantly lighted apartment, with all its rich appointments of plate-laden sideboard, of snowy, damask-covered table, decked with flowers and bravely set forth with its array of carved decanters, cut glass, and costly china. It was a strange sight, that of the veteran trooper with his scarred face and bristling, grizzled moustache, standing there rigidly erect and scrupulously buttoned in his best cavalry jacket, brave with yellow lace, the broad chevrons of the standard-bearer and the glistening shoulder-scales, blushingly holding the wine-glass that his host was hospitably filling to the brim, while two gallant men in the garb of major-generals of the Union, a third in the simple, single-breasted frock of the line officer, but with the gold leaves of a major on his infantry shoulder-straps, looking, despite his modest uniform and pallid face, as though he might be the brother of the younger general officer, a fourth man, youngest of all, and soldier, too, despite the evening dress of civil life,—these four standing with uplifted glasses to drink health and happiness and prosperity to Sergeant Morrissey of the old army, while three fair women, one with silvery hair, hovered smiling at the broad door-way.

"By Jove!" cried Major Jack, his blue eyes sparkling with delight, "what wouldn't I give if Fairfax could but be here!"

"I saw Gineral Fairfax in Richmond, sorr," said the sergeant, promptly, "and he gave me this, sorr, for the meejor," he added with the quick recognition of the Celtic soldier of new rank and title, and then

Blushingly holding the wine-glass.

produced from an inner pocket a letter which he handed to Jack as he would have presented an orderly's despatch. "There's no answer, sorr, but I was not to fail to deliver it," and Lowndes turned red as he tucked it in an inner pocket. It was late before he could read it at all, and when he did the girls had gone, much earlier than usual, to their rooms, whereat there were others to look disappointed.

But Madam Heatherwood, with fond interest in her soft eyes, stood at the door-way of her sitting-room as Lowndes reached the second story, and with all the old trust and faith he hastened to her side, and she led the way within.

"Read it yourself," he said, "and tell me what it means." But his heart was throbbing hard as he handed her the open sheet. And this was what she read:

"You told me to ride for Belle Heatherwood's sake the night you set me free and saved my neck. It was like you, Jack Lowndes, but it wasn't fair. You made me believe it was she who planned the whole escape,—that you were but her instrument. I went with hope I had never known before, and that hope was killed long months ago, long before we lost all hope for the cause of our blessed South. Only after you disappeared, leaving no trace behind, did I learn the whole truth. Only after Appomattox did I hear through Belden of your safe and glorious return.

"I am glad no Virginians were in your front that December day at Nashville. I have often wished I had died with Garnett and Armistead that grand, but fatal afternoon at Gettysburg, and had been buried there where I lay among your guns, but it pleased God to order that I should be with Pickett to the last.

"Say to dear Aunty Heatherwood that, so long as I live, I shall remember her loving-kindness. Tell her that friends in England offer me an opening there, and that within a few weeks I shall be on my way to London, it appearing that I am no longer 'wanted' to answer to the charge of being a spy. Tell her I saw the Waddells at their old home, reunited and, except Laura, reconcilable. Between you and me, that young woman is the worst Reb I ever saw. Frank is a manly fellow, who will soon restore the family fortunes, but as for Laura she declaims against you Yankees from morn till night, despite the New England blood that flowed in her mother's veins and twangs at times in the tones of her otherwise melodious voice; despite the more damaging fact that she is believed to hold prisoner a New Hampshire heart, that of one Lieutenant Pettingill, whom we captured wounded at Cold Harbor; and so loyal a Rebel is she that, following the example of your government, she refuses to exchange her prisoner for a Virginian of equal rank who, in the interest of harmony between the sections, is said to be willing to offer himself. At this moment Mr.

Pettingill is believed to be home on parole, but within easy call of that kittenish *patte de velours* at Leesburg. It is my belief that, in her longing to whip the whole Yankee nation as it deserves, Miss Waddell has determined to hold him for life, leaving the whippings to be administered in the by and by to a generation yet unborn.

"And now, to yourself—the man who gave me life and liberty and saved me from a shameful fate —I have no words with which to say how deep is my gratitude, or with what full heart I pray God's blessing on you—on you and Belle.

"Fairfax."

They were standing under a gas-jet by her dressing table, her silvering head bowed over the page, the soft lines about her lips betraying the emotion with which she read, now quivering with tender sympathy as the letter told of the writer's sorrow and coming exile, now curving almost merrily as it spoke of Laura; but it was the final paragraph of which Jack had so impulsively spoken, of which alone he was thinking, and when at last she raised her head and looked up with swimming eyes into his face, the fond woman whispered, "Wait here one moment," and then, moved to sudden resolution, left the room.

A moment he stood there alone. He seemed to realize what was coming. There was a bounding in his pulses, a throbbing in his heart, that recalled the wild ecstasy of the charge, yet *there* there was no trembling. Impatient he turned to the door as though to follow, but there came a light footfall, and at the very threshold he met the girl he had loved so long, and long so hopelessly. Her eyes, startled, fell before his eager gaze.

"Mother sent me——" she faltered, but with sudden movement he seized her trembling hands and drew her within before she could complete the words.

"I have such strange news," he hurried to say. "Floyd Fairfax tells me he goes abroad to live. He tells me practically that my renunciation was—wasted. Belle, what does it mean?"

Her head was bowed so near his breast that his pleading lips almost swept her fair white forehead. For a moment she could not answer. "Tell me," he whispered, bending lower still, and she felt the quiver of his strong, nervous hand and heard the loud throbbing of his brave heart. One quick glance up into his glowing eyes, and then the long lashes swept her cheeks again.

"I never told you—I never meant," at last she whispered, "that you should renounce—me."

FINIS.

By John Strange Winter.
(Mrs. Arthur Stannard.)

A Magnificent Young Man.
12mo. Paper, 50 cents; cloth, $1.00.

"There is a happy mingling of comedy and tragedy in *A Magnificent Young Man*. It is a story with an original plot, involving a secret marriage, the mysterious disappearance of a bridegroom, and the experiences of a young girl, who refuses to clear her reputation, even to the mother of her unacknowledged husband, until such a time as he shall give permission. The plot is well sustained, the incidents and dialogue are entertaining, and the mystery is kept up long enough to hold the close attention of the reader to the last chapter."—*Boston Beacon*.

Every Inch a Soldier.
12mo. Paper, 50 cents; cloth, $1.00.

"Of the incidents of the work before us, the plot is highly entertaining, and incidentally we meet the Bishop of Blankhampton, whose matrimonial affairs were ably discussed in a book previously written. It is a very pleasant and readable book, and we are glad to see it."—*Norristown Herald*.

Aunt Johnnie.
12mo. Paper, 50 cents; cloth, $1.00.

"Mrs. Stannard preserves her freshness and vivacity in a wonderful way. 'Aunt Johnnie' is as bright and amusing a story as any that she has written, and it rattles on from the first chapter to the last with unabated gayety and vigor. The hero and heroine are both charming, and the frisky matron who gives the story its name is a capitally managed character. The novel is exactly suited to the season, and is sure to be very popular."—*Charleston News and Courier*.

The Other Man's Wife.
12mo. Paper, 50 cents; cloth, $1.00.

"The hero and heroine have a charm which is really unusual in these hackneyed personages, for they are most attractive and wholesome types. Indeed, wholesomeness may be said to be the most notable characteristic of this author's work."—*N. Y. Telegram*.

Only Human.
12mo. Paper, 50 cents; cloth, $1.00.

"A bright and interesting story. . . . Its pathos and humor are of the same admirable quality that is found in all the other novels by this author."—*Boston Gazette*.

J. B. LIPPINCOTT COMPANY, PHILADELPHIA.

By Elizabeth Phipps Train

ISSUED IN THE LOTOS LIBRARY.
ILLUSTRATED. 16MO. POLISHED
BUCKRAM. 75 CENTS PER VOL.

THE AUTOBIOGRAPHY OF A PROFESSIONAL BEAUTY.

"It is an interesting confession, admirably written, and the story throughout is delightfully fresh and vivacious."—*Philadelphia Evening Bulletin.*

"The author gives in this handsome little book a charming glimpse of ultra-fashionable English society. It has an air of truth which makes its moral the more impressive, and the characters are well drawn."—*Columbus Evening Dispatch.*

"This is a profoundly interesting love story. Its plot is simple, natural, and life-like—often approaching the tragic. The dangers from the abuse of the powers of hypnotism are strikingly illustrated."—*Chicago Inter-Ocean.*

A SOCIAL HIGHWAYMAN.

"There is a consistency of bold purpose in the book which makes it the reverse of mawkish. It is a kind of modernized Dick Turpin."—*Chicago Times-Herald.*

"'A Social Highwayman,' a small and dainty volume in Lippincott's Lotos Library, is a distinctly interesting, almost a fascinating, story."—*Brooklyn Daily Eagle.*

"The J. B. Lippincott Company has issued in the Lotos Library, in a handsome little volume, with illustrations, 'A Social Highwayman,' by Elizabeth Phipps Train, which originally appeared in *Lippincott's Magazine*. This thrillingly dramatic story, always intensely absorbing, has acquired a new interest since it was turned into a play, and many will be anxious to compare it with the drama which bears the same name. The tale has abundant life and movement, and commands and retains attention."—*Boston Saturday Evening Gazette.*

J. B. LIPPINCOTT COMPANY, PHILADELPHIA.

www.ingramcontent.com/pod-product-compliance
Lightning Source LLC
Chambersburg PA
CBHW022135300426
44115CB00006B/192